I M A G E S
of America

BOONE HALL PLANTATION

Michelle Adams

ARCADIA PUBLISHING

ISBN 978-0-7385-6725-9

Published by Arcadia Publishing
Charleston, South Carolina

Printed in the United States of America

Library of Congress Catalog Card Number: 2008926397

For all general information contact Arcadia Publishing at:
Telephone 843-853-2070
Fax 843-853-0044
E-mail sales@arcadiapublishing.com

Visit us on the Internet at www.arcadiapublishing.com

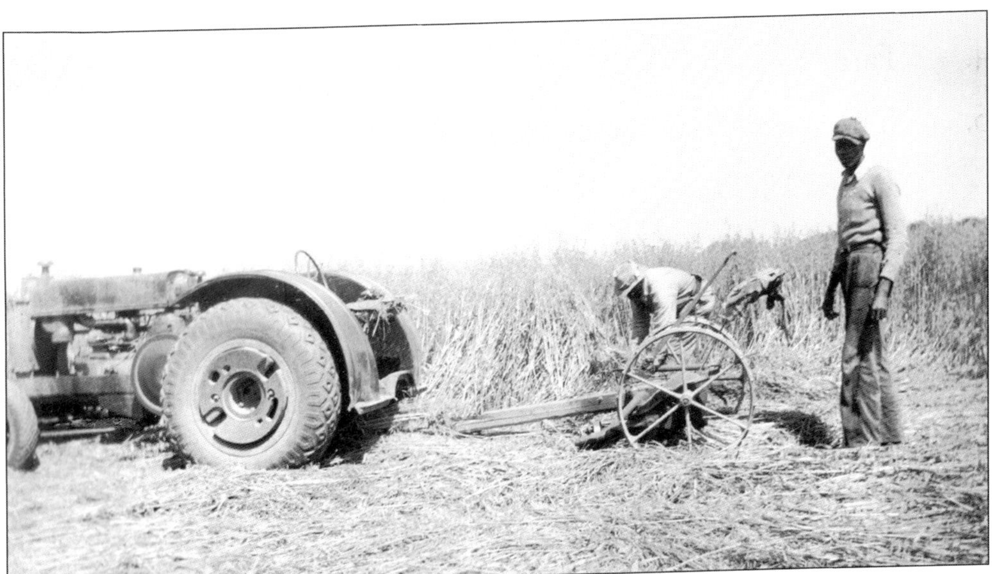

The plantation could not be what it is today without the surrounding community. The uniqueness of the community itself has helped shape the plantation with its strong culture and heritage. The Gullah culture is still celebrated on the plantation through educational programs and the sweetgrass baskets that can be seen throughout the Lowcountry. (Courtesy of the South Carolina Historical Society.)

Contents

ACKNOWLEDGMENTS

Discovering all the images needed for this book was a great undertaking, and I would like to thank several people for their assistance and direction in obtaining these photographs. I am most appreciative to Mike Coker with the South Carolina Historical Society for his wonderful help in scanning the majority of the photographs found within these pages and directing me to many more I was unaware existed. Also, thanks to Nic Butler with the Charleston County Public Library for researching all the e-mail requests I sent him.

I also appreciate the help of the families involved, including Ellen Stone Devine and John Howell and our many wonderful discussions about Thomas Stone. Willie McRae of Boone Hall Plantation has also been most helpful, as has Abby Sensenbaugh, who never tired of the questions I sent her and was a great editorial source. Ann Gelwicks of the Scottish Society of Charleston and Tony Libby shared their photographs of the festivals held at Boone Hall.

Lastly, thanks to Maggie Bullwinkel with Arcadia Publishing for encouraging me when I hit a few walls with my searches and my family for putting up with my endless hours at libraries and working on the computer. I hope I was able to create an interesting glimpse into the history of Boone Hall Plantation through all this work for guests and the surrounding community to enjoy.

INTRODUCTION

Boone Hall was primarily a cotton plantation that also produced brick in the colder months, like many other plantations in the area. Pecans, cattle, and vegetables have also been raised here at different times. John Boone arrived in Charleston in approximately 1672. Boone Hall was received in a land grant in 1681 from the English Lords Proprietors. He did not plant cash crops such as cotton, rice, and indigo but was more involved with the local government and militia, as well as with his sawmill and producing cattle for the naval stores. Five generations of Boones lived on the plantation, building three different homes during that time. The last and longest standing of these homes was built around the mid to late 1700s, with the first succumbing to fire and the second damaged by a hurricane. John Boone's son, Thomas, is credited with starting the planting of the avenue of oaks in 1743 and is buried along the avenue. His sister, Sara Hext, married Andrew Rutledge, and they had two famous grandsons: John Rutledge was the first governor of South Carolina, and Edward Rutledge was a signer of the Declaration of Independence. The house was sold briefly in 1811 to Thomas Vardell, who tried to build a brick-making business. He was unsuccessful, and the plantation was then sold to local builders Henry and John Horlbeck Jr. in 1817.

The Horlbecks were the sons of German immigrant John Adam Horlbeck, who with his brother, Peter, built the Old Exchange Building and several churches in downtown Charleston. Henry and John Horlbeck Jr. also built many buildings in Charleston between 1812 and the Civil War. They created a successful business from the brick kilns, producing brick for many of the homes in downtown Charleston and the building of Fort Sumter. The clay material was dug from pits in the creek beds, and the brick making was often done in the winter months when the cotton crops were not grown. Little is known of the family during this time, but it is known that they began planting the pecan groves in 1890, planting 15,000 trees on 600 acres. The groves grew to be the largest in the world by the early 1900s. The plantation was briefly sold to a pecan company but returned to the Horlbeck family until the 1930s.

In 1935, the plantation was again sold, this time to the Honorable Thomas Stone, a Canadian ambassador. When he purchased the plantation, he found that the Horlbecks had not lived in the home for quite some time, and the house was falling apart from neglect. This was before the era of preservation, so he decided to tear down the structure and rebuild it using material from the previous home, brick made on the plantation, and material from other old homes in the area. The Stones entertained several famous people, including writer DuBose Heyward and composer George Gershwin. Stone was called back to serve his country at the beginning of World War II, and the plantation was sold for a brief time to Prince Dimitri Djordjaze of Russia and his wife, Audrey Emory. When the couple divorced in 1945, the plantation was purchased by Dr. Henry Deas, who used it to raise Hereford cattle. The last time the plantation was sold was in 1955 to the current owners, the McRaes. They decided to live on the top two floors and opened up the main floor to the public for the first time in 1956 during the spring garden tours. The McRaes continued to give tours of the home as well as to farm the property and to restore the gardens throughout the next few decades. Today many events take place on the plantation, such as the Scottish Games, the reenactment of the Battle of Secessionville, and the Taste of Charleston, as well as the annual spring strawberry patch and fall pumpkin patch.

One

The Boones

John Boone arrived in South Carolina early in the 1670s. The exact date of his arrival has been in dispute. According to State of South Carolina historian A. S. Salley Jr., John Boone arrived with the first fleet in 1670. The Boone family history at the South Carolina Historical Society indicates John Boone's arrival in 1672 aboard the *Three Brothers*. However, a warrant for land given to John Boone for a servant arriving in December 1671 shows that John Boone must have arrived by then. Finally, the *Biographical Directory of the House of Representatives* states Boone's arrival as 1673.

Although he eventually became a planter, Boone began his career in the province as a trader with Native Americans, a dealer in native slaves, and a fence for the pirates who plagued the Carolina coast. John Boone was also involved in other activities, such as accumulating land and participating in local politics as a tax assessor, highway commissioner, and parish vestryman. He and his wife, Elizabeth Patey, had seven children, with his descendants following in his footsteps in local politics. His son, Capt. Thomas Boone, was elected to the Royal Assembly in 1730. Other descendants also served in the General Assembly and supported the militia during the American Revolution.

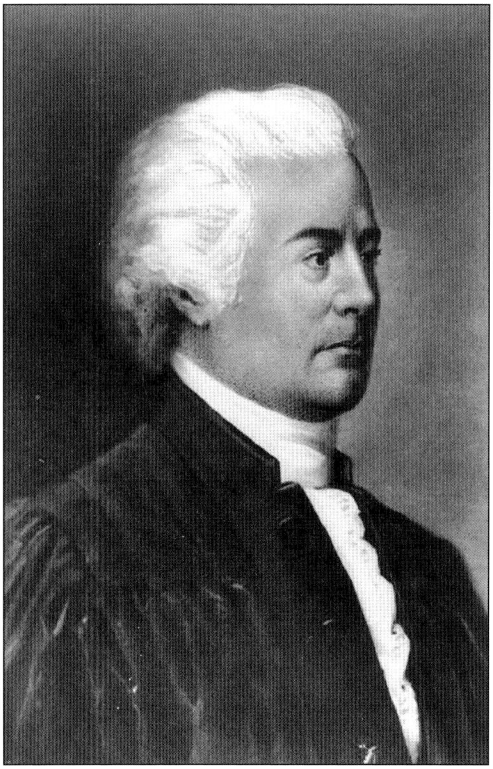

John Rutledge was the great-grandson of John Boone. Rutledge studied law between 1755 and 1760 in Charleston and then in London. Upon his return to South Carolina in 1761, he became a successful lawyer and politician. He served as a delegate to the Stamp Act Congress and the Continental Congresses, and as governor of South Carolina. He helped write the U.S. Constitution in 1787 and supported its ratification. He also sat on the first Supreme Court. (Courtesy of the Library of Congress.)

Christ Church started as a small wooden building. It was built on its current site in 1708 but was accidentally destroyed by a fire in 1725. The church was finished in 1727 but was burned by retreating British troops in 1782. It was rebuilt six years later. At the end of the Civil War, a company of Union cavalry used the building as a stable and burned the pews for firewood in the bitter winter of 1865. (Courtesy of the South Carolina Historical Society.)

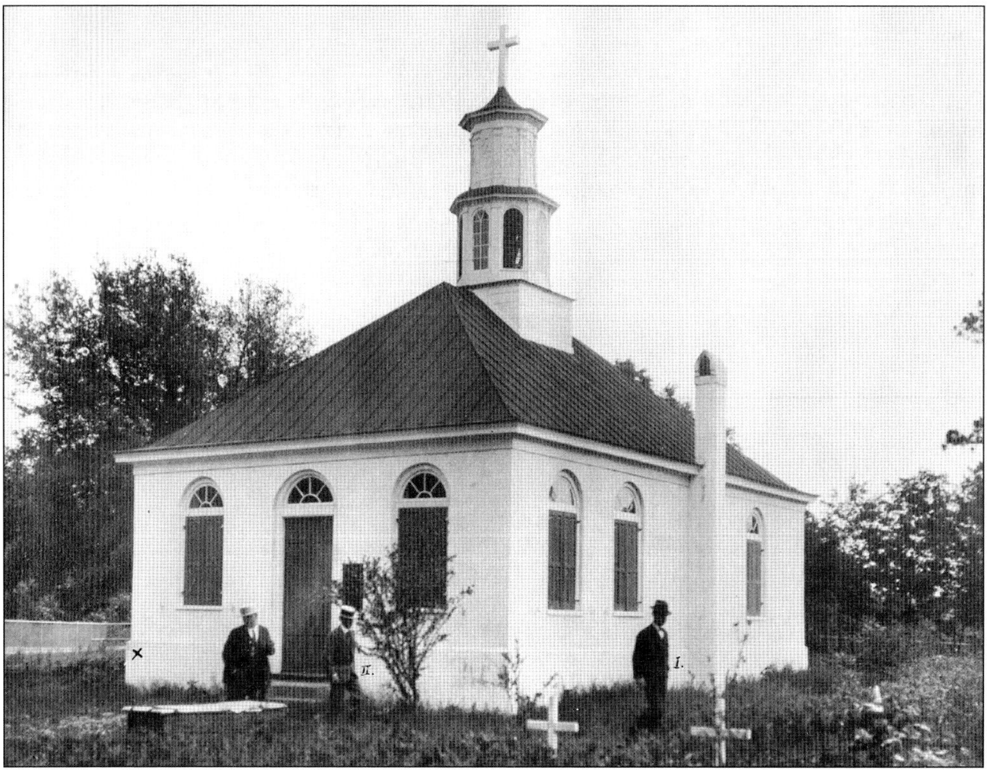

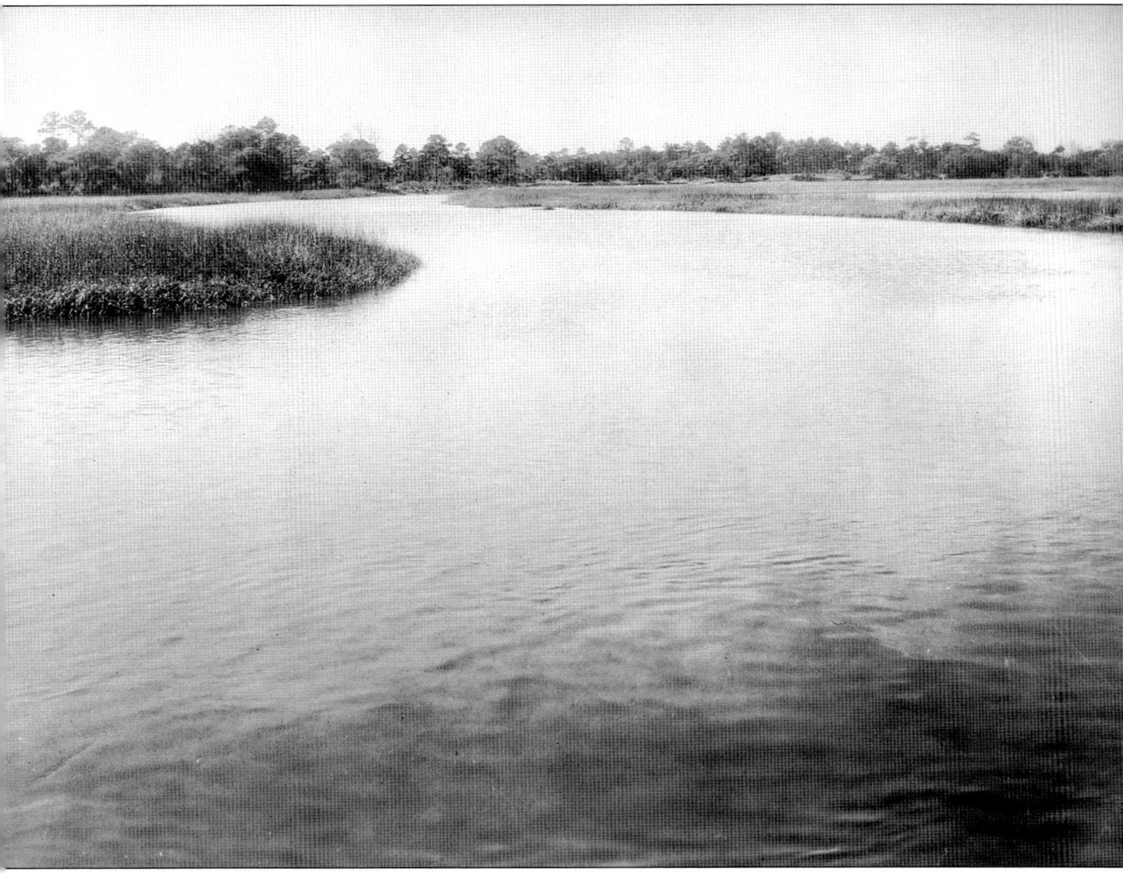

Plantations were often placed next to a waterway for the ease of transporting crops and people to and from Charleston. Boone Hall Plantation is located next to the Wampancheone Creek, which flows into Horlbeck Creek and then into the Wando River. The Wando River then flows into the Cooper River, on which a traveler would ride the tide right into Charleston. (Courtesy of the South Carolina Historical Society.)

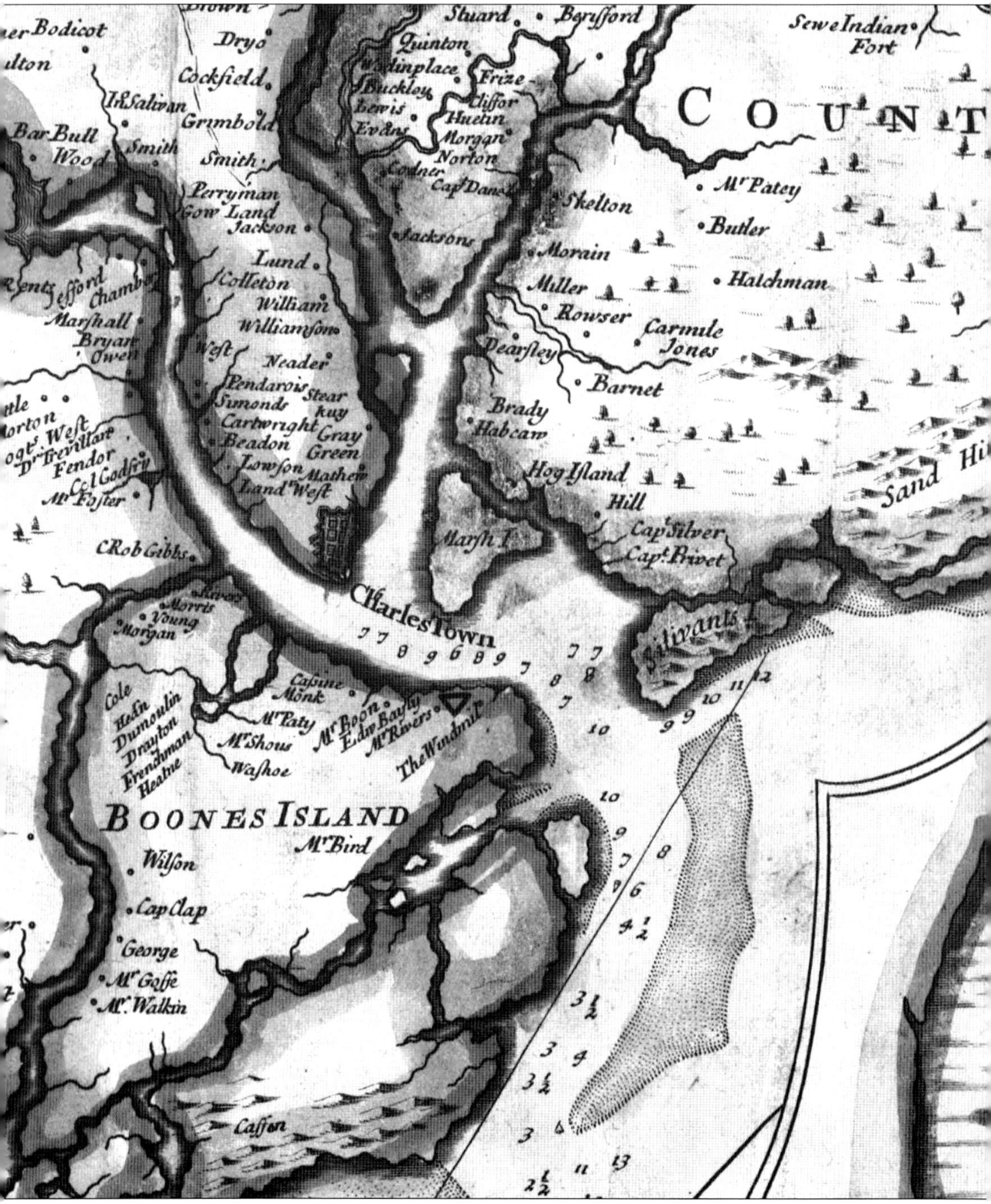

There is a legend that states that James Island was originally named Boones Island after a John Boone, possibly a relative of the Boones at Boone Hall. He is reported as living in this area during the 1670s. This early map shows that area as Boones Island. Watchtowers were placed strategically around the Charleston harbor, and John Boone is listed as the first tower watcher on the island. (Courtesy of the Library of Congress.)

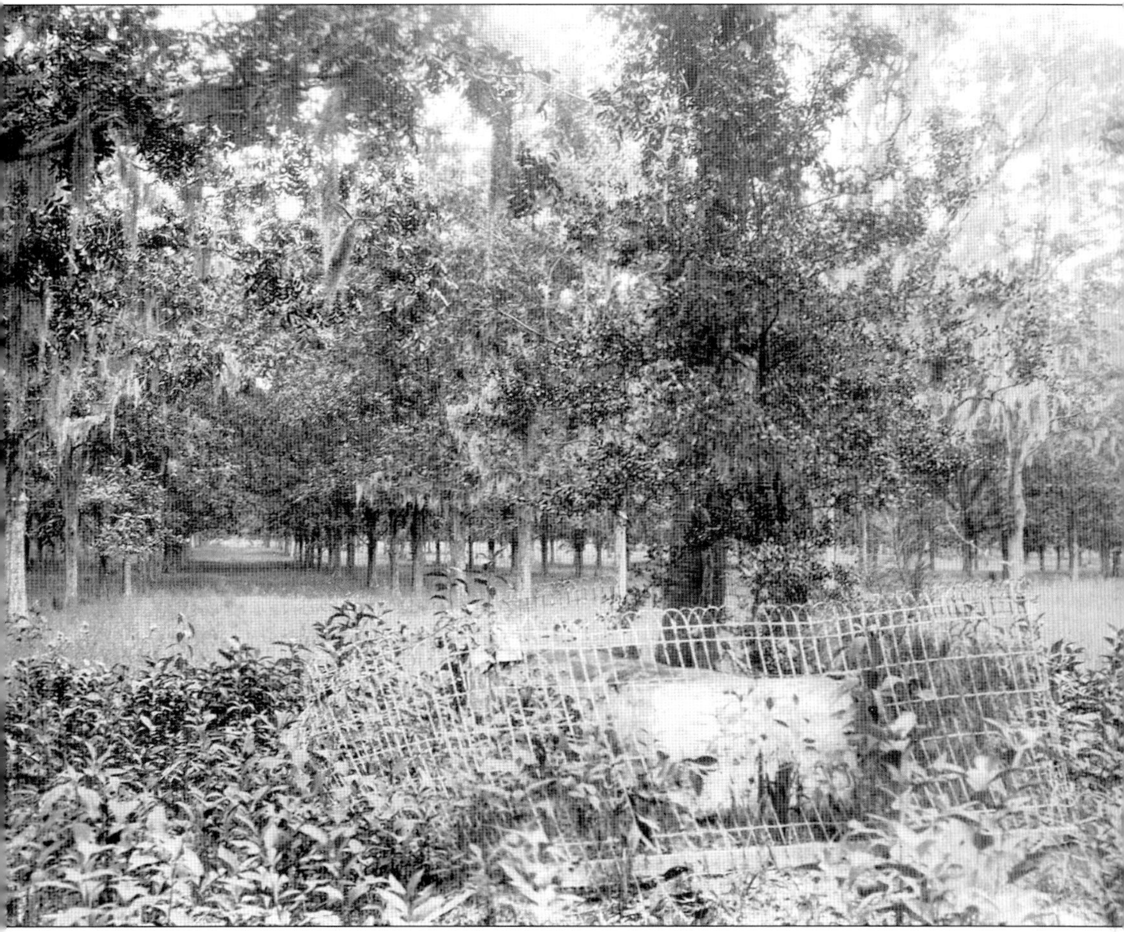

Capt. Thomas Boone, the son of John Boone who inherited Boone Hall after John Boone's death, was elected from Christ Church Parish to the Eighth Royal Assembly in 1730. Thomas Boone's grave resides along the drive under the magnolia trees. His is the only grave marked on the plantation. (Courtesy of the South Carolina Historical Society.)

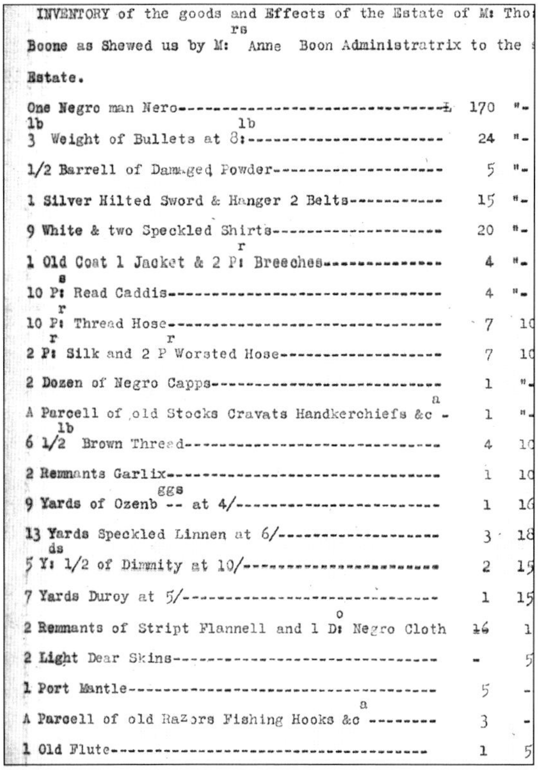

INVENTORY of the goods and Effects of the Estate of Mrs Thos Boone as Shewed us by Mr Anne Boon Administratrix to the Estate.

One Negro man Nero---------------------------------£	170	"-
3 lb Weight of Bullets at 8d------------------------	24	"-
1/2 Barrell of Damaged Powder---------------------	5	"-
1 Silver Hilted Sword & Hanger 2 Belts-----------	15	"-
9 White & two Speckled Shirts---------------------	20	"-
1 Old Coat 1 Jacket & 2 Pr Breeches--------------	4	"-
10 Prs Read Caddis----------------------------------	4	"-
10 Pr Thread Hose-----------------------------------	7	10
2 Pr Silk and 2 Pr Worsted Hose------------------	7	10
2 Dozen of Negro Capps----------------------------	1	"-
A Parcell of old Stocks Cravats Handkerchiefs &ca -	1	"-
6 1/2 lb Brown Thread------------------------------	4	10
2 Remnants Garlix----------------------------------	1	10
9 Yards of Ozenbggs -- at 4/----------------------	1	16
13 Yards Speckled Linnen at 6/-------------------	3	18
5 Yds 1/2 of Dimmity at 10/-----------------------	2	15
7 Yards Duroy at 5/---------------------------------	1	15
2 Remnants of Stript Flannell and 1 Do Negro Cloth	16	1
2 Light Dear Skins---------------------------------	-	5
1 Port Mantle--------------------------------------	5	-
A Parcell of old Razors Fishing Hooks &ca --------	3	-
1 Old Flute--	1	5

John Boone's son, Thomas, left a total of 55 slaves in his will—30 percent are men, 23 percent are women, 25 percent are boys and 22 percent are girls. Ages are not given but are determined by references to "Three men" or "Three women." Everything is listed, right down to his tools, furniture, and clothes. It is also interesting to note that the slaves are listed as material wealth, along with household goods such as brown thread, an old flute, and deerskins. (Courtesy of the Charleston County Public Library.)

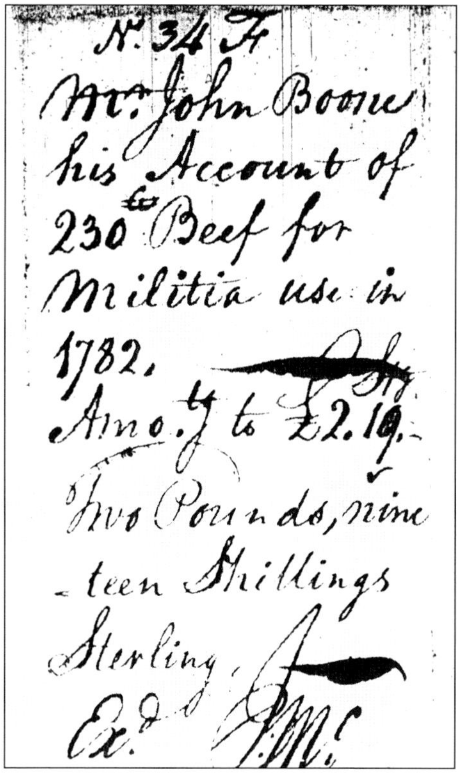

No. 34 F
Mr. John Boone
his Account of
230 lb Beef for
Militia use in
1782,
Amo.t to £2.19.-
Two Pounds, nine
-teen Shillings
Sterling,
Ex.d

Boone Hall Plantation played a supportive role in the Revolutionary War. John Boone supplied the army with beef, as is seen in this receipt to the government. Legend also has it that John Boone hid his cousin John Rutledge, governor of South Carolina, as he escaped northward from approaching British troops. (Courtesy of the South Carolina Department of Archives and History.)

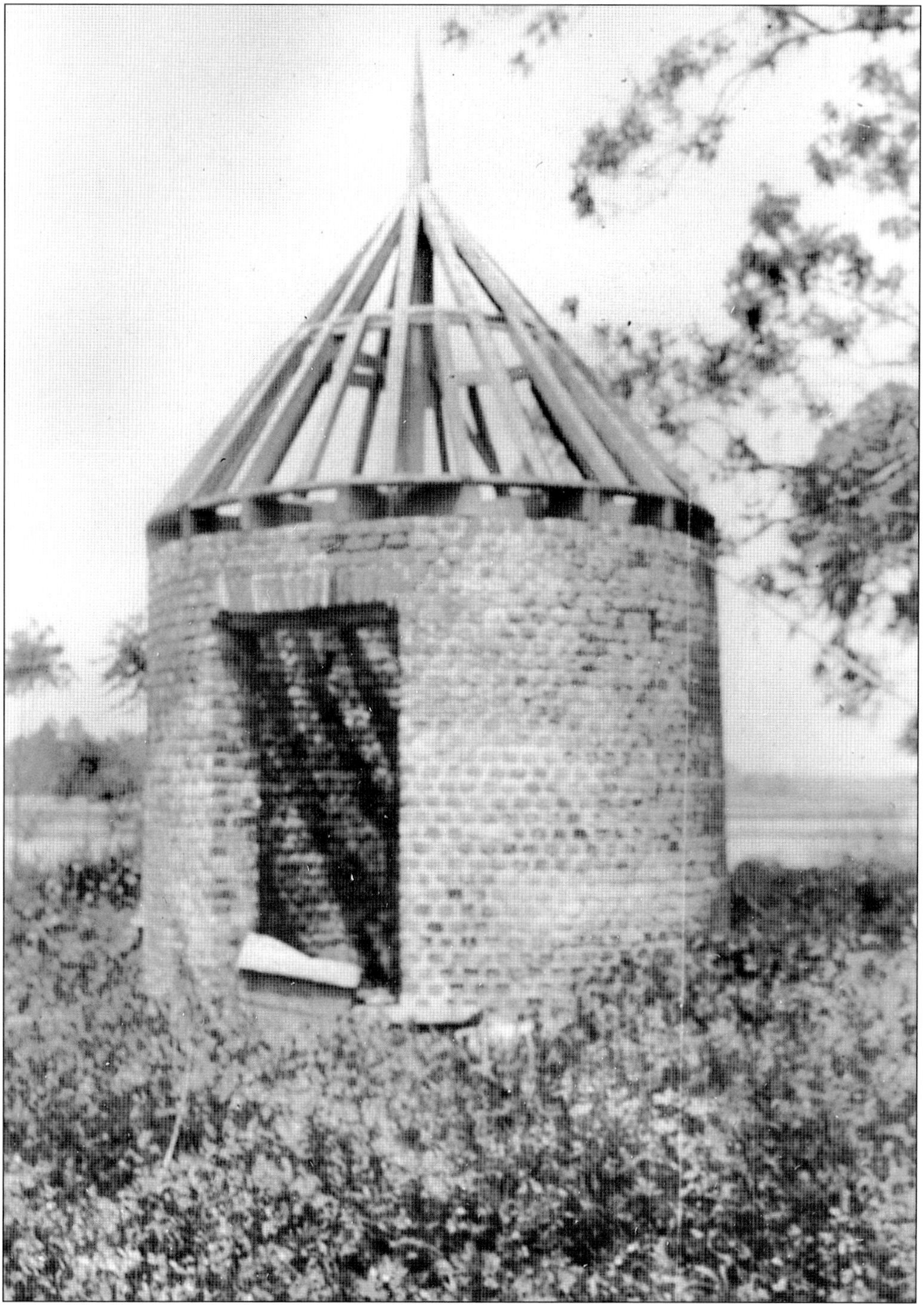

The smokehouse is the oldest building on the plantation and in the state, dating to the mid-1700s. A fire would be built in the center, and the smoke would drift out through a hole in the roof. The meat was hung from the roof and cured to preserve it for later use. A diamond pattern, which can be seen in the walls, was created by using bricks that are darker in color, which were closer to the fire in the kiln. (Courtesy of the South Carolina Historical Society.)

HEADS OF FAMILIES—SOUTH CAROLINA. 33

CHARLESTON DISTRICT, DORCHESTER COUNTY, ST. GEORGES PARISH—Continued.

CHARLESTON DISTRICT, CHRIST CHURCH PARISH.

NAME OF HEAD OF FAMILY.	Free white males of 16 years and upward, including heads of families.	Free white males under 16 years.	Free white females, including heads of families.	All other free persons.	Slaves.
Arther, Georg (Est*)					17
Arther, Nat (Est.)	1				24
Airs, Georg	1		2		8
Airs, Wm	1	1	1		7
Barksdale, Thos	1	1	5		89
Barksdale, Go	1	2	5		82
Buckel, Go	2		4		
Brown, C	2		1		11
Bonhoste, Jacob	1	1			17
Bonhoste, Wm (Est)	1	3	2		17
Baldwin, Esther	1		1		49
Bonneau, H. (Est*)	1				2
Bullock, Stephin	1		7		14
Bollough, James	2		1		32
Barton, Thomas (Est)	1	2	1		65
Barton, George	1	1			
Boon, John	1	1	4		40
Bennett, Henry	1		3		3
Bennett, Elizth	1	2	1		
Boldman, Obrh	1				
Capers, Gabrial	1		8		82
Capers, George	1	4	1		15
Cook, William	1	2	3		11
Cole, Sarah	1		3		3
Clealand, William	1	2			20
Crosby, Timth	1				9
Darr, Vallentine	1		3		5
Darr, Peter	1		2		7
Dunn, James	1	1	4		
Dorrill, John	1	3	1		8
Dorrill, William	1		4		12
Dorrill, Jonth (Est)	1	2	1		11
Dorrill, Joseph	3	3	2		20
Dorrill, Robt (Est)					19
Dewees, Andr	1	4	4		34
Dubose, Jonathan (Est)					1
Dubose, Isaac	1				6
Cooper, Dick		3	4		3
Eden, James, Junor	1	2	5		14
Eden, James	1	2	5		5
Eden, M. C	1		2		11
English, John	1	2	2		14
Evans, John	2	2	2		5
Evans, James	1	3	2		8
Eden, Rebeccah				1	12
Fowler, Joseph (Est)					9
Fowler, Richd. & Jo	3				2
Fowler, Michal	1				5
Froget, Adden	1		1		1
Flowrah (freewhench)				1	
Gowdy, William					5
Hibben, Andr (Est)	1	1	3		29
Hibben, James	1	2	2		7
Huggins, Eli	1	1	2		4
Huggins, William	1		3		12
Hartman, John	2		4		16
Hamlin, Hanner			2		5
Hamlin, William	1	4	4		26
Hamlin, Thomas	1		5		14
Hamlin, Mary			2		1
Huggins, Jos (Est)		4	1		33
Jon, Jacob B	1				134
Jeffords, Danl, Senr	1	2	5		12
Jeffords, Danl, Junr	1		2	1	15
Jeffords, Joseph (Est)					1
Joy, Richd (Est)			6		
Joy, Thomas	1	2	1	1	7
Joy, Cathariner	2		1	1	2
Joy, James	2		1	1	4
Legare, Isaac (Est)	3	1	1		12
Legare, Ann	1	1	2		23
Legare, John	1	1	2		4
Legare, Nathan	1		3		37
Leggett, John	1		1		1
Murrell, Thomas	1		1		7
Murrell, Sarah			1		3
Murrell, J. Jno	1		1		40
Murrell, John	1	3	4		58
Murrell, Robt Eo, Junr	1		1		14
Moon, Patrick	4	3	7		5
Maybank, Jos. (Est)			3	1	23
Guerin, Dr. Henry	1			1	5
Murrell, Hanner			1		2
McNellage, Allixd	1	4	1		10
Osendine, John	1	1			3
Player, Thomas	1	1	2		46
Player, Wm	2	3	2		2
Price, Wm (Est)	1			1	24
Rutledge, Sarah (Est)	1	1	1		64
Rowser, Richd	1		3		4

*Illegible.

The 1790 census is the first census record of the newly formed United State of America. Under John Boone's name is listed one free white man over 16, one free white man under 16, four free white women, and 40 slaves. In comparison to the other plantations in the parish, Boone Hall slaves are somewhere in the middle as far as number. (Courtesy of the Charleston County Public Library.)

Two

THE HORLBECKS

One family that exists in the footnotes of Charleston history is the Horlbeck family, which owned Boone Hall Plantation in the 19th century. The Horlbecks literally helped build the city with one of the largest and longest running brickyards in the Charleston area, but little is known of the family. The Charleston Horlbeck family began in Leibnitz, Germany. John Adam Horlbeck was born on February 11, 1729. It is unknown when he arrived in Charleston, but he and his brother, Peter, established a construction business in Charleston by 1754. John married 29-year-old Elizabeth Geiger on February 25, 1769. John and Peter both joined the German Friendly Society and supported the patriots during the Revolutionary War. John was cited in family genealogy as fighting at the Siege of Savannah. He had two sons: John Jr., born in 1771, and Henry, born in 1776. These brothers also became involved in the family business. John Sr. and Peter continued to help Charleston grow, with their business building notable structures such as the Old Exchange Building. The younger Horlbeck brothers also built significant structures such as St. John's Lutheran Church and St. Stephen's Episcopal Church. The brothers also purchased a plantation in Christ Church Parish previously owned by the Boone family for five generations. The Boones sold the plantation due to an internal squabble over inheritance. The plantation was left to a minor son, and his older sisters and their husbands sued the estate for equal shares. The plantation was sold as a result.

There are few photographs of the Horlbecks and fewer of the slaves the Horlbecks owned. Most of what is known about any of the inhabitants of the plantation throughout the 19th century is through documents, whether it be census records, inventory lists, wills, or bills of sale. These documents are the key to unlocking the stories of the lives that passed through Boone Hall. The included photographs illustrating brick production are from the Charleston Brick Company around 1950.

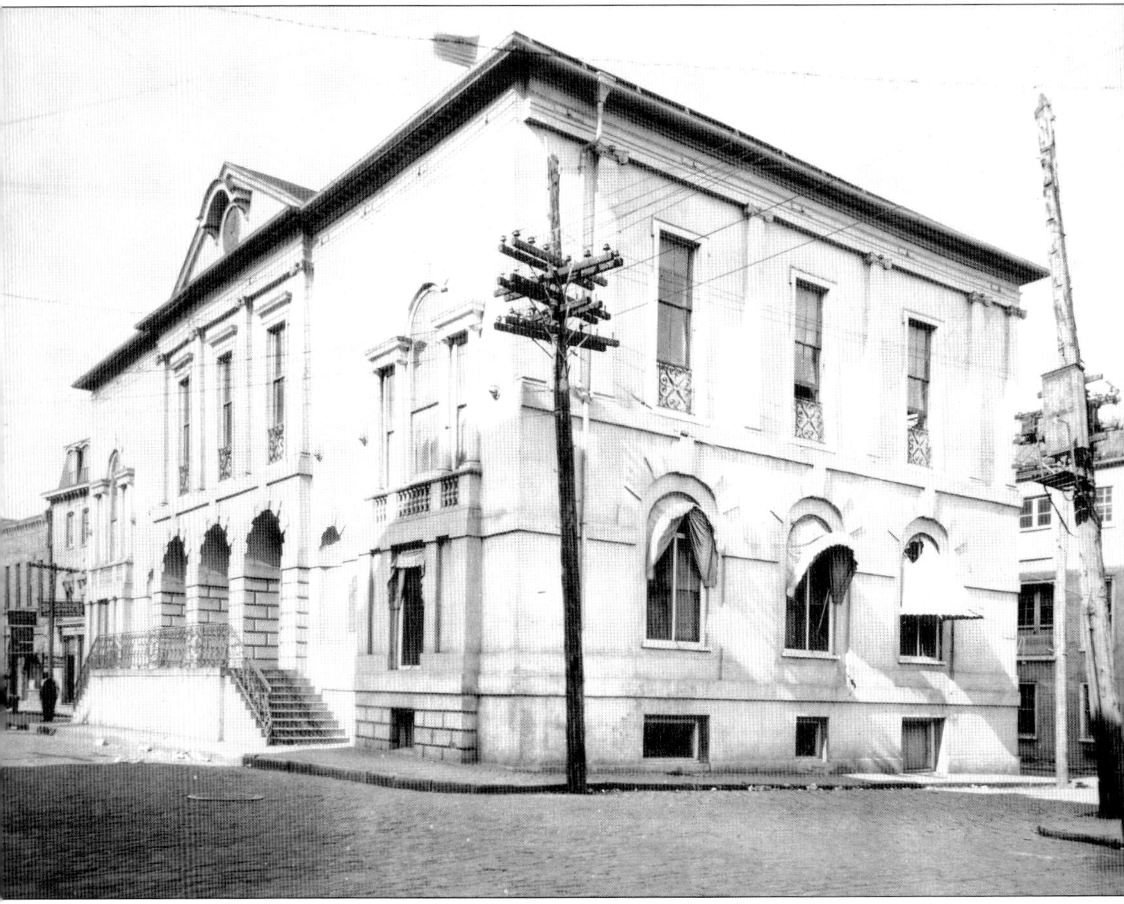

The Old Exchange Building and Custom House was built in 1767–1771. William Naylor was the architect, and it was constructed by brothers Peter and John Adam Horlbeck, German-born masons. The Exchange is built on the site of the Court of Guard, where Stede Bonnet, the "Gentleman Pirate," was imprisoned in 1718. (Courtesy of the Charleston County Public Library.)

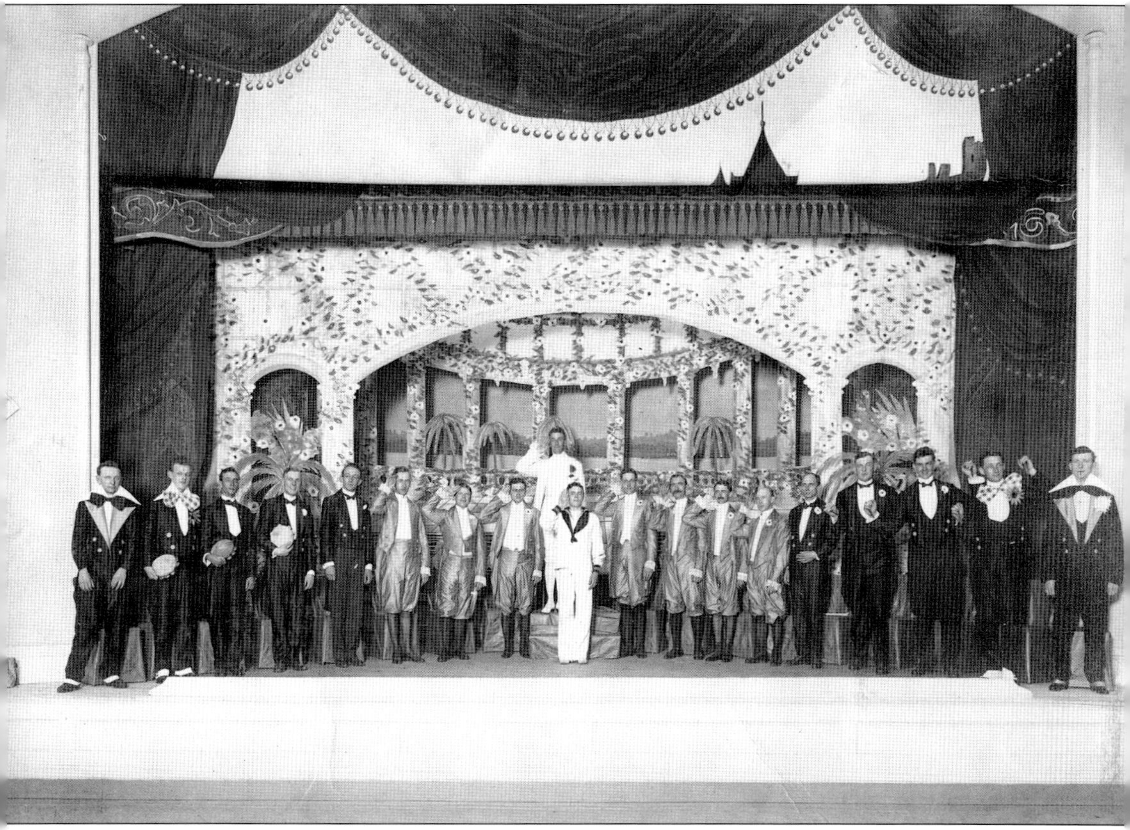

The Horlbeck brothers were members of the German Friendly Society and also built the society hall. Founded by members of St. John's Lutheran Church in 1766, the German Friendly Society gave assistance to new immigrants and aid to orphans and widows. The original society hall was located at 27 Archdale Street until 1864 when it burned in a fire believed to have been started by a Federal shell. Pictured are members of the society in their hall. (Courtesy of the South Carolina Historical Society.)

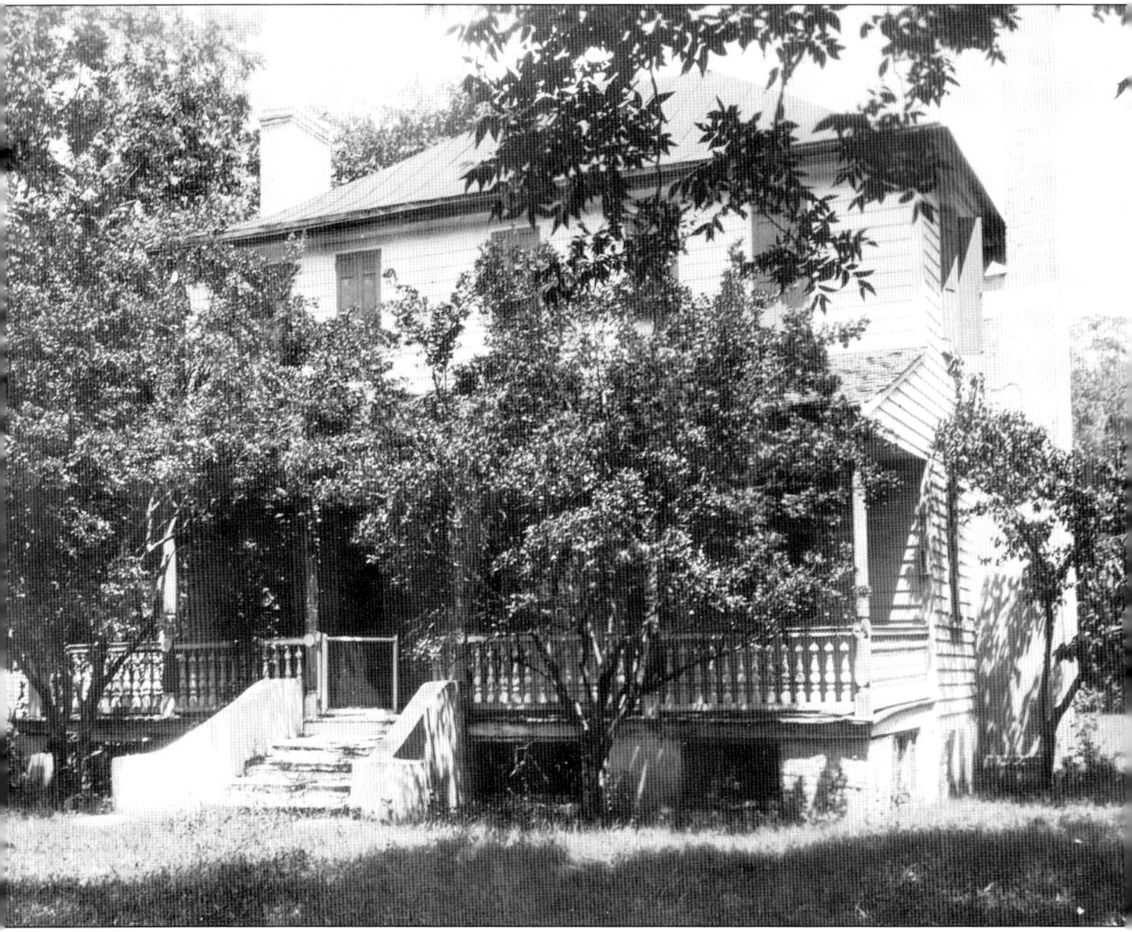

The previous plantation house at Boone Hall was a typical Southern farmhouse. Many of the earlier plantation homes found in the Lowcountry were similar in style. This house is characteristic of the time period and not as grand as the houses often portrayed in movies. The exact date of the house in unknown, but it probably dates to the mid to late 18th century. (Courtesy of the South Carolina Historical Society.)

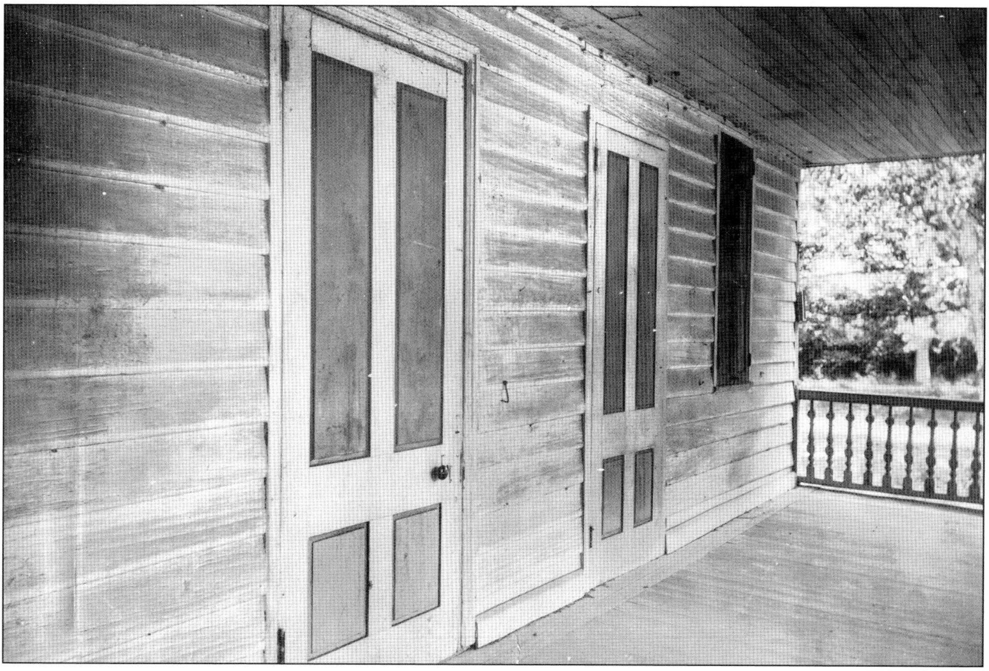

Double front doors can also be found on many Southern plantation homes. The simplicity of the plantation house can be felt from this view of the porch. The doors lack the ornate woodwork one would expect of a Southern plantation. The home illustrates a rural farmhouse where little entertaining is done. (Courtesy of the South Carolina Historical Society.)

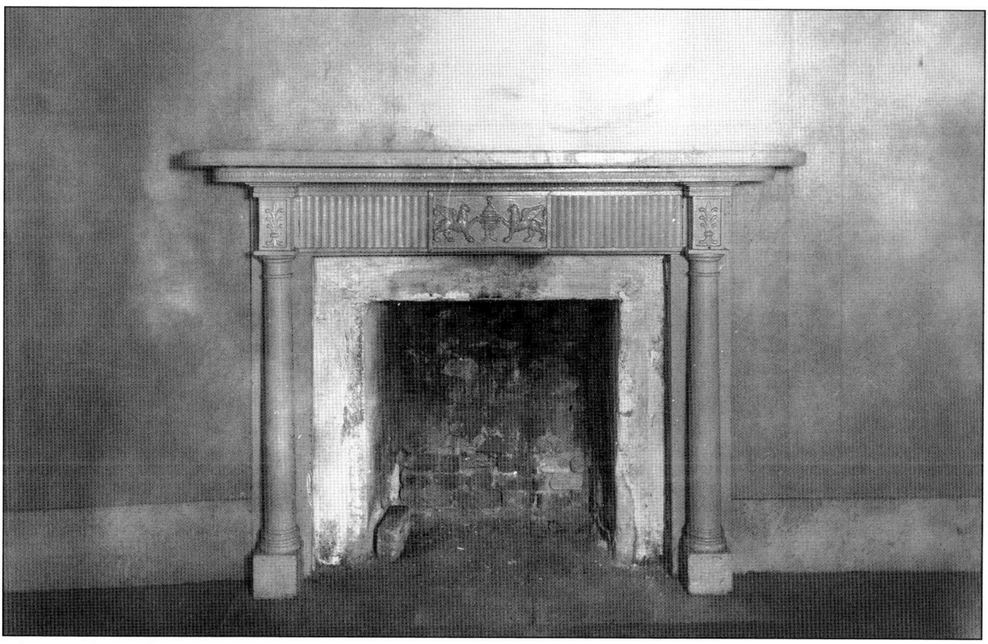

This is the only photograph of the inside of the previous plantation house. It is unknown how much the house itself was used. It is possible that the family may have only occasionally used the house, if at all. According to census records, the house continued to be listed as the Frederick Horlbeck Estate. (Courtesy of the South Carolina Historical Society.)

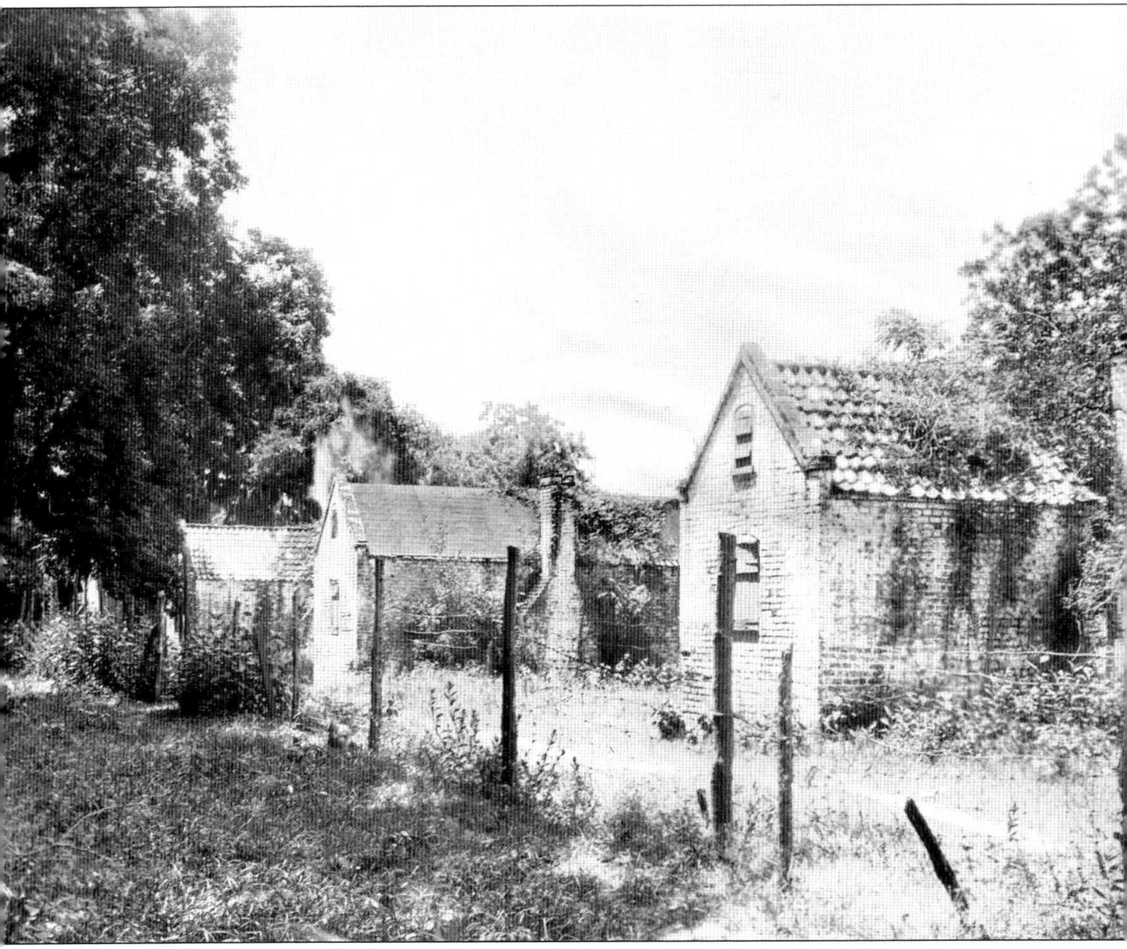

The slave cabins were built around 1800. They are built in front of the plantation house as a sign of wealth, since this is also the entrance to the plantation. Many plantations had the front of the house facing the waterway because that was the normal entry location. Boone Hall's dock has always been in the same location, so the house has always faced the way guests would arrive. (Courtesy of the South Carolina Historical Society.)

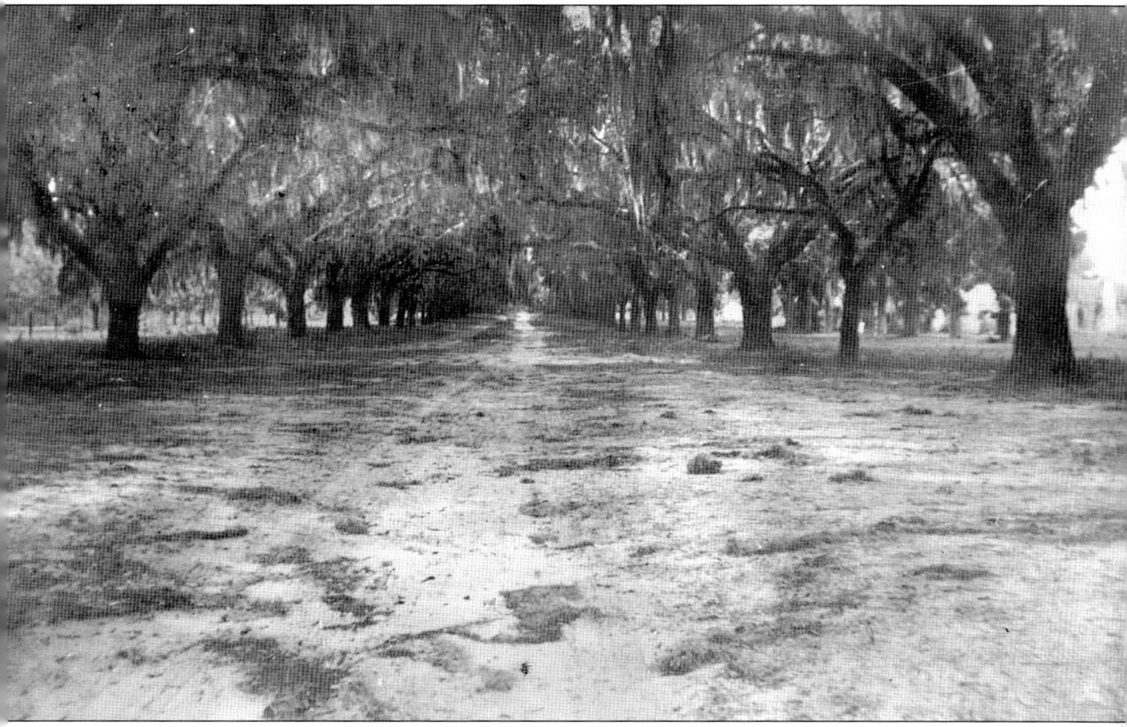

The initial planting of the avenue is credited to Thomas Boone. Many of the oaks are considerably larger closer to the house, indicating their advanced age. The Horlbecks continued the planting in the mid-19th century, creating a stunning drive that is still enjoyed today. (Courtesy of the South Carolina Historical Society.)

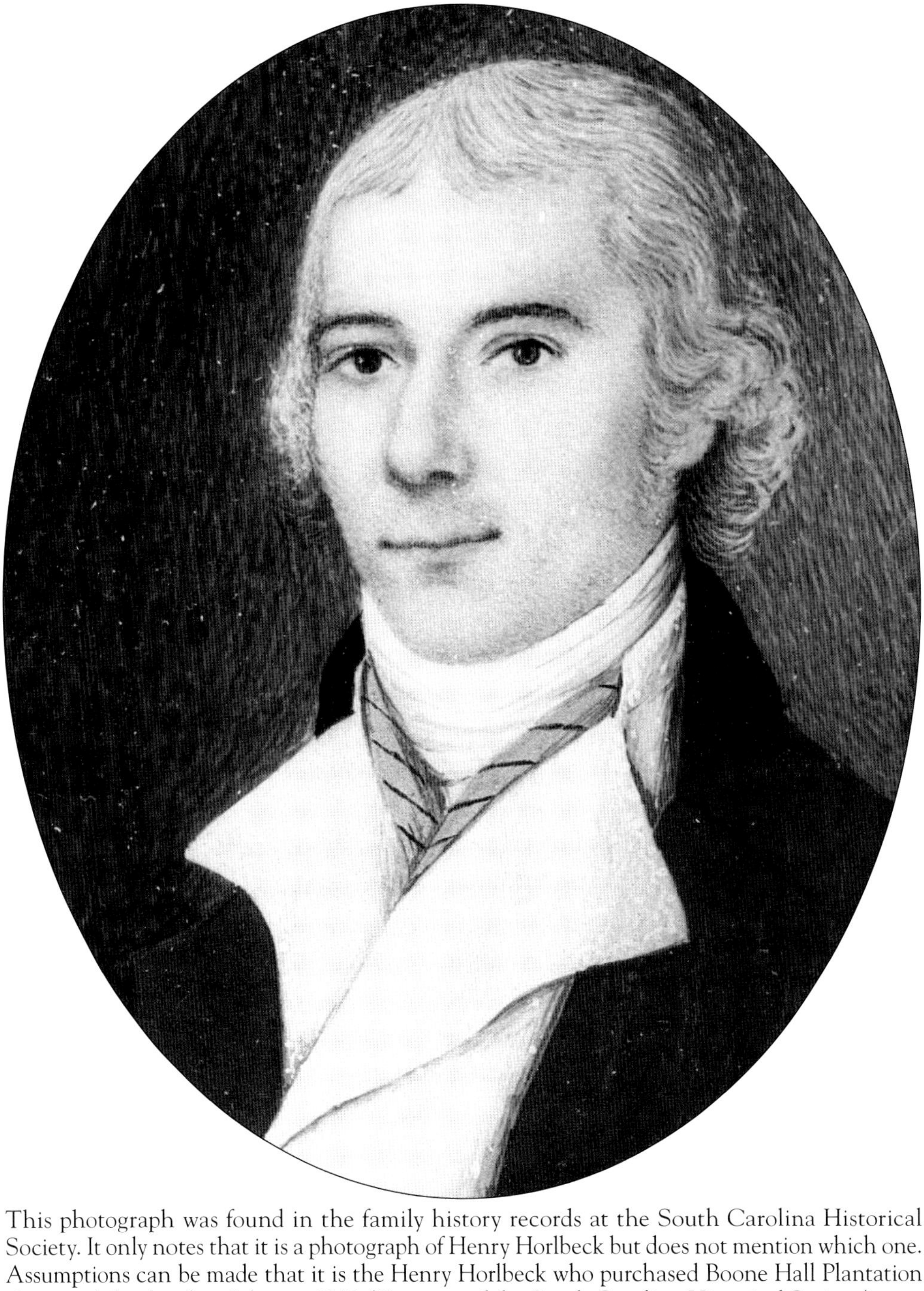

This photograph was found in the family history records at the South Carolina Historical Society. It only notes that it is a photograph of Henry Horlbeck but does not mention which one. Assumptions can be made that it is the Henry Horlbeck who purchased Boone Hall Plantation along with his brother, John, in 1817. (Courtesy of the South Carolina Historical Society.)

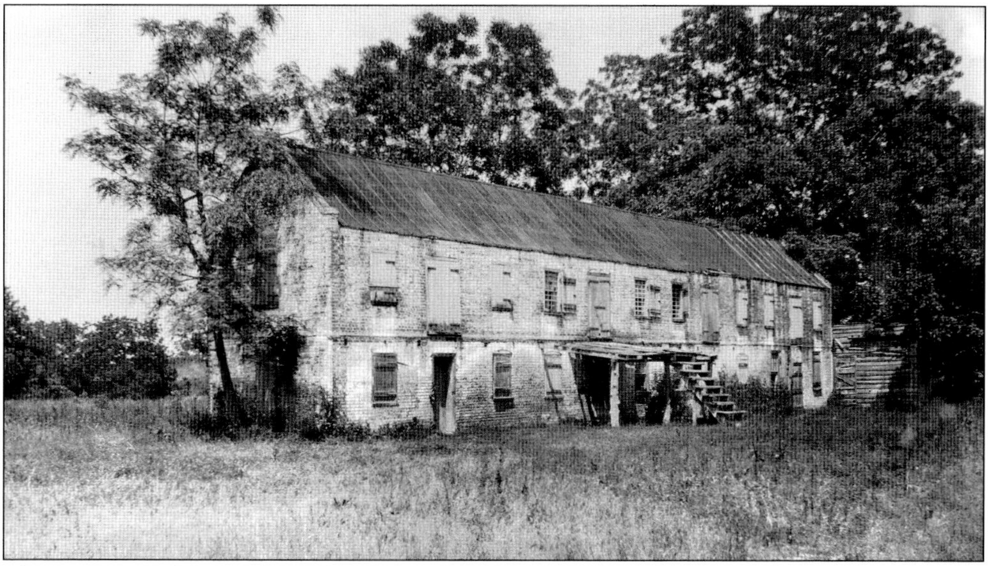

The Gin House dates to the mid-1800s. This building was originally used to gin the cotton grown on the plantation. Over the years, this building has been used to store cotton and as a guesthouse, a restaurant, and a gift shop. (Courtesy of the South Carolina Historical Society.)

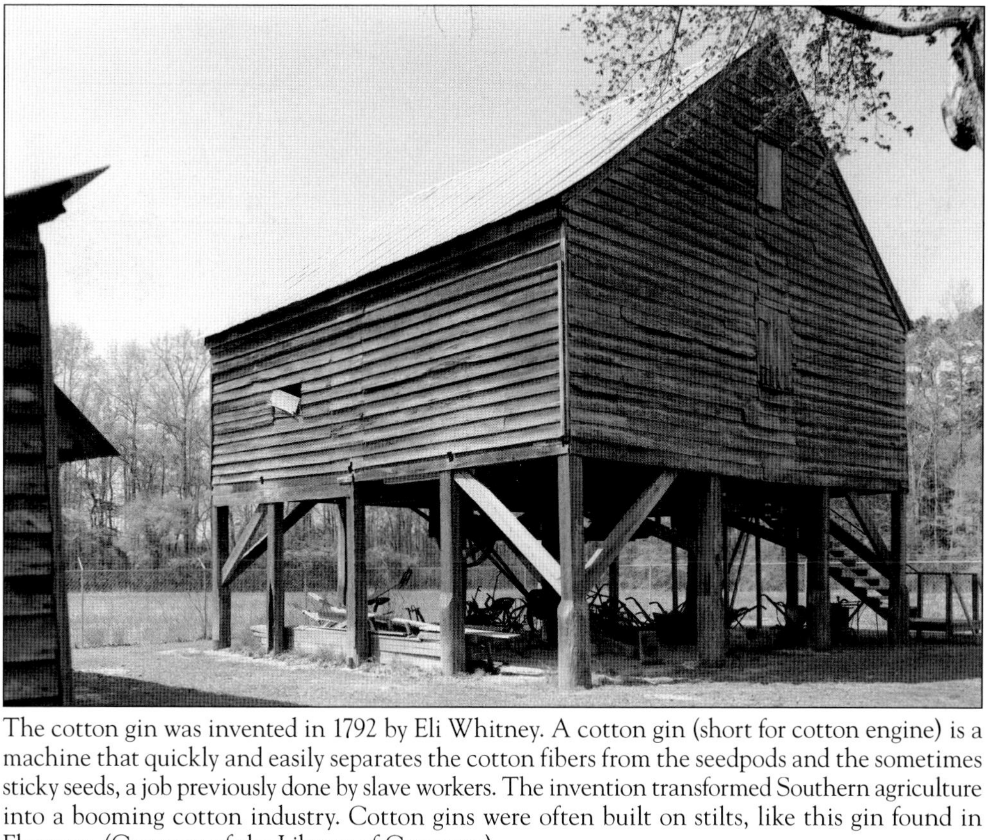

The cotton gin was invented in 1792 by Eli Whitney. A cotton gin (short for cotton engine) is a machine that quickly and easily separates the cotton fibers from the seedpods and the sometimes sticky seeds, a job previously done by slave workers. The invention transformed Southern agriculture into a booming cotton industry. Cotton gins were often built on stilts, like this gin found in Florence. (Courtesy of the Library of Congress.)

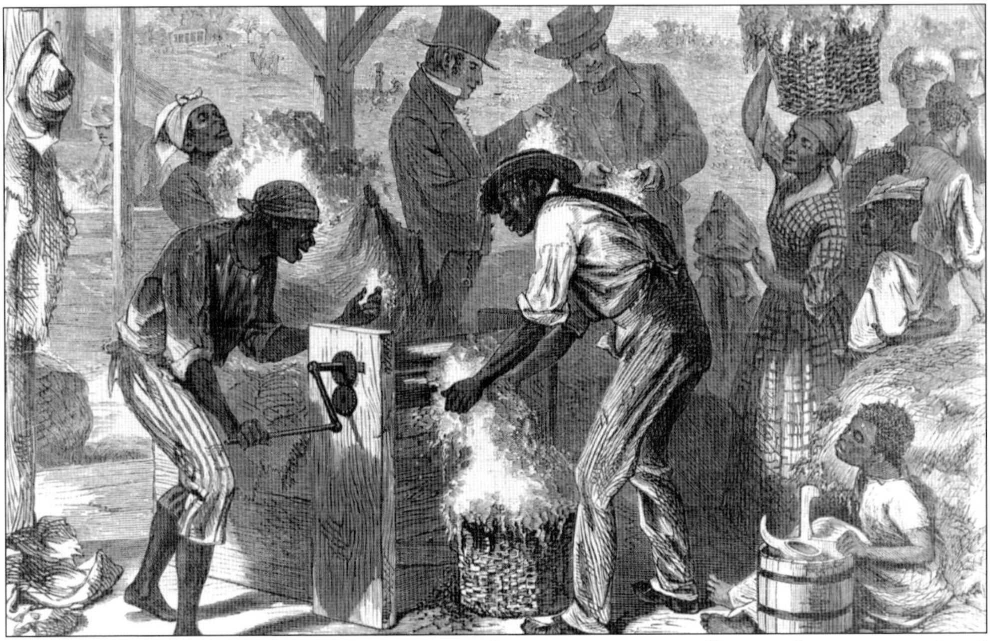

Eli Whitney failed to profit from his invention because imitations of his machine appeared and his 1794 patent for the cotton gin could not be upheld in court until 1807. Whitney could not stop others from copying and selling his cotton gin design. He spent many years in court attempting to enforce his patent against planters who made unauthorized copies. A change in patent law ultimately made his claim legally enforceable—too late for him to make much money off of the device in the single year remaining before the patent's expiration. (Courtesy of the Library of Congress.)

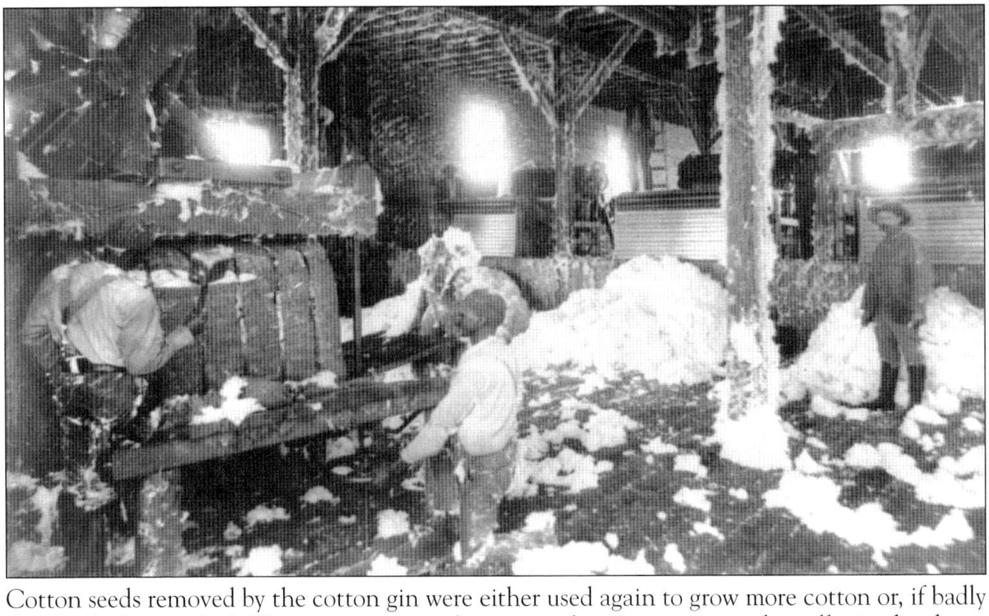

Cotton seeds removed by the cotton gin were either used again to grow more cotton or, if badly damaged, disposed of. The gin uses a combination of a wire screen and small wire hooks to pull the cotton through the screen, while brushes continuously remove the loose cotton lint to prevent jams. This photograph is an example of a cotton gin from Mississippi. (Courtesy of the Library of Congress.)

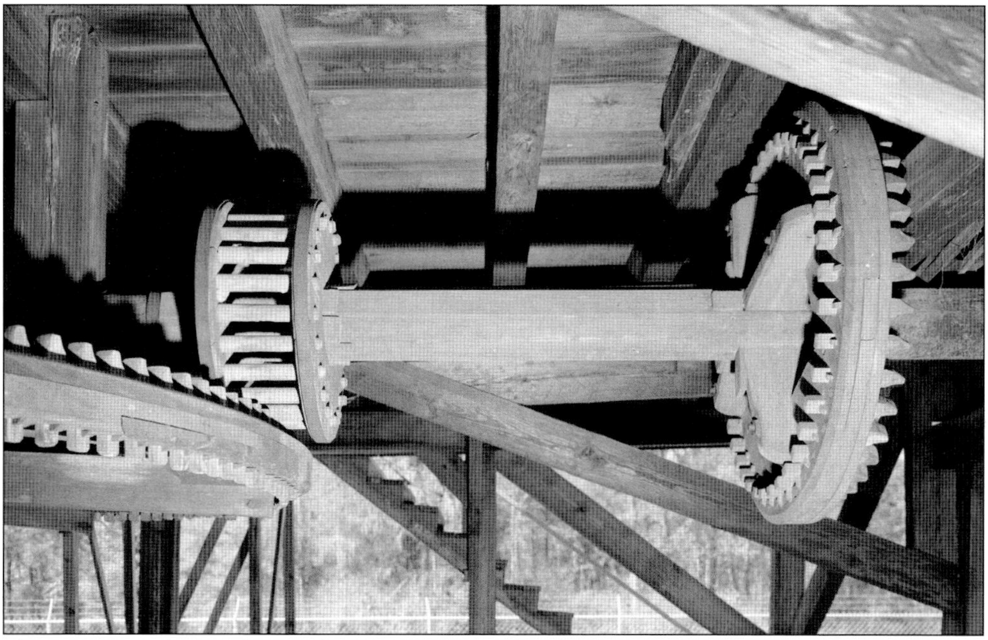

Plantation gins before the Civil War were primarily sold to farmers who installed them on their own property and used them to gin their own cotton. The newspapers of the time were full of the testimonials of planters discussing the merits of particular gins and how the processed fiber graded for price in the market. The machinery pictured here is found at the Browntown Cotton Gin in Florence. (Courtesy of the Library of Congress.)

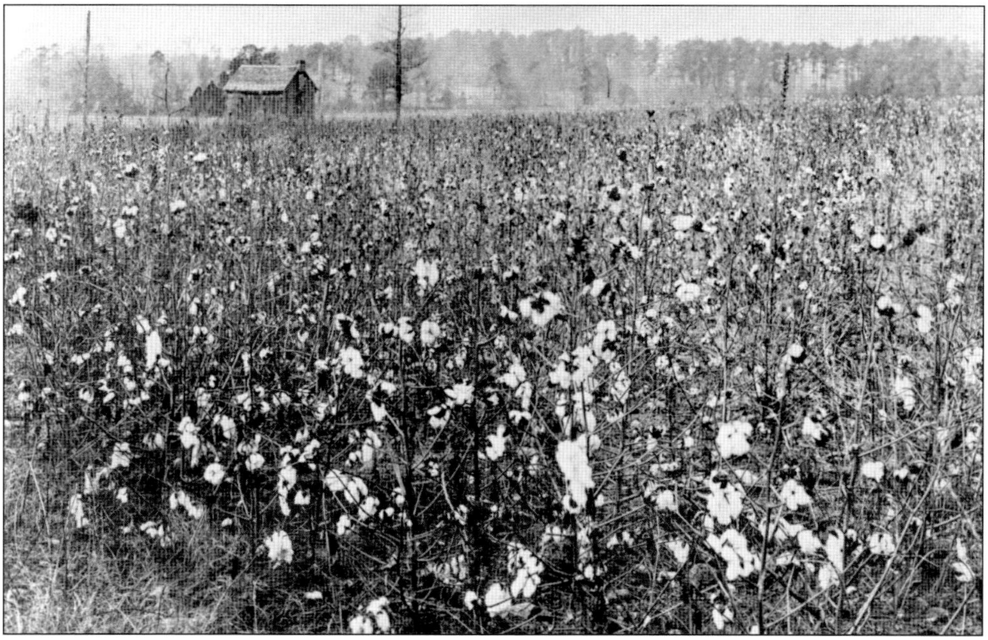

Cotton was a labor-intensive crop that required long days for slaves, usually about 12 hours working in the fields and even longer during harvest times. Both men and women worked in the cotton fields, as well as children. Children were considered half hands until they turned 12, at which time they were considered full hands. (Courtesy of the Library of Congress.)

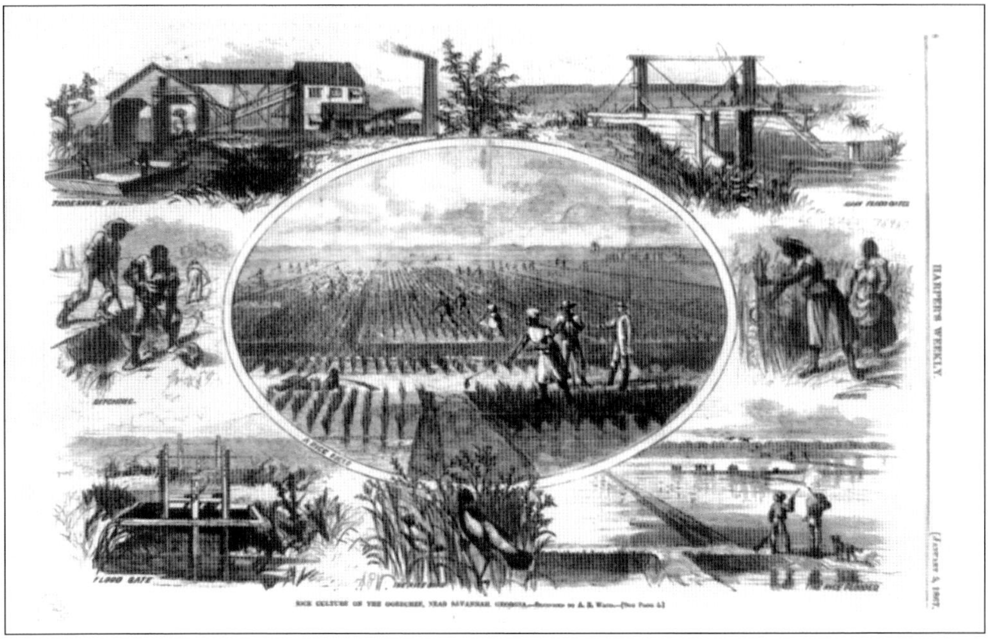

From the slaves, plantation owners learned how to dike the marshes and periodically flood the fields to grow rice. At first the rice was milled by hand with wooden paddles, then winnowed in sweetgrass baskets (the making of which was another skill brought by the slaves). The predominant strain of rice in the Carolinas was from Africa and was known as Carolina Gold. (Courtesy of the Library of Congress.)

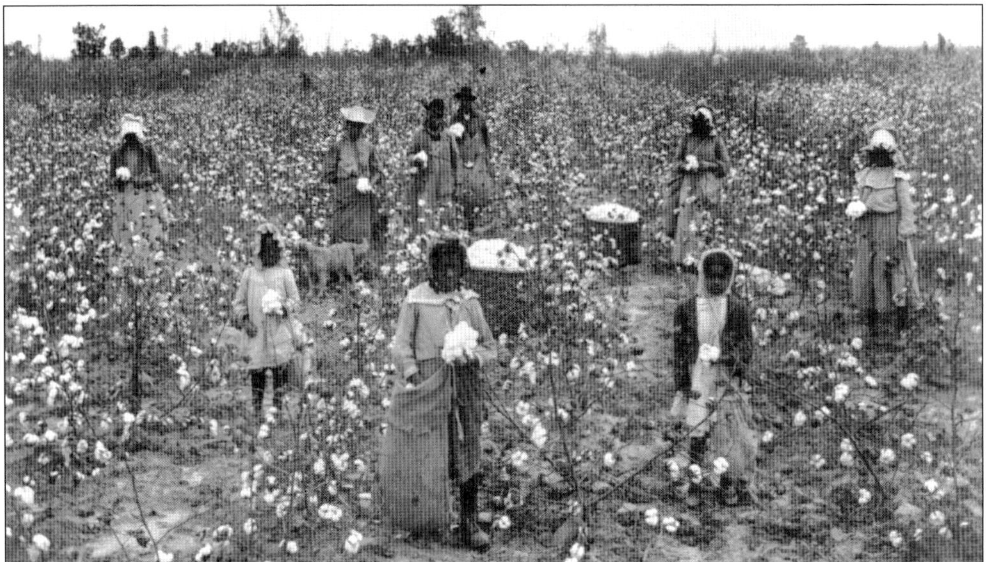

After the Civil War, sharecropping evolved, as illustrated here by this Georgia cotton field. Free black farmers worked on white-owned cotton plantations in return for a share of the profits. Cotton plantations required vast labor forces to hand-pick cotton fibers, and it was not until the 1950s that reliable harvesting machinery was introduced into the South. During the early 20th century, employment in the cotton industry fell as machines began to replace laborers and as the South's rural labor force dwindled during the world wars. (Courtesy of the Library of Congress.)

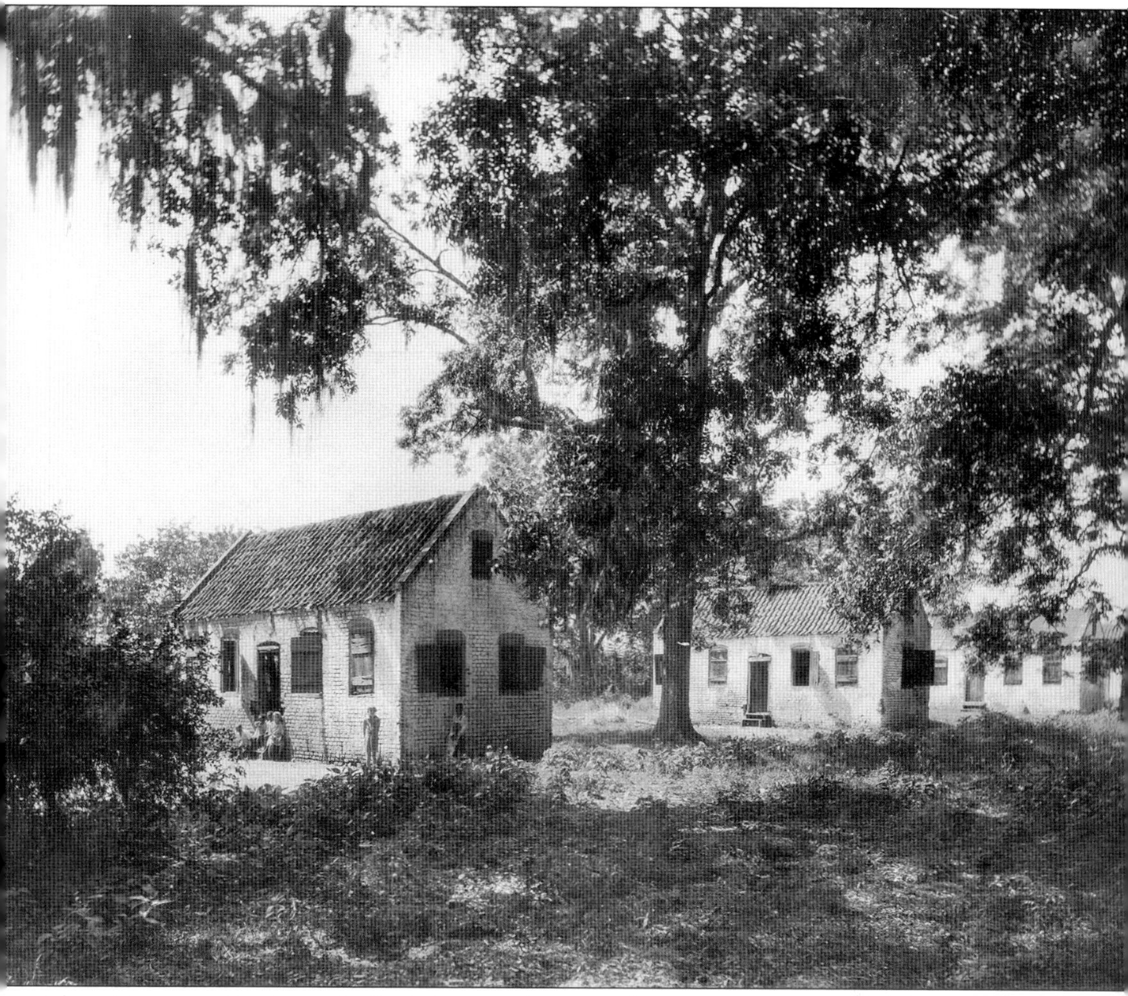

The 1820 census lists both Horlbeck brothers living in Charleston County, with John owning 25 slaves and Henry owning 40. Interestingly enough, both brothers own the same amount of female slaves, while John's male slaves are twice the number of his female slaves. Henry lists 10 manufacturers in his household, and John lists 29. It is possible that Henry is in residence at Boone Hall, since sex ratios are generally equal among workers at plantation brickyards. Pictured are slave cabins made of brick. (Courtesy of the South Carolina Historical Society.)

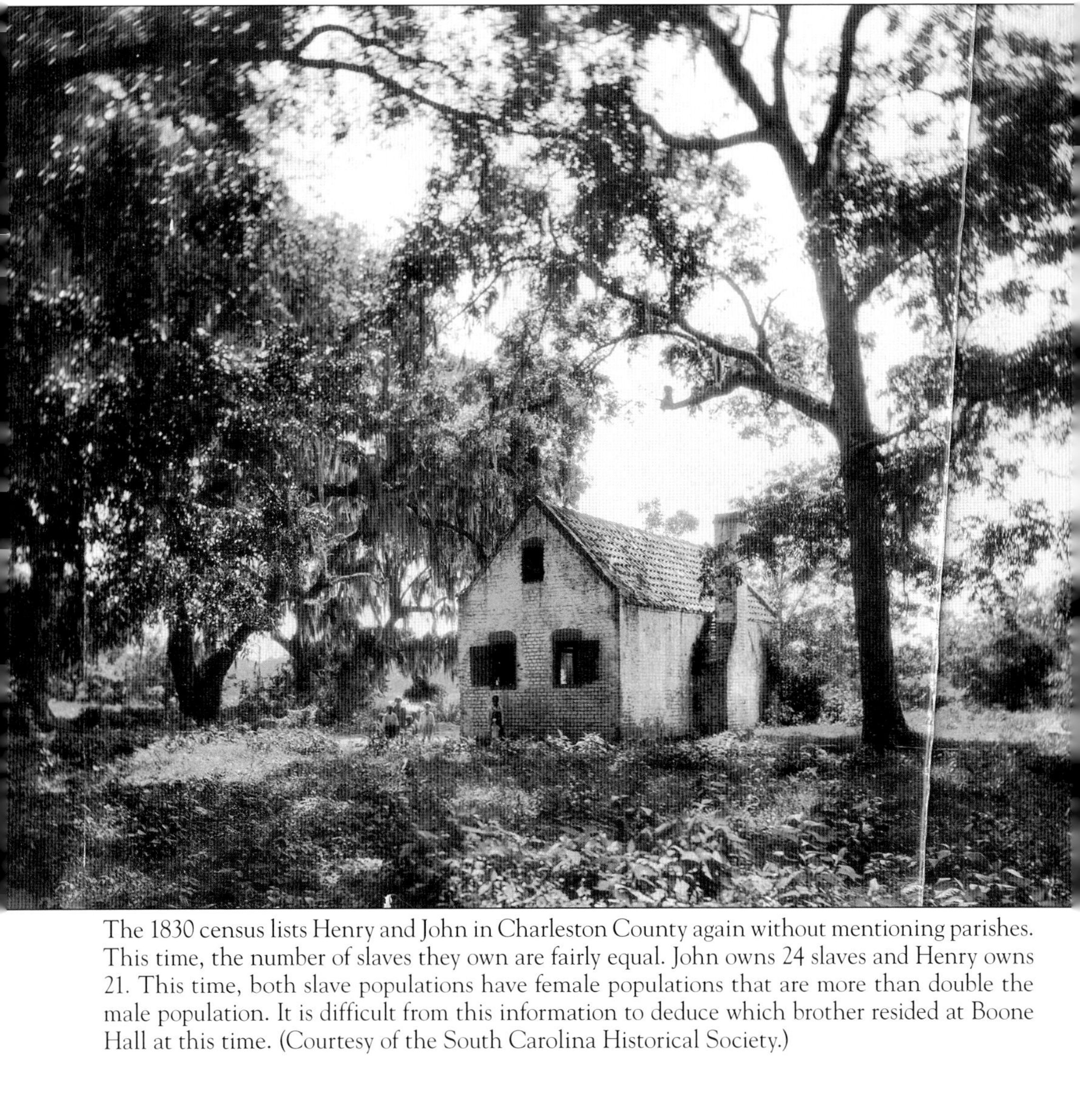

The 1830 census lists Henry and John in Charleston County again without mentioning parishes. This time, the number of slaves they own are fairly equal. John owns 24 slaves and Henry owns 21. This time, both slave populations have female populations that are more than double the male population. It is difficult from this information to deduce which brother resided at Boone Hall at this time. (Courtesy of the South Carolina Historical Society.)

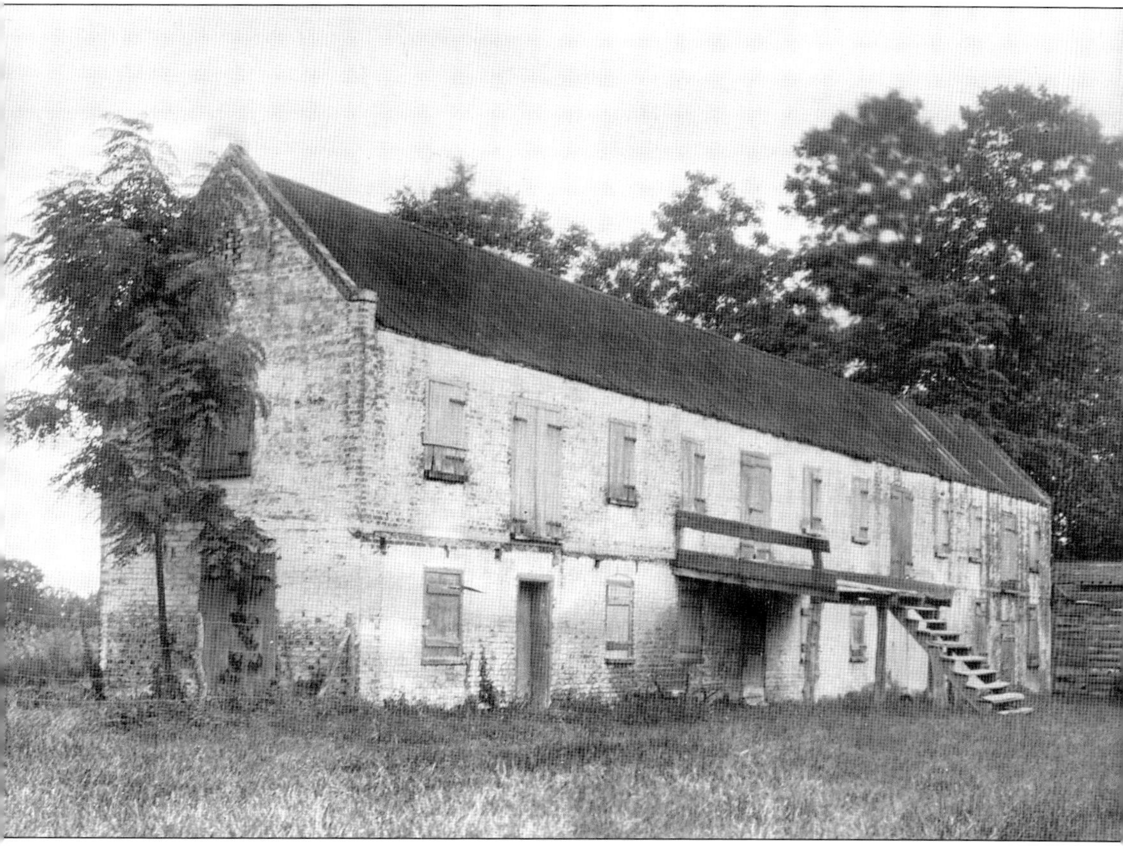

John and Henry have died by the 1840 census. John Horlbeck Jr. dies without children, but Henry has 11. The property goes to four of Henry's sons: John, Henry, Daniel, and Edward. The slaves now number 113 for the estate, and this is a consistent number for the plantation for the next few years. (Courtesy of the South Carolina Historical Society.)

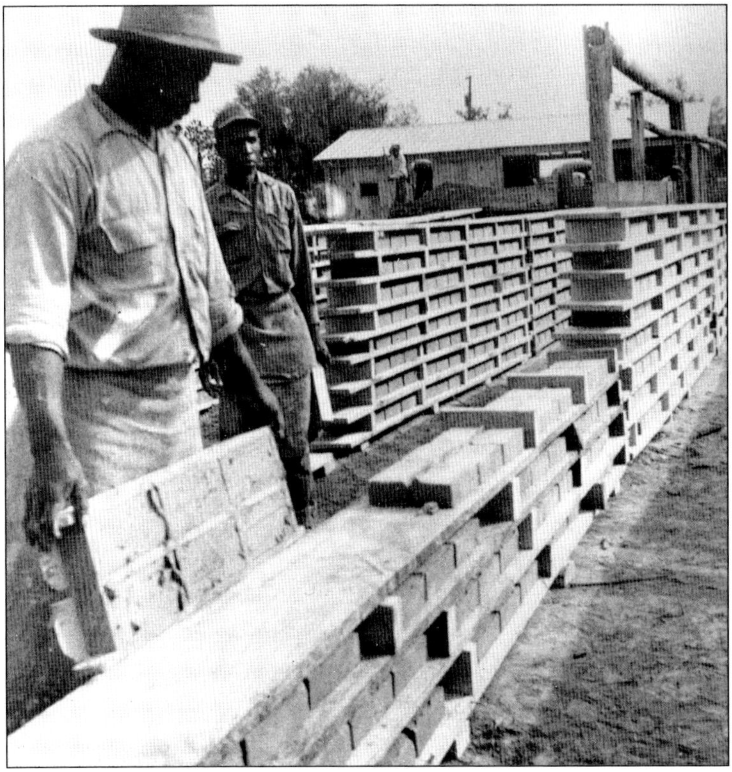

Over 50 brickyards existed in the Charleston area along the Ashley, Cooper, and Wando Rivers, and almost half of these brick makers were located along the Wando River by the late 18th century. The soil had all the necessary requirements to produce brick, including easy access to the Charleston market. The brick industry was a seasonal production that could easily be worked into an agricultural schedule. (Courtesy of the South Carolina Historical Society.)

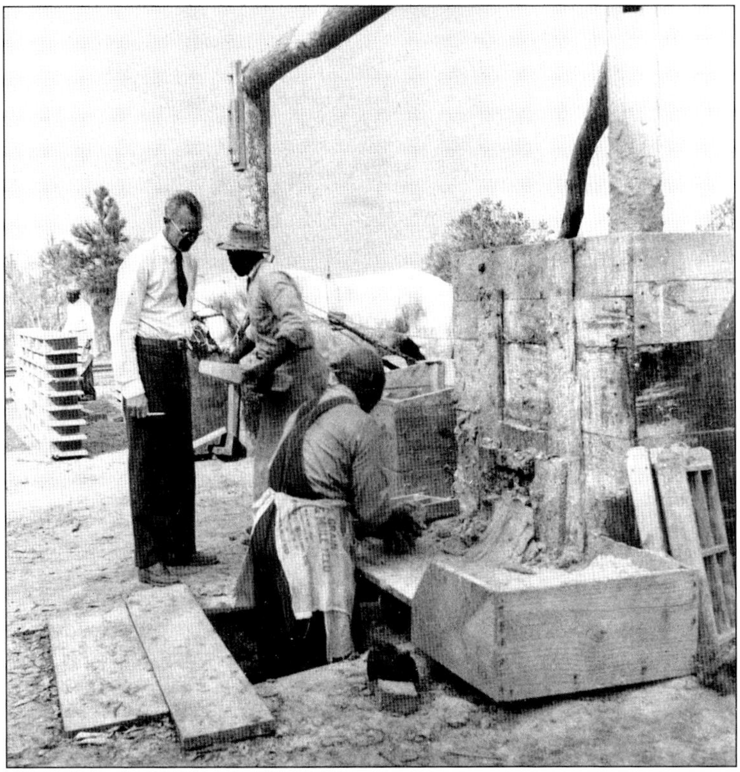

Bricks were created from clay found along the creek beds mixed with sand and water. After being placed in single and double molds to dry in the sun for several days, the bricks were placed into kilns to bake and were fired for several more days. Mortar was then created from clay, sometimes with crushed shells, or tabby, mixed in. Modern-day cement has been found to cause deterioration in the soft brick. (Courtesy of the South Carolina Historical Society.)

By the census of 1850, only nine brickyards existed from the original 50 in the Charleston area, producing over nine million bricks in 1849 alone using a total of 288 slaves. The Horlbeck brickyard employed 50 male hands and 35 female hands, producing four million bricks valued at $28,000. Between the years of 1850 to 1860, the average annual production was 2,266,551 bricks valued at an annual average $15,558.54. (Courtesy of the South Carolina Historical Society.)

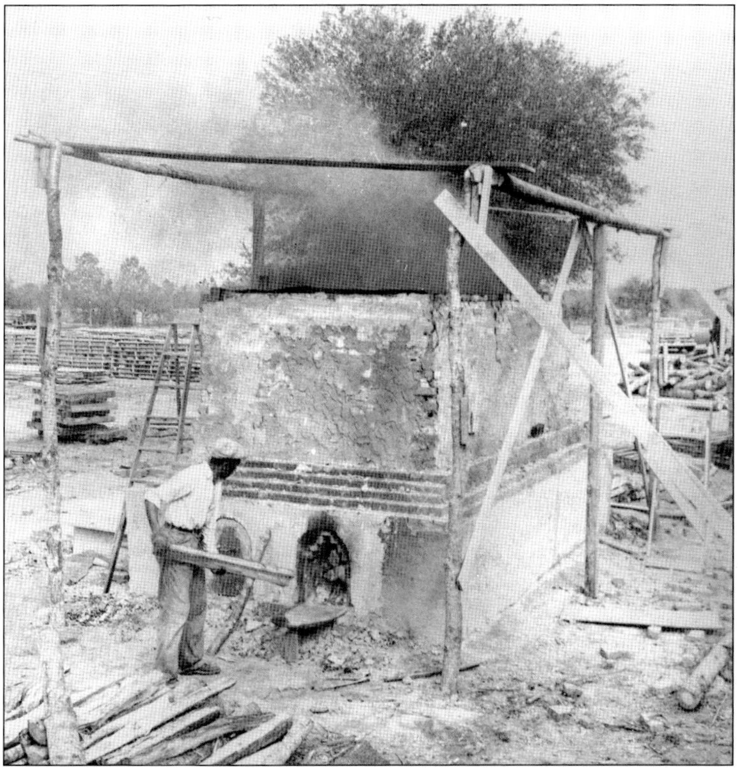

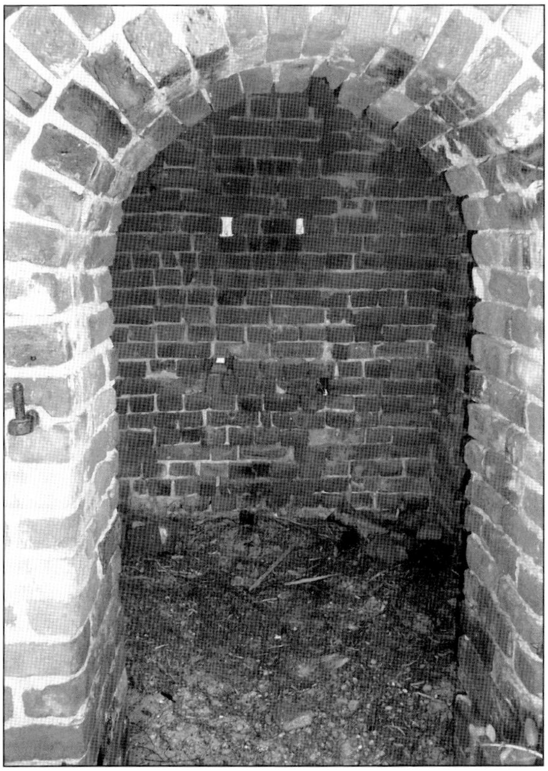

Boone Hall was the longest running brickyard in the region, operating until the late 19th century, and the high production of bricks at Boone Hall may have shut down the other businesses. After the Civil War, John Horlbeck purchased an additional brickyard on Parker Island to increase production. This image is of an existing chimney of a brick kiln at Boone Hall. (Courtesy of Michelle Adams.)

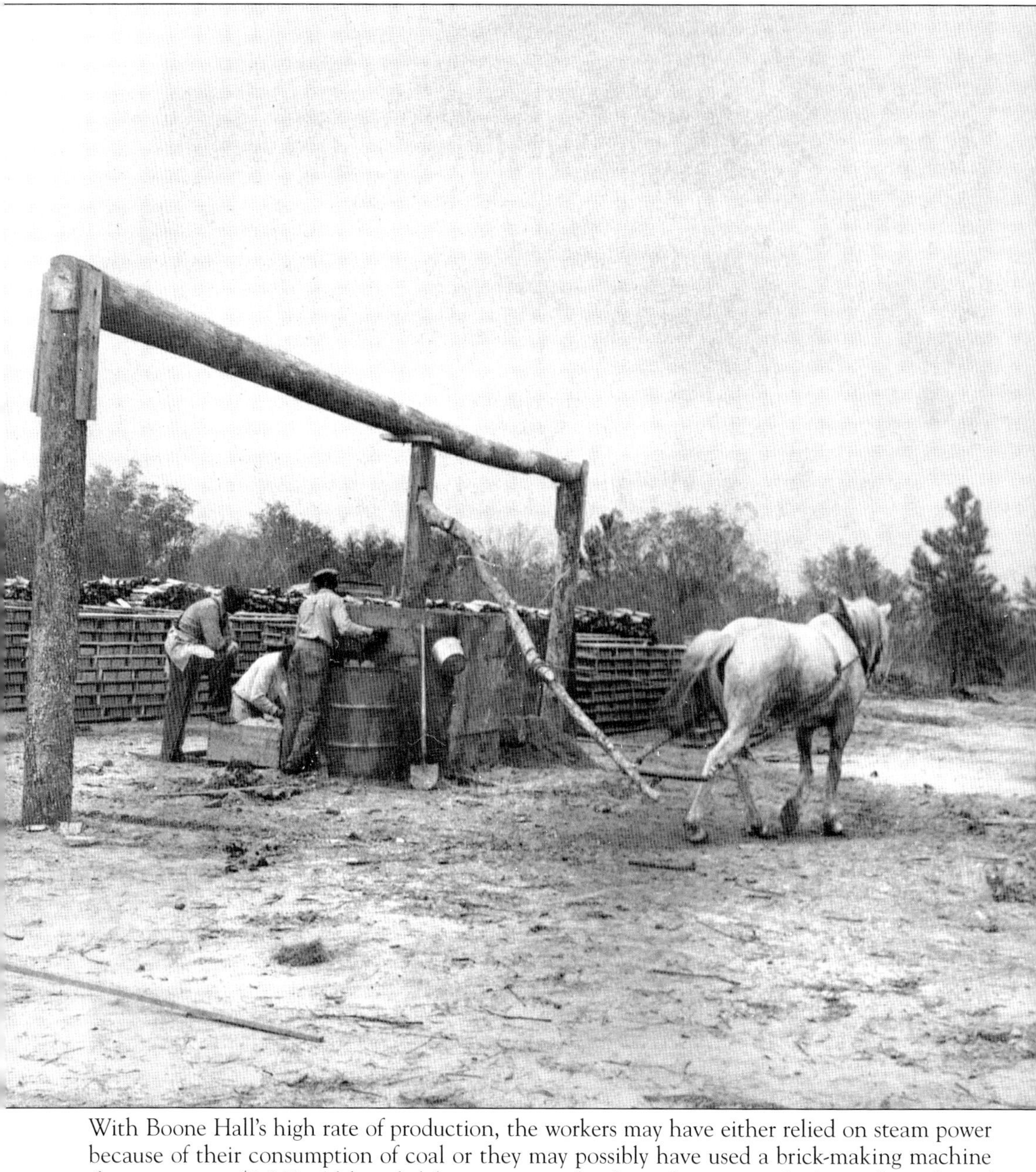

With Boone Hall's high rate of production, the workers may have either relied on steam power because of their consumption of coal or they may possibly have used a brick-making machine that costs over $1,000. Although labor intensive, brick production used a limited number of slaves, could be done seasonally, and financially equaled plantation cash crops. Daily activities included molding, hauling wood, carting clay, and loading and unloading the kiln. Pictured is a brick oven. (Courtesy of the South Carolina Historical Society.)

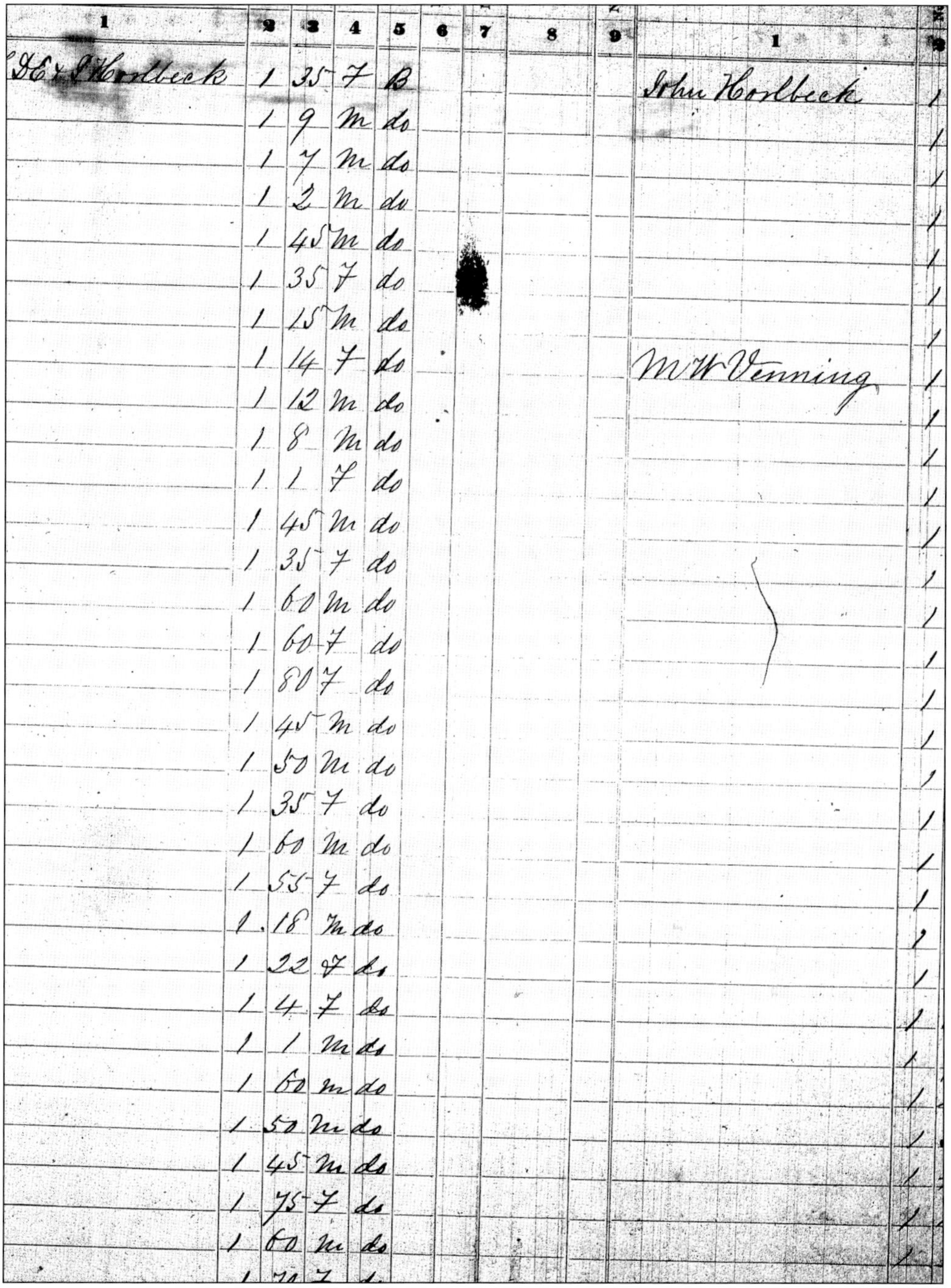

1	2	3	4	5	6	7	8	9
D E & S Horlbeck	1	35	F	B				
	1	9	M	do				
	1	7	M	do				
	1	2	M	do				
	1	45	M	do				
	1	35	F	do				
	1	15	M	do				
	1	14	F	do				
	1	12	M	do				
	1	8	M	do				
	1	1	F	do				
	1	45	M	do				
	1	35	F	do				
	1	60	M	do				
	1	60	F	do				
	1	80	F	do				
	1	45	M	do				
	1	50	M	do				
	1	35	F	do				
	1	60	M	do				
	1	55	F	do				
	1	18	M	do				
	1	22	F	do				
	1	4	F	do				
	1	1	M	do				
	1	60	M	do				
	1	50	M	do				
	1	45	M	do				
	1	75	F	do				
	1	60	M	do				

1	2
John Horlbeck	1
M W Venning	1

The 1850 census has a slave schedule that lists Boone Hall's slaves under the name of Henry's son John—John Horlbeck III—so he must be in residence at the plantation. The slaves total 121, and the schedule lists ages and gender as well. The slave population is almost equal along gender lines: 55 percent male and 45 percent female. They range in age from a one-year-old to two 80-year-old slaves and one 90-year-old slave. (Courtesy of the Charleston County Public Library.)

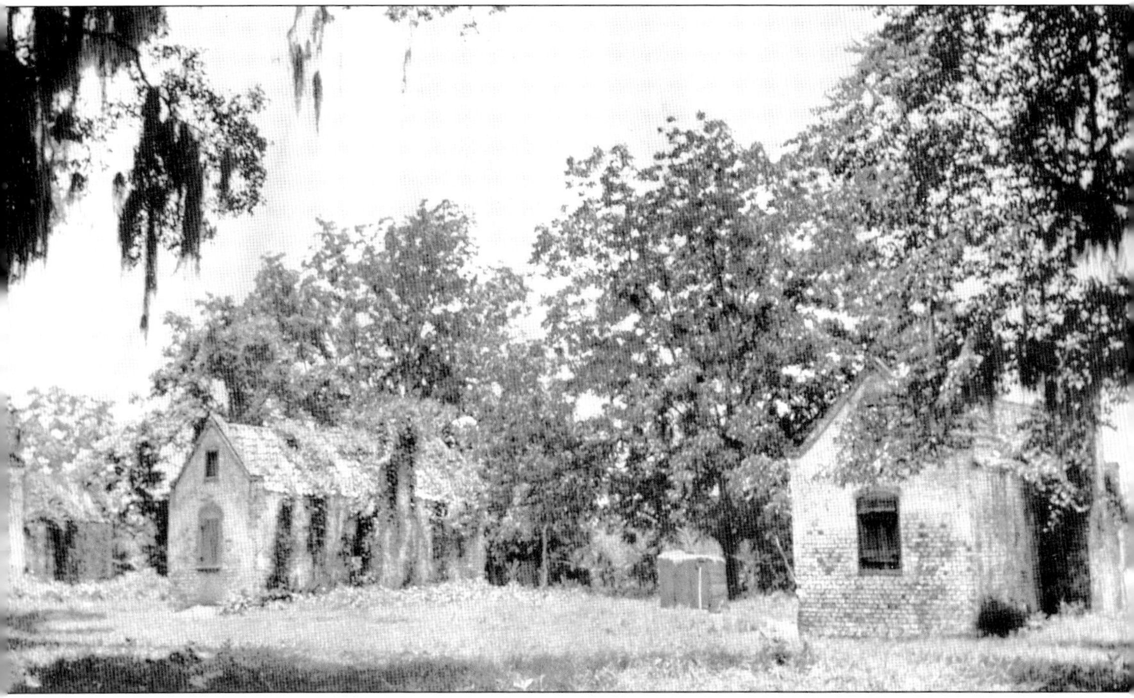

Two hundred ninety slaves are listed in the 1852–1853 inventory book of Boone Hall. The increase in the slave population may be attributed to increased brick production. The ages and gender of the slaves are fairly equal, not accounting for several infants that are listed without gender or the slaves that are listed without age, generally because they have died or have been sold, and they make up 25 percent of the population. (Courtesy of the South Carolina Historical Society.)

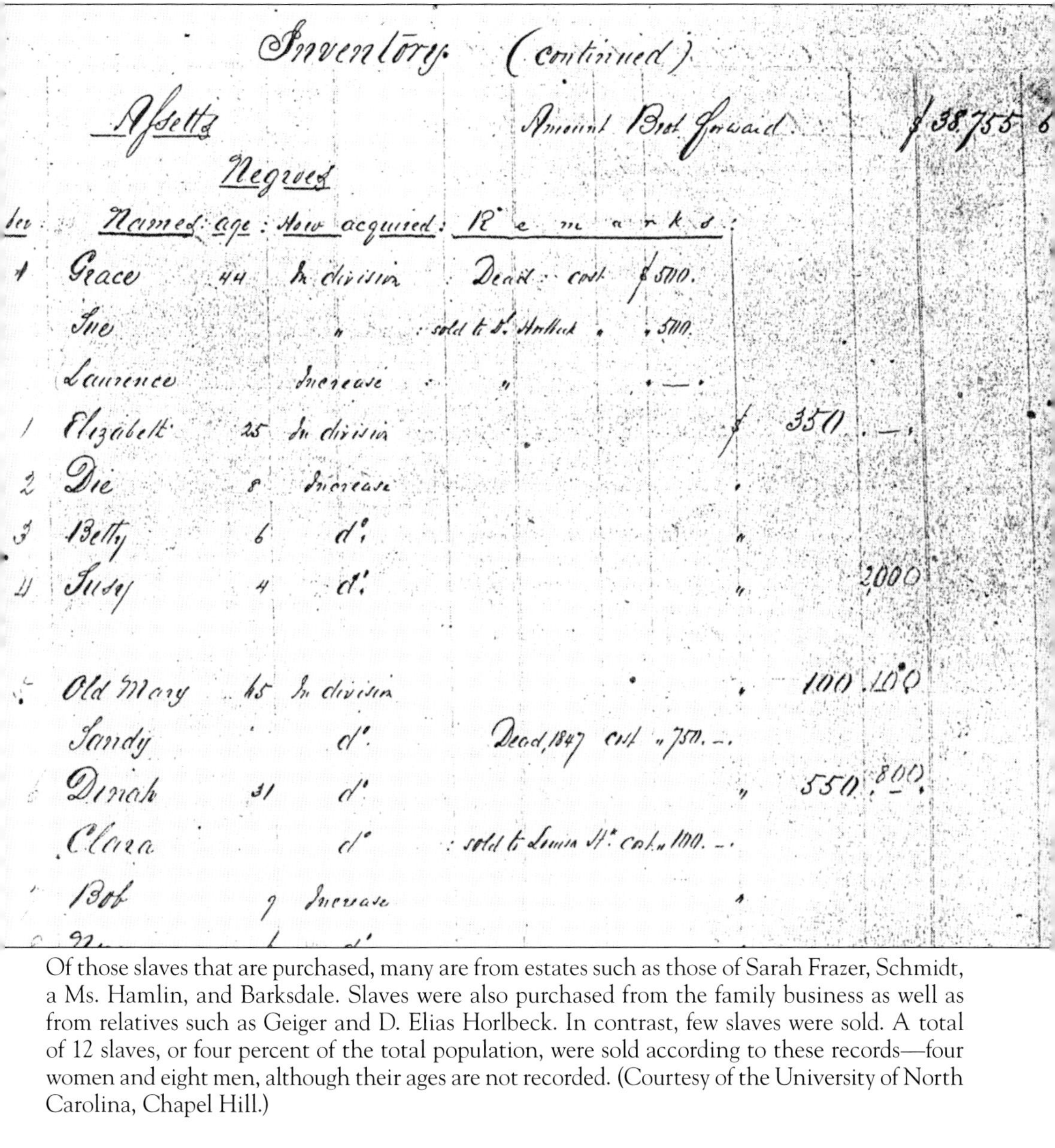

Inventory (continued)

Assetts — Amount Brot. forward — $38,755 6

Negroes

	Names	age	How acquired	Remarks		
1	Grace	44	In division	Dead: cost $500.		
	Sue		"	sold to D. Horlbeck " 500.		
	Laurence		Increase	" —.		
1	Elizabeth	25	In division		$ 350.—.	
2	Die	8	Increase			
3	Betty	6	d.o			
4	Susy	4	d.o			2000
	Old Mary	65	In division		100	100
	Sandy		d.o	Dead, 1847 cost " 750.—.		
	Dinah	31	d.o		550.	800
	Clara		d.o	sold to Lewis H.o cost " 100.—.		
	Bob	7	Increase			

Of those slaves that are purchased, many are from estates such as those of Sarah Frazer, Schmidt, a Ms. Hamlin, and Barksdale. Slaves were also purchased from the family business as well as from relatives such as Geiger and D. Elias Horlbeck. In contrast, few slaves were sold. A total of 12 slaves, or four percent of the total population, were sold according to these records—four women and eight men, although their ages are not recorded. (Courtesy of the University of North Carolina, Chapel Hill.)

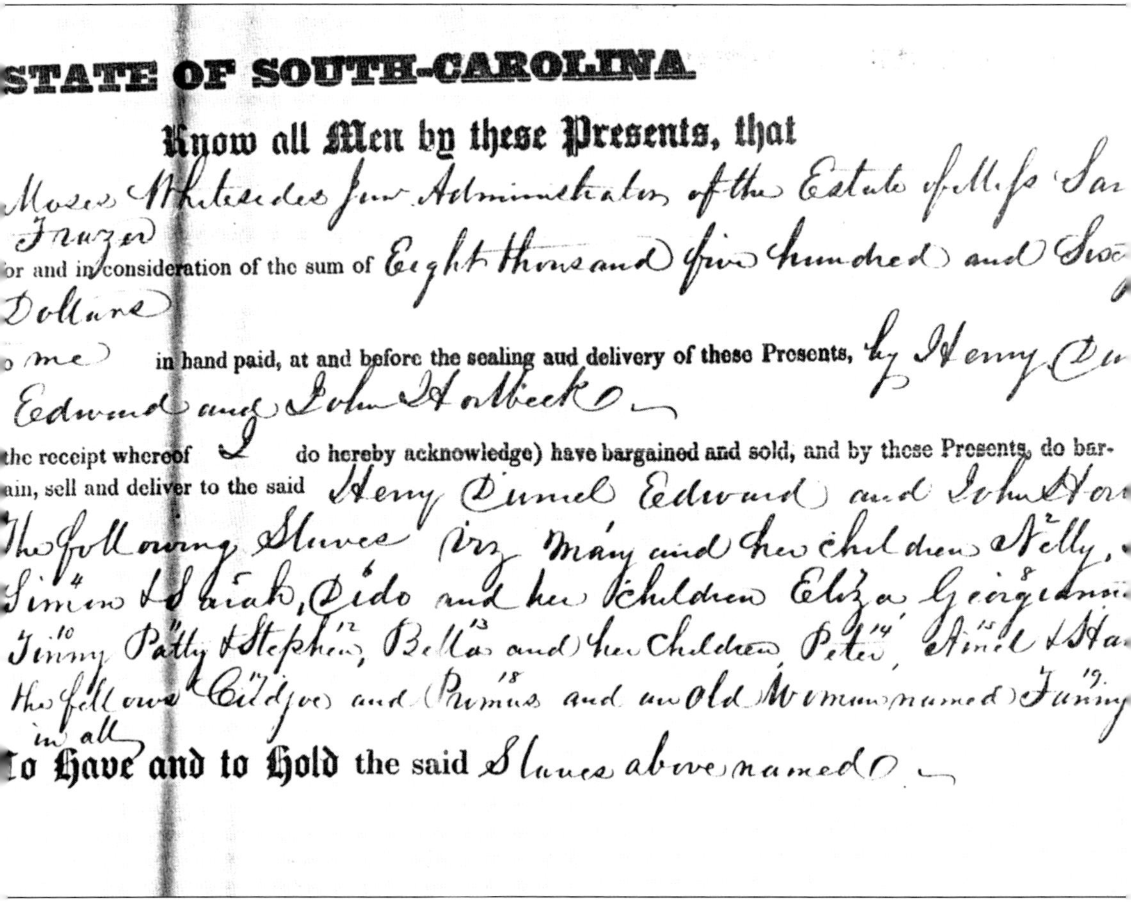

STATE OF SOUTH-CAROLINA

Know all Men by these Presents, that Moses Whitesides Jun Administrator of the Estate of Miss Sarah Frazer

for and in consideration of the sum of Eight thousand five hundred and Sixty Dollars

to me in hand paid, at and before the sealing and delivery of these Presents, by Henry Daniel Edward and John Horlbeck

the receipt whereof I do hereby acknowledge) have bargained and sold, and by these Presents, do bargain, sell and deliver to the said Henry Daniel Edward and John Horlbeck

the following Slaves viz Mary and her children Nelly, Simon & Sarah, Dido and her children Eliza Georgianna Jinny Patty & Stephen, Bella and her children Peter, Ainel & Ha the fellows Cudjoe and Primus and an old Woman named Fanny in all

To Have and to Hold the said Slaves above named

The Horlbeck brothers purchased many slaves during the early 1850s. The above bill of sale for 19 slaves from the estate of Sarah Frazer reflects the wholesale purchasing at Boone Hall. The Horlbeck brothers were obviously enjoying a prosperous time and raised the number of their slaves substantially early in this decade. (Courtesy of the South Carolina Department of Archives and History.)

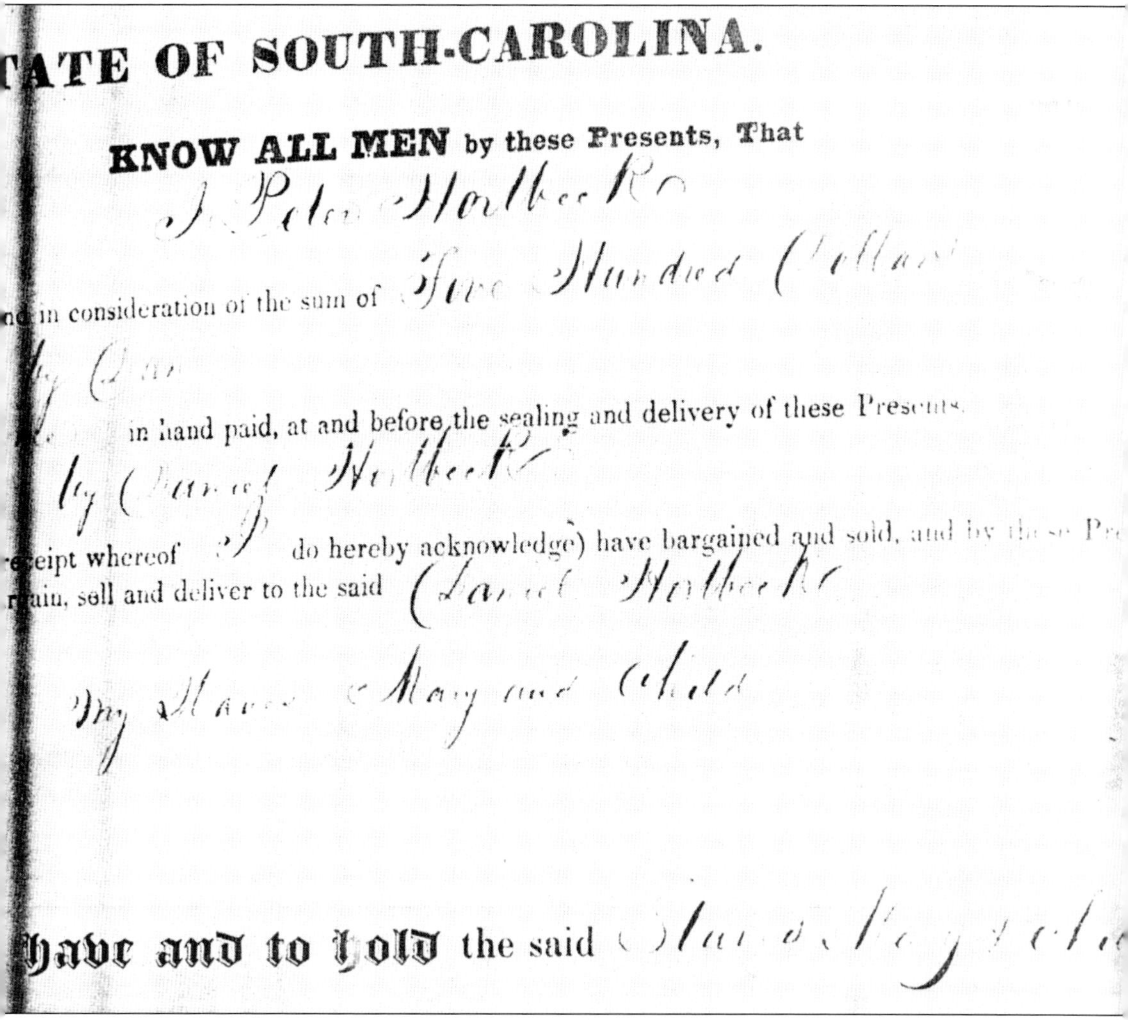

TATE OF SOUTH-CAROLINA.

KNOW ALL MEN by these Presents, That

J. Peter Holbeck

nd in consideration of the sum of Five Hundred Dollars

by Dan

in hand paid, at and before the sealing and delivery of these Presents

by Daniel Holbeck

receipt whereof I do hereby acknowledge) have bargained and sold, and by these Pre

rgain, sell and deliver to the said Daniel Holbeck

My Slave Mary and Child

Have and to Hold the said Slave Mary & child

Family units were considered mother and child. The status of a child born to a slave was determined by the mother's status. If the father was a free man but the mother was a slave, the child would also become a slave. The above sale reflects a common occurrence of the sale of a mother and her child. (Courtesy of the South Carolina Department of Archives and History.)

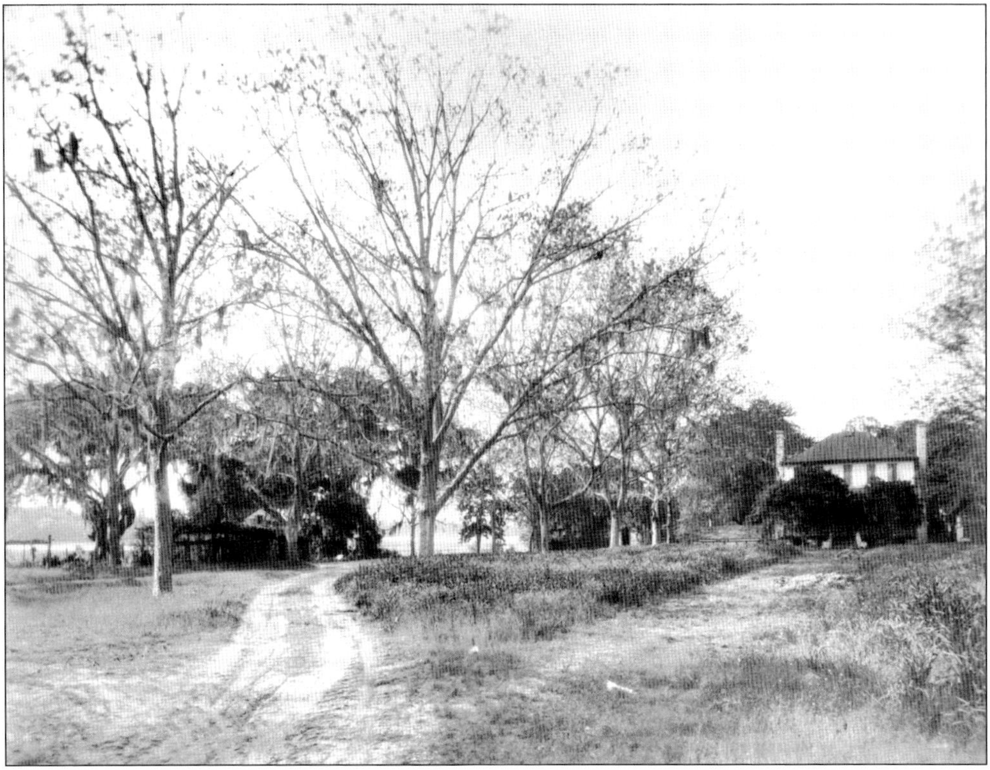

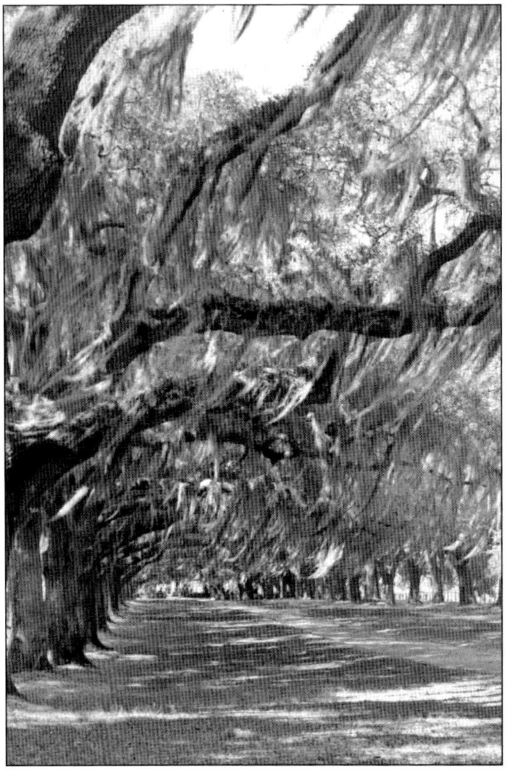

Several of the young Horlbeck men fought in the Civil War. Dr. Elias Buckingham Horlbeck, the 21-year-old son of Edward and Ainsley Horlbeck who had just received his medical degree from the Medical University of South Carolina, fought with the Lancaster Greys, Company A, 9th Infantry. James Moultrie, son of Elias Horlbeck, M.D., and brother of Dr. Elias, served with Company L, 1st Infantry, as a first sergeant and with Company D, 1st Infantry, as a first lieutenant. (Courtesy of the South Carolina Historical Society.)

Margaret Horlbeck, daughter of Henry, displayed an adamant fervor for the Southern cause in a letter to her uncle Daniel dated January 10, 1863. "The second year has dawned on our Confederacy and that kind hand that has kept us thus far, and has caused our noble sons of Carolina to achieve such heroic and Confederacy be established on a foundation as strong and lasting, that we may know war no more." (Courtesy of the South Carolina Historical Society.)

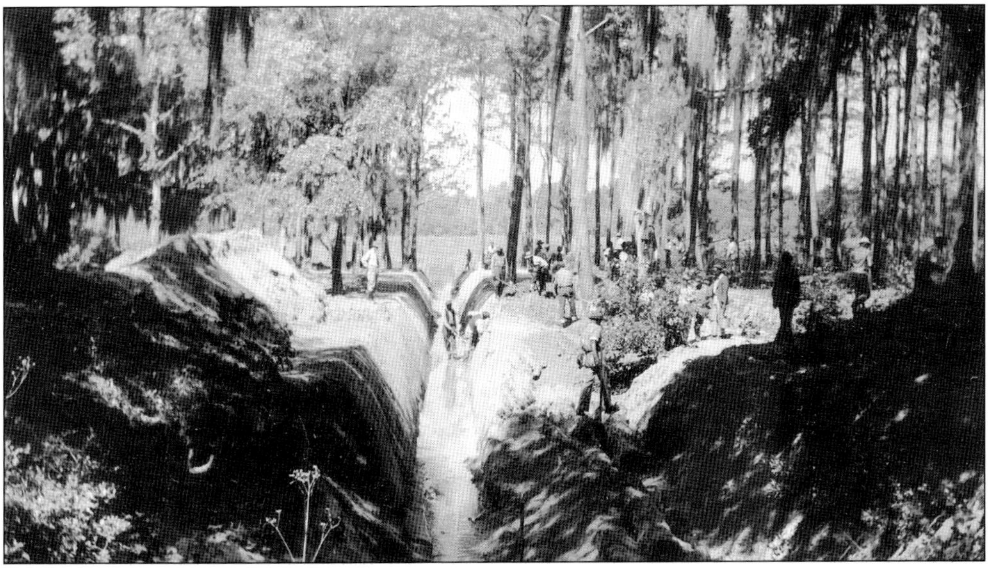

Boone Hall did not suffer any damage as a result of the war, but local slaves built fortifications on the property to defend the town they had built (seen on the left of image). Boone Hall was left untouched by the Union troops, but a company of Union cavalry from the 21st Massachusetts Colored Regiment camped in the churchyard, using the building as a stable and burning the pews for firewood in 1865. (Courtesy of the South Carolina Historical Society.)

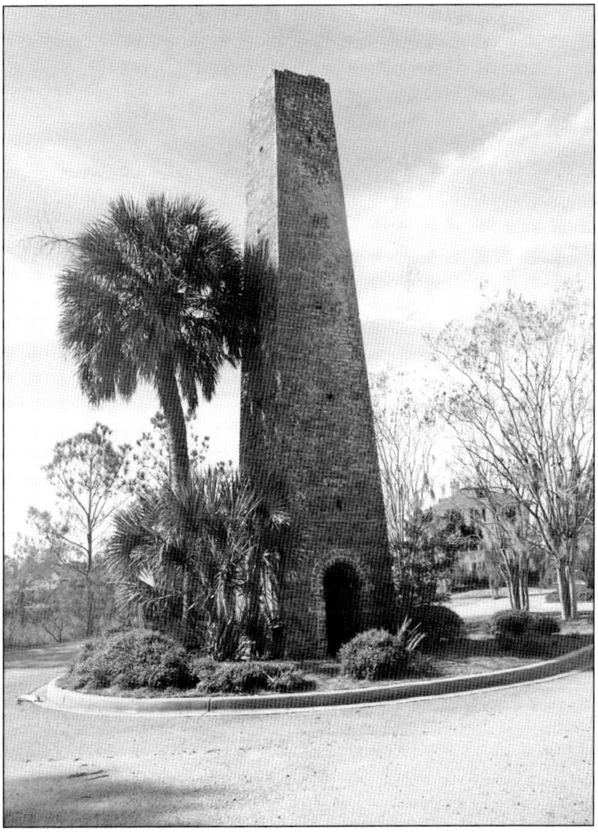

Brick making continued at Boone Hall until the late 19th century. As previously mentioned, larger scale operations weeded out smaller brickyards. John S. Horlbeck purchased more land on Parker Island to expand the brick-making operations at Boone Hall. This photograph is of an existing brick-kiln chimney found in the Brickyard subdivision behind Boone Hall plantation. (Courtesy of Michelle Adams.)

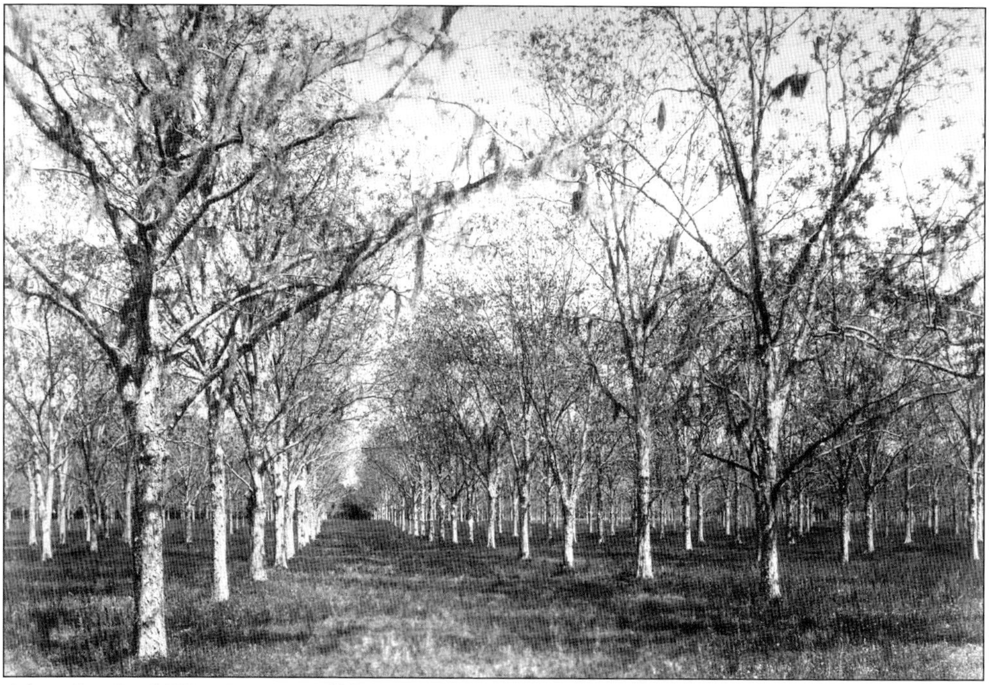

After the Civil War, Boone Hall became a pecan orchard. Pecans commonly grew in the wild in the southeast. After cotton fields were unable to produce cotton any longer, it was discovered that pecans could be grown commercially on the tired out cotton fields and could produce a crop within five years. By 1900, six hundred acres were planted with more than 15,000 trees, which became notable as the largest pecan groves in the world. (Courtesy of the South Carolina Historical Society.)

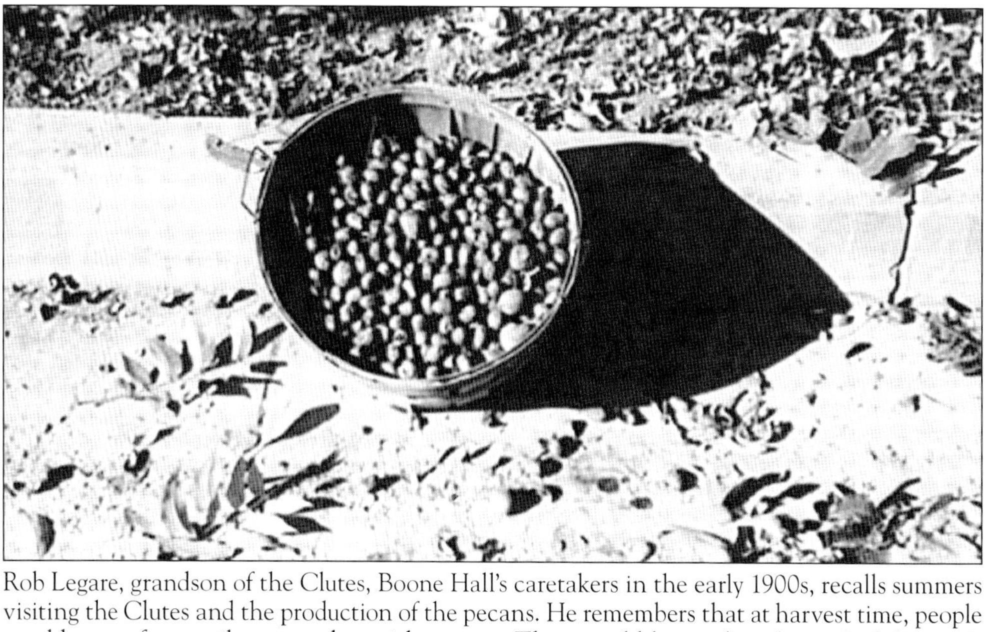

Rob Legare, grandson of the Clutes, Boone Hall's caretakers in the early 1900s, recalls summers visiting the Clutes and the production of the pecans. He remembers that at harvest time, people would come from miles around to pick pecans. They would be paid at the end of the week depending on the amount of pecans picked. (Courtesy of the Library of Congress.)

Three

THE STONES REBUILD

The Horlbecks sold the Boone Hall property in 1902 but retained the timber rights; John S. Horlbeck leased the timber rights to the Dorchester Land and Timber Company for five years. The company was allowed to cut any oak and pine trees measuring 10 inches or more in diameter except for the oaks and any ornamental trees near the house. After the original buyer was foreclosed, the property was returned to the Horlbecks. Then the Horlbecks sold the property to the South Atlantic Pecan Company in 1912, but the property was also returned to the Horlbecks in 1916 after the company was unable to pay the mortgage. John S. Horlbeck died in 1916, leaving his son and daughter in charge of his estate.

The Horlbeck family finally sold the property to Thomas and Alexandra Stone in 1935. The Stones were from the North and had driven through Charleston where they stopped at a roadside pecan seller. They were intrigued with the man's story and became convinced that they could become successful at growing pecans. They scoured the area, looking for just the right plantation. After viewing many up and down the coast, the Stones purchased Boone Hall Plantation in 1935. They immediately set their plans into full swing, hiring new staff and laborers to pull down the old house, erect the current brick structure, and prepare the fields for planting. Thomas Stone kept a detailed scrapbook of these events, from which many of the pictures and captions for this book were taken. William Seabrook and his son, Bill, ran the farming aspect of the plantation, while Charlie Schroeder oversaw the financials and the selling of the produce.

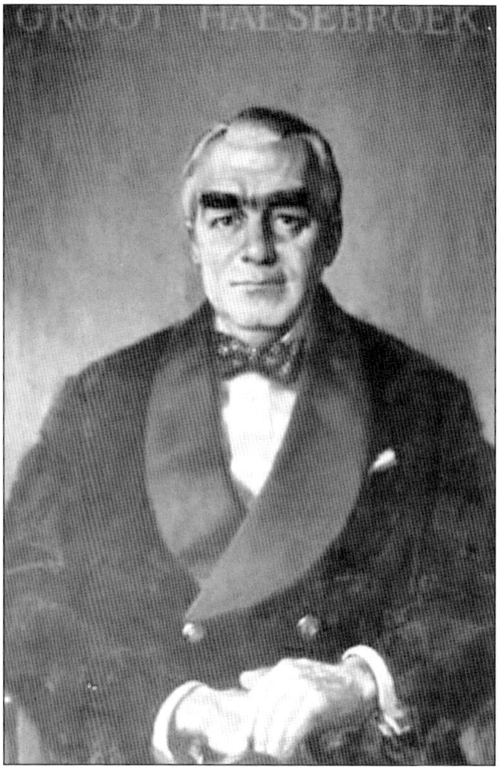

As a young diplomat, Thomas Stone once spent a crossing from New York to London playing backgammon with Winston Churchill. They played daily, and by the end of the journey, Churchill had lost £50 to Stone. Later, upon Stone's request, a signed photograph arrived from Churchill along with a note stating there was no way he could forget the young Canadian who had won £50 from him. (Courtesy of Ellen Stone Devine.)

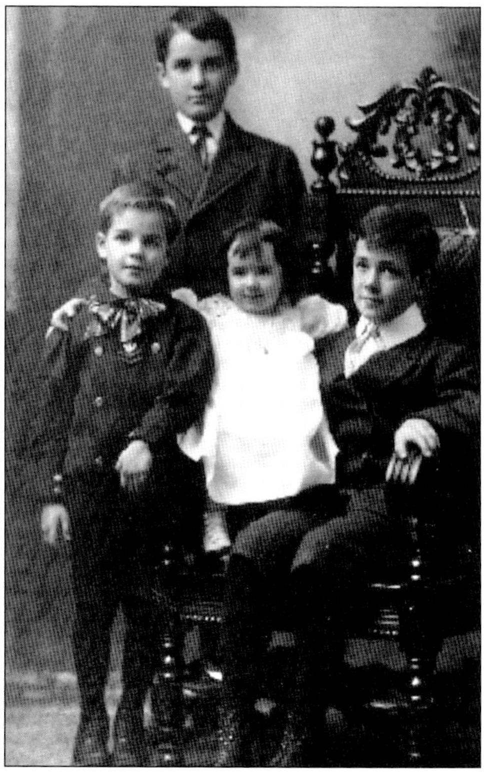

This picture is from around 1907 and shows, from left to right, Thomas Stone (standing) with his siblings John, Elizabeth, and Robert. He was the oldest child of Flora Maude Campbell Stone and Spencer Stone. Thomas was born in Chatham, Ontario, and attended school in Ontario and Paris. He received his degree from the University of Toronto. (Courtesy of Ellen Stone Devine.)

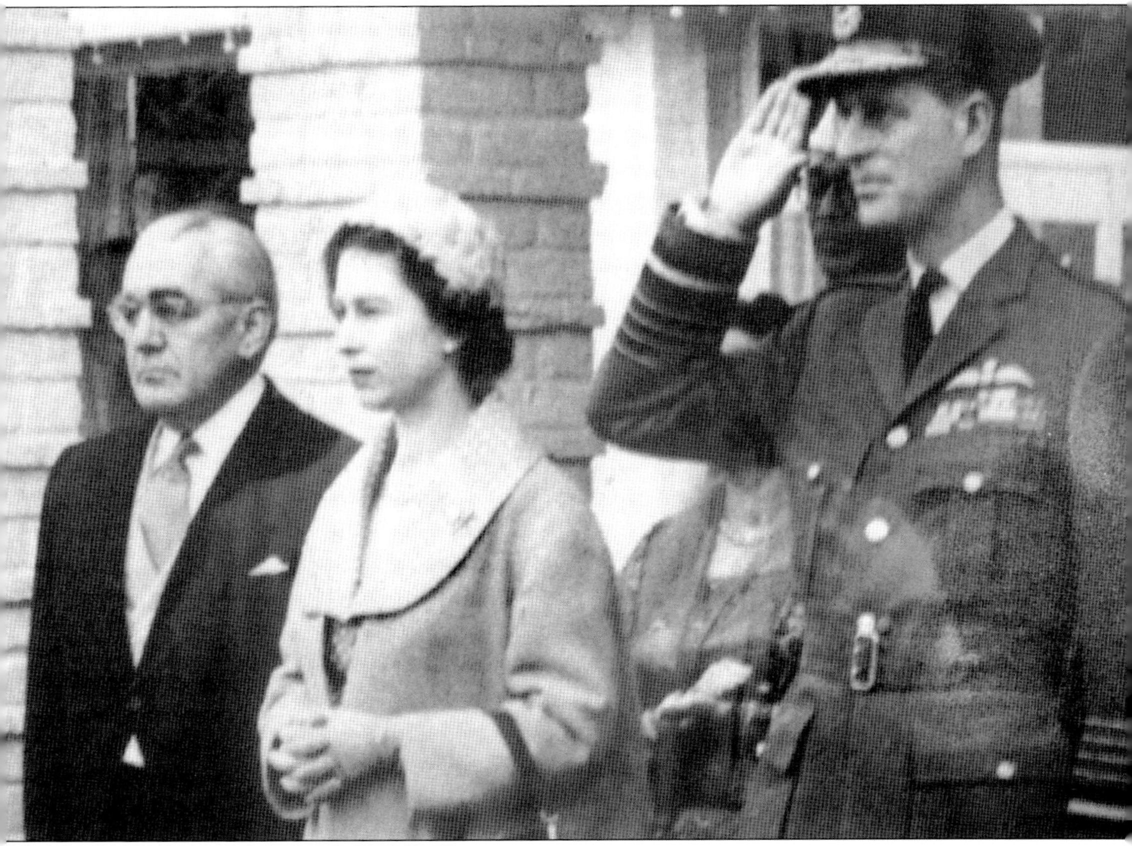

Stone was the Canadian ambassador to exiled governments, including France, Belgium, and Holland during World War II. Afterwards, he was the Canadian ambassador to Sweden and then Holland. This photograph reflects Stone's status in Europe. He is shown on the left next to Queen Elizabeth II of the United Kingdom and her husband, His Royal Highness Prince Philip, Duke of Edinburgh. Stone's duties as ambassador took him from Mexico to Europe throughout his career. (Courtesy of Ellen Stone Devine.)

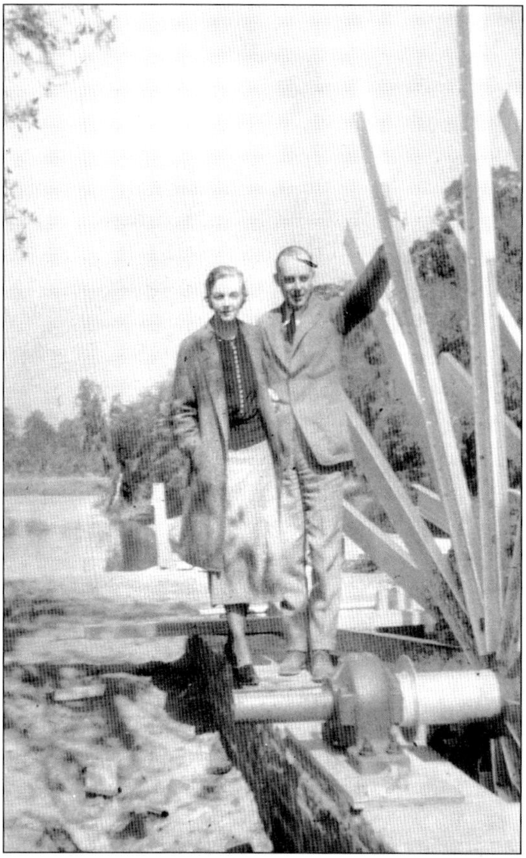

In 1935, Thomas and his wife, Alexandra, (pictured) purchased and restored Boone Hall. After first becoming intrigued with pecan production in the Charleston area, the Stones saw several plantations in the area that were for sale. The Stones ultimately decided upon Boone Hall and immediately set to work clearing the fields and hiring new workers. (Courtesy of the South Carolina Historical Society.)

On October 7, 1395, Thomas Stone wrote, "This time we remained in Charleston about ten days, Alex joining us four days after our arrival. During these ten days we did not once stop thinking about plantations. . . . Alex favoured Boone Hall: I favoured Dixie. Boone Hall finally won and as I write . . . I am more pleased than ever that it did. We paid for it and took title on July 5th." (Courtesy of the South Carolina Historical Society.)

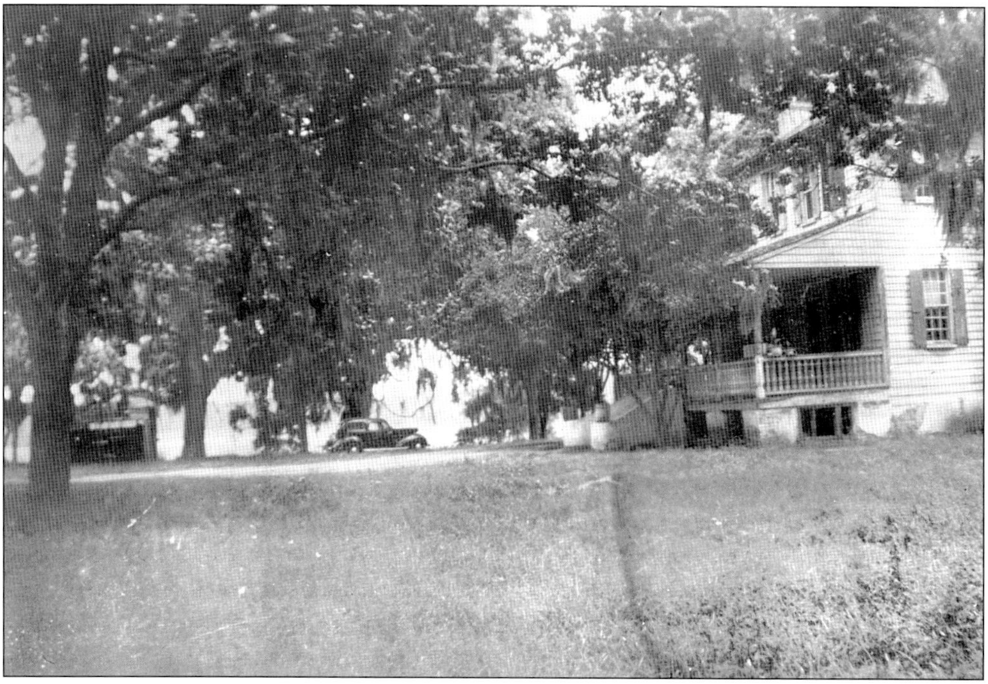

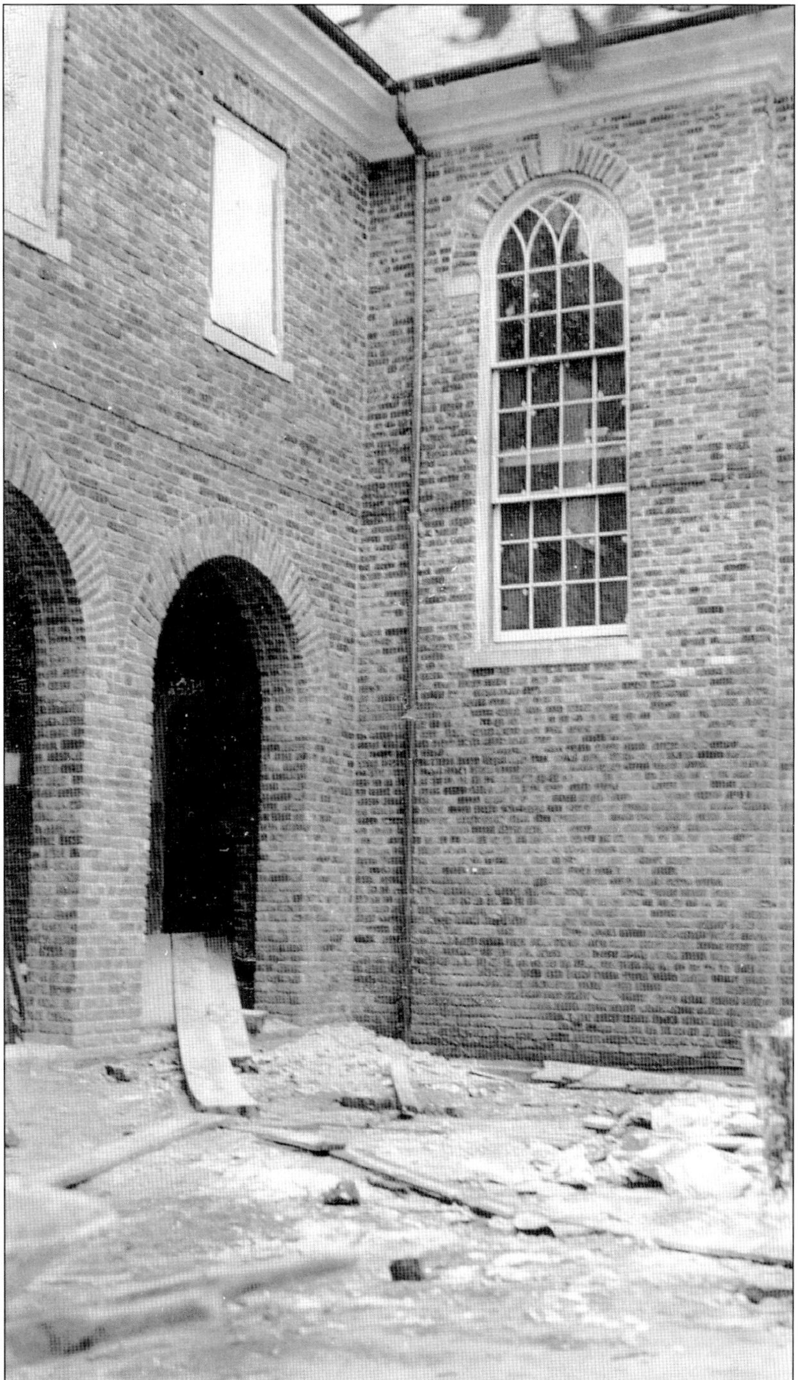

Stone continued, "The old building started to come down, trees came down, we speeded up work on Wampancheone, commenced work on the roads, and the whole place generally became a hive of activity. We purchased a Case tractor, harrow plough, harrow, mower, and rake, two horses and two mules. The farm work got immediately under way and now the main ditches are almost cleared. Last week our payroll was 56 men." (Courtesy of the South Carolina Historical Society.)

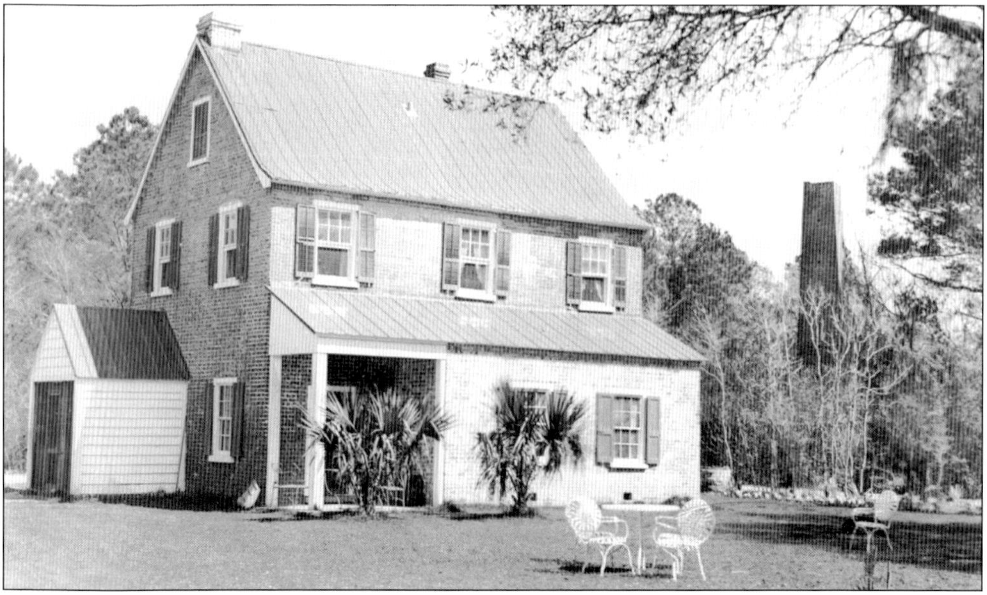

The Stones were able to quickly renovate and move into an existing house on the plantation. They named the building Wampancheone, and it was used by the Stones as their main residence throughout the remaining part of 1935 and 1936. After that, the Stones would use this building for plantation guests. (Courtesy of the South Carolina Historical Society.)

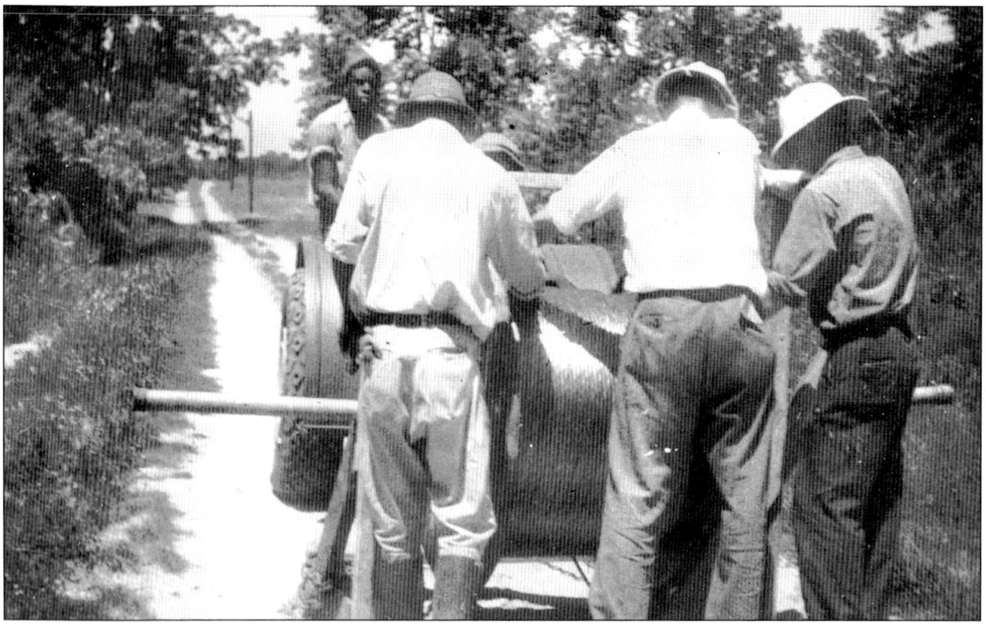

On October 8, 1935, Stone wrote, "Working on ditches, cutting bushes on Savannah ditches principally. Began clearing . . . trees . . . and continued clearing new ground. . . . Cut, raked and piled hay . . . [and] finished preparing cabbage bed. Cleaned some bricks . . . and filled old pecan tree holes around house. Finished pulling down Clute house and began clearing away old cistern. Cut up vegetable garden with tractor but have not yet found tiles for the draining. Hauled some bricks with team and piled compost from old barn." (Courtesy of the South Carolina Historical Society.)

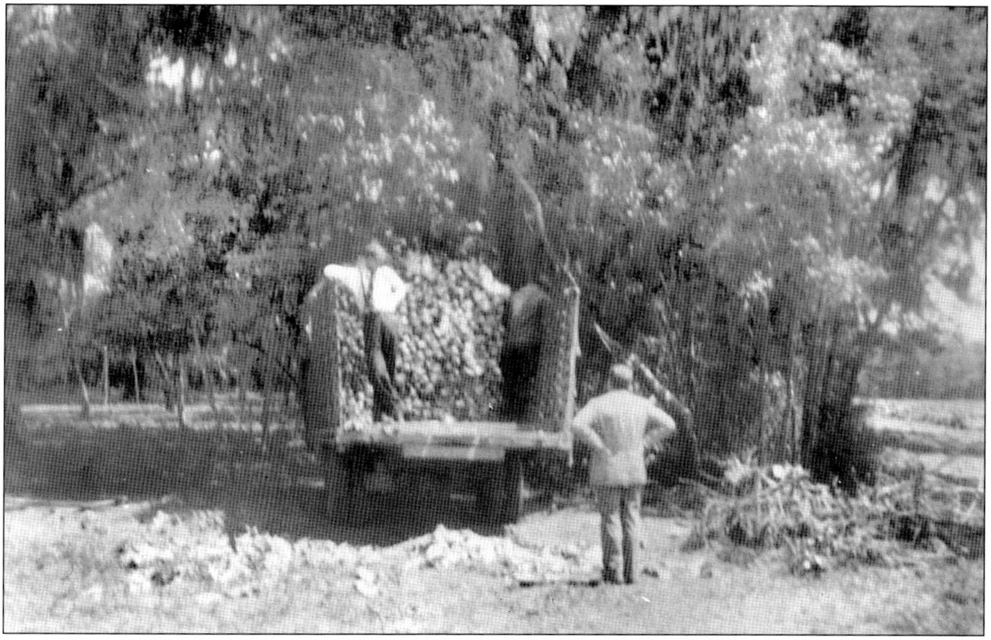

At first, a large amount of labor was required to complete the Stones' vision. Initial payrolls included approximately 40 men employed at such tasks as tearing down the old house, hauling and stacking hay, and working in the fields or on the old stable. Women were also employed but usually for field work, such as picking pecans. (Courtesy of the South Carolina Historical Society.)

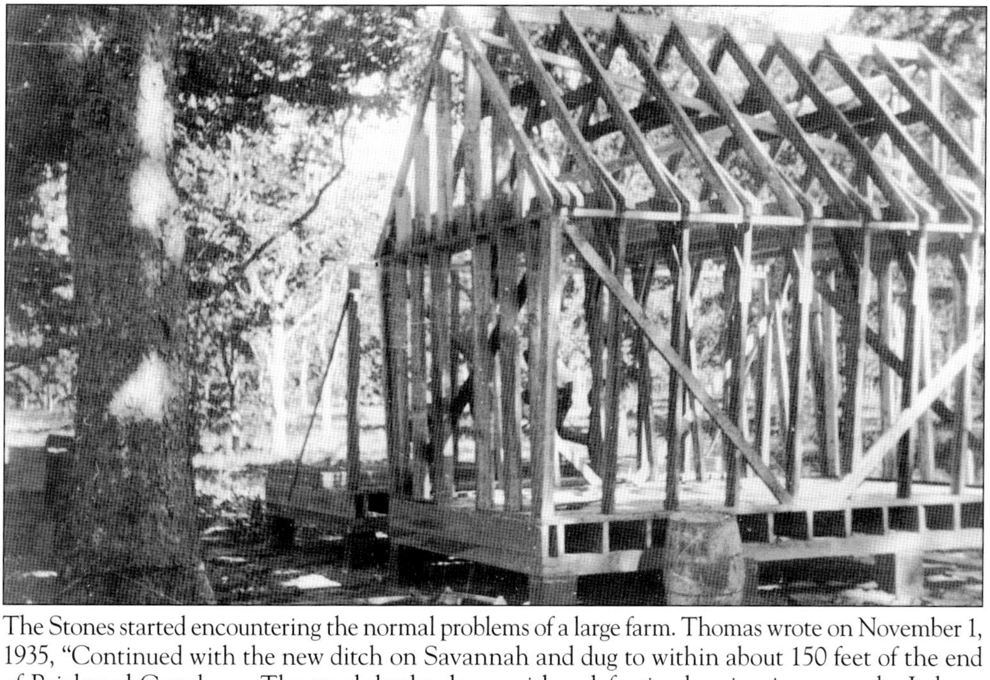

The Stones started encountering the normal problems of a large farm. Thomas wrote on November 1, 1935, "Continued with the new ditch on Savannah and dug to within about 150 feet of the end of Brickyard Canal. . . . The truck broke down with a defective bearing in rear axle. Labour distribution about same as rest of week. Trott finished pouring foundations for the new stable, which, strangely enough, is on the exact site of what was probably the first stable on Boone Hall." (Courtesy of the South Carolina Historical Society.)

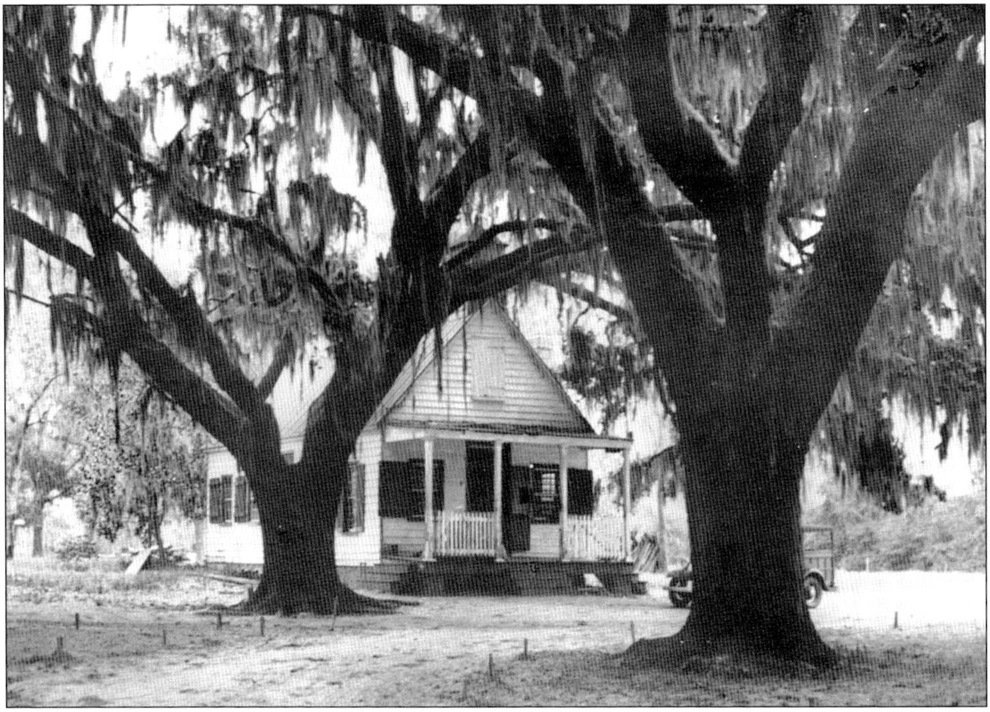

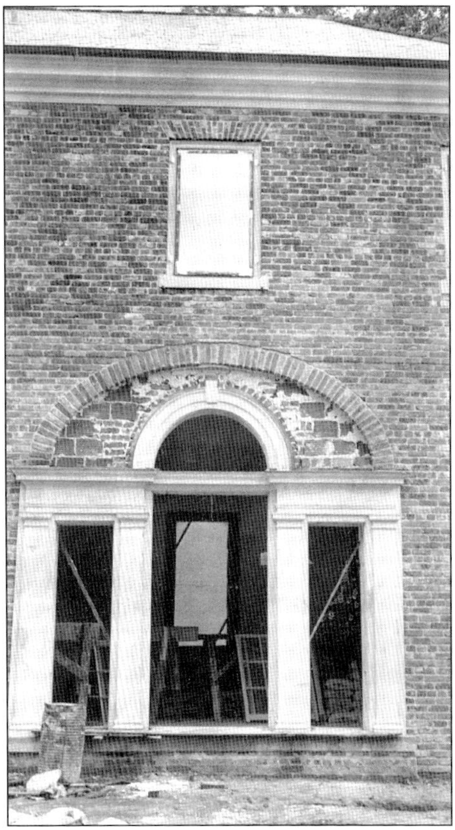

Building a new house on the site of the old was high on the Stones' list of priorities, but it was not as easy as they had hoped. Thomas Stone wrote on November 14, 1935, "The contractors and the architect were disappointing; the former's bids on the new house were all too high and the latter refused, with the best will in the world, to understand that his house could not be built for less. . . . Bill Beers went back to N.Y. to figure how to reduce costs." (Courtesy of the South Carolina Historical Society.)

On January 27, 1936, Stone wrote, "Bill Beer's original plans put the dining room floor 5'9" above the present ground level which would have set the house up in the air like a pimple at the end of the avenue and called for a stupendous amount of grading. (The little grading which we did around the stable cost us $450—This other would have run into thousands!)" (Courtesy of the South Carolina Historical Society.)

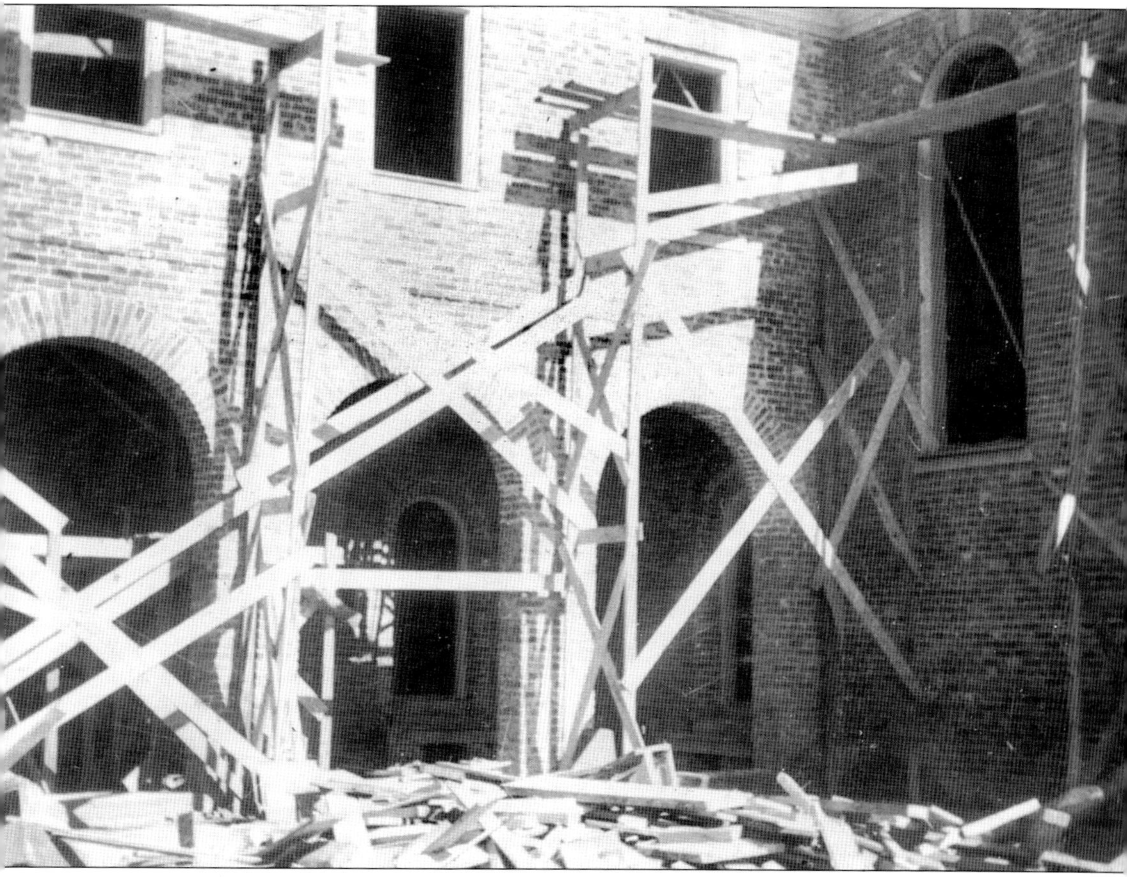

Stone continued, "Excavation for the cellar . . . is about finished and they are now building the forms for the cement foundation. We had considerable discussion as to the depth of the cellar. . . . We dug test pits and found the water table at this season 9' down so we decided that we were perfectly safe in excavating about seven feet. We shall be finished getting bricks out of the kilns on Laurel Hill tomorrow." (Courtesy of the South Carolina Historical Society.)

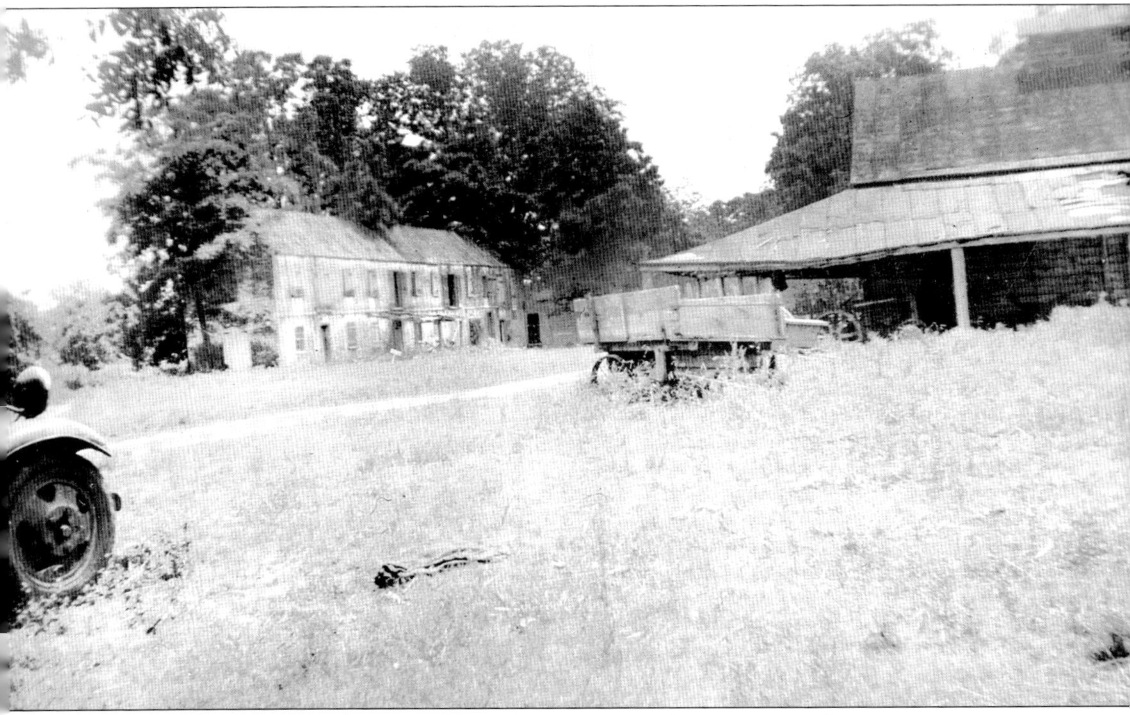

On January 26, 1937, Thomas Stone wrote, "We moved at once into the cotton gin, where we were extremely comfortable until about (November 1), when we moved into the Big House when we did, it would probably not have been finished yet. We literally shoved the workmen out, although not quite as fast as we would liked to have done. . . . We had a very successful housewarming, which I am sure had much to do with the charm of the house now." (Courtesy of the South Carolina Historical Society.)

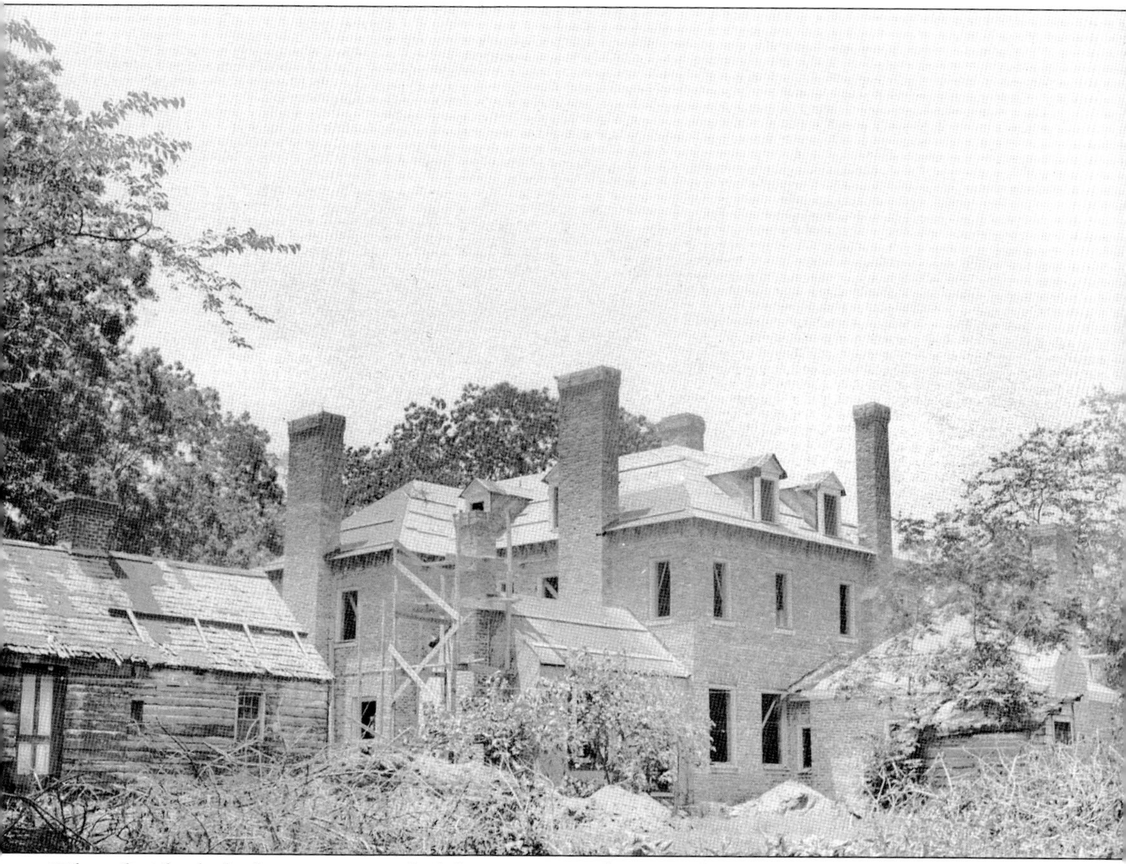

When finished, the house consisted of three stories. The main floor housed the library or living room; a gun room; the dining room, kitchen, and pantry; a storage room; and a maid's room. The second floor consisted of two bedrooms, a ballroom, a sitting room, two servants' rooms, and a pressing room, with two bedrooms and a bath on the third floor. (Courtesy of the South Carolina Historical Society.)

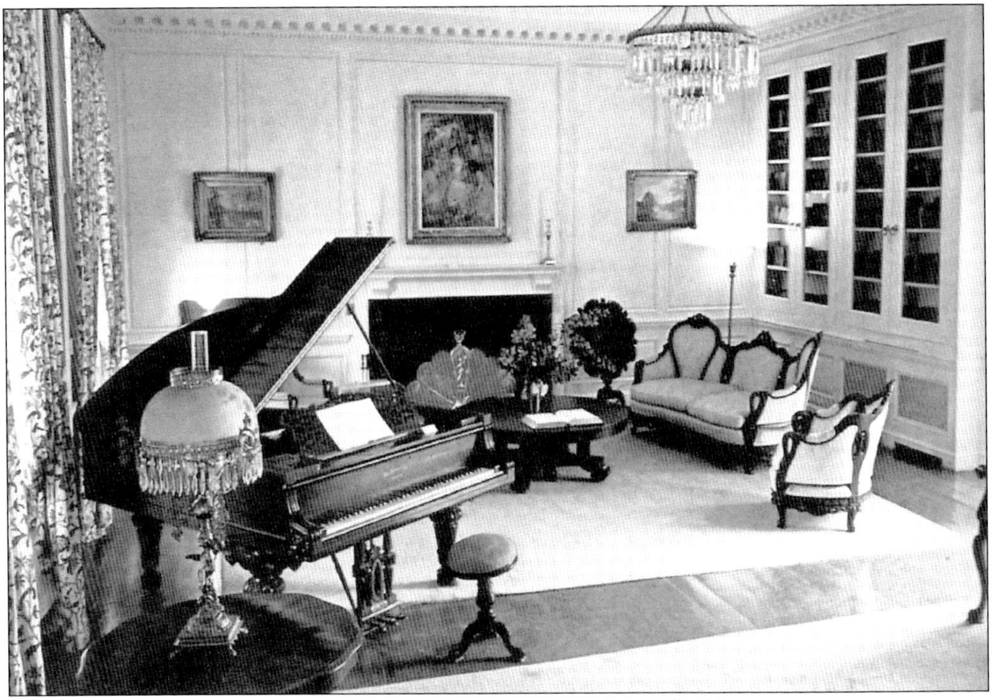

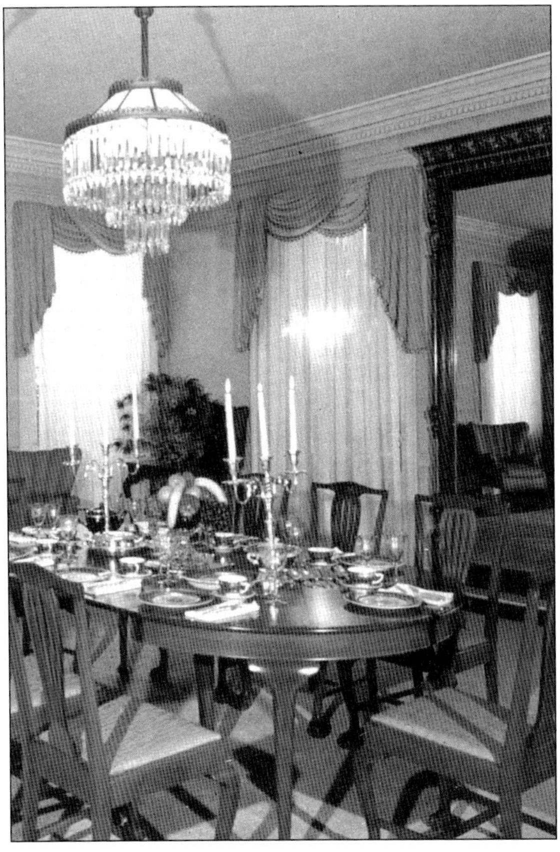

This is the library or music room, where the ladies and children would come after dinner. Entertainment such as piano playing or singing might be enjoyed, or possibly just talking while doing their embroidery. The floors are made of random wide oak planks that are assembled with handmade nails and wooden pegs. The walls are made of cypress, which at one time was considered a cheap wood and would often be painted over. (Courtesy of Boone Hall Plantation.)

In the 19th century, it was customary to have the largest meal in the middle of the day; the fashionable hour would be 3:00 p.m. These dinners would often last several hours and consist of several courses, such as fish, soup, meats, and vegetables, and then pies and puddings. Dessert usually consisted of fruit, with the rarer fruit such as pineapples and oranges placed in the center and more common fruits placed on the edges of the serving plate. (Courtesy of Boone Hall Plantation.)

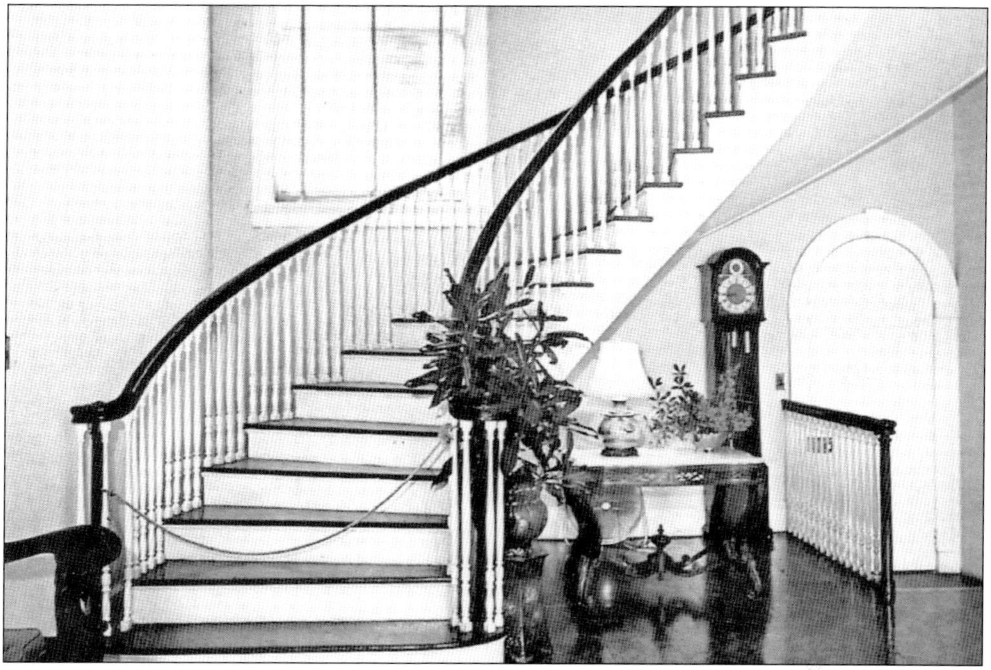

The staircase is a free-flying, or cantilever, staircase. It is attached at the bottom and the top with no support in between. It has been reinforced with a block of wood along the wall to make it more stable. This is one of three cantilever staircases in the Charleston area; the others can be found at the Nathaniel Russell House and the Thomas Bennett House. (Courtesy of Boone Hall Plantation.)

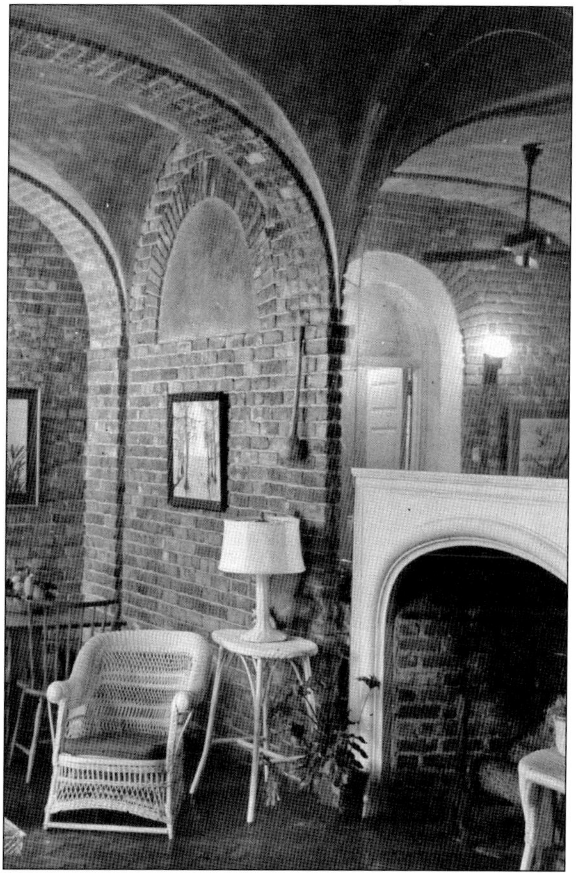

Loggia is an Italian word meaning a roofed open porch as well as an open gallery enclosed with columns on a ground floor. The Boone Hall loggia was originally open but was later enclosed in glass and given French doors to allow access to the back patio, where the brickwork and patterns are continued. (Courtesy of Boone Hall Plantation.)

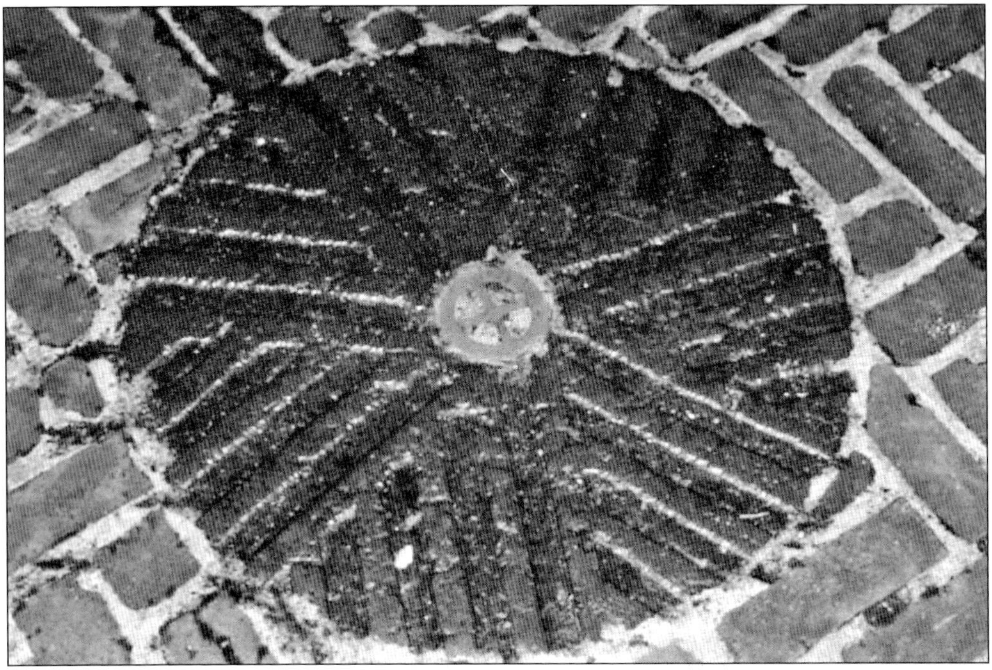
Millstones used to grind grits are also included in the floor's design. This brick was made on the plantation, and in the floor, it creates a herringbone pattern that has been sanded down and covered with polyurethane to keep it from wearing. Both elements from the plantation add to the charm and uniqueness of the loggia. (Courtesy of Boone Hall Plantation.)

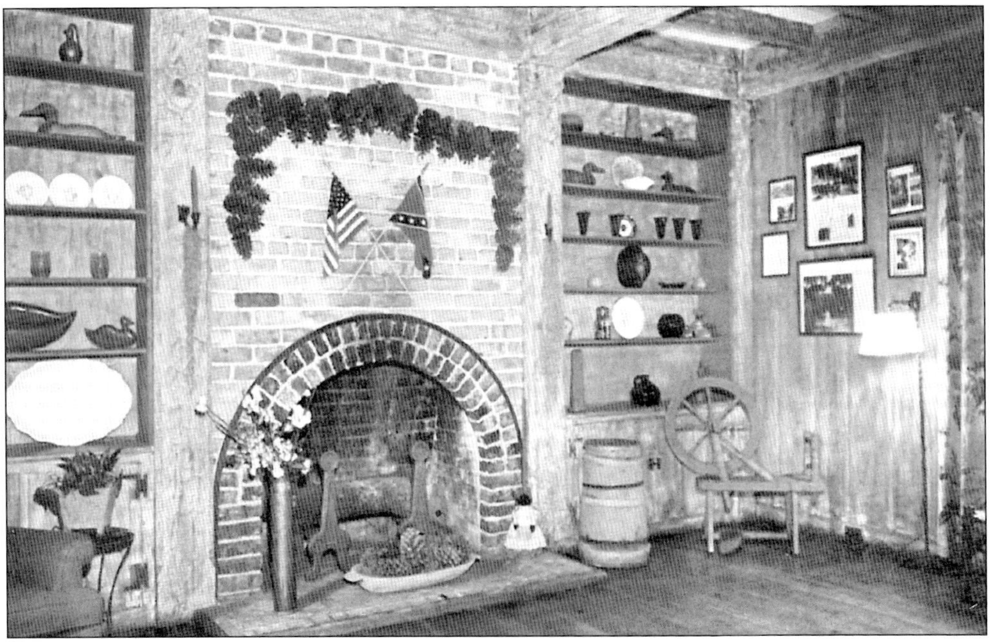
This is the room where the men would go after dinner to smoke, drink, and play poker. Gambling was a favorite sport of the men, and they would often gamble for high stakes, where plantations were won and lost. There is a smaller room where the bar is located with stairs leading to the wine cellar. (Courtesy of Boone Hall Plantation.)

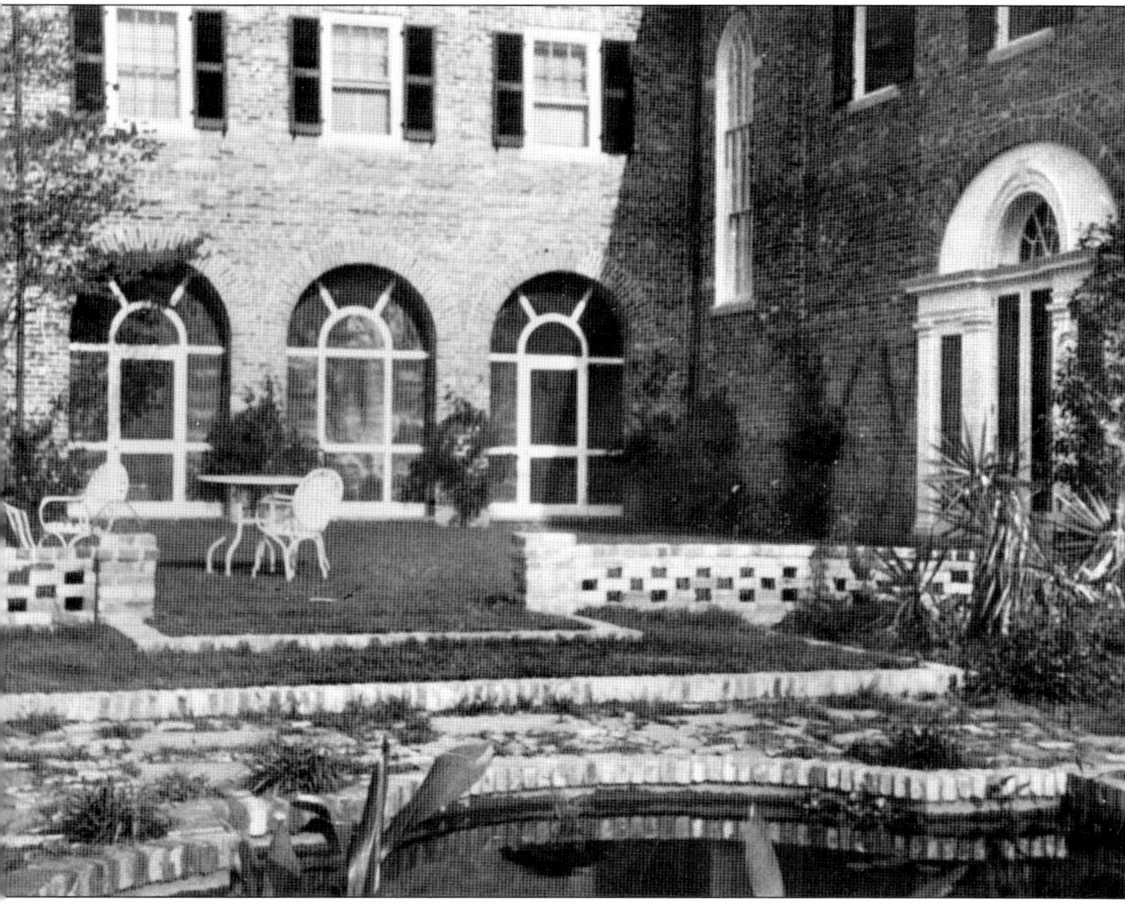

The back of the house was manicured and designed for the family's enjoyment. Near the loggia was a reflection pool, and the terrace was covered with plants. The pool has since been filled in, and French doors were installed into the loggia. A covered trellis and serpentine walls were installed into the patio, reflecting the current look today. (Courtesy of the South Carolina Historical Society.)

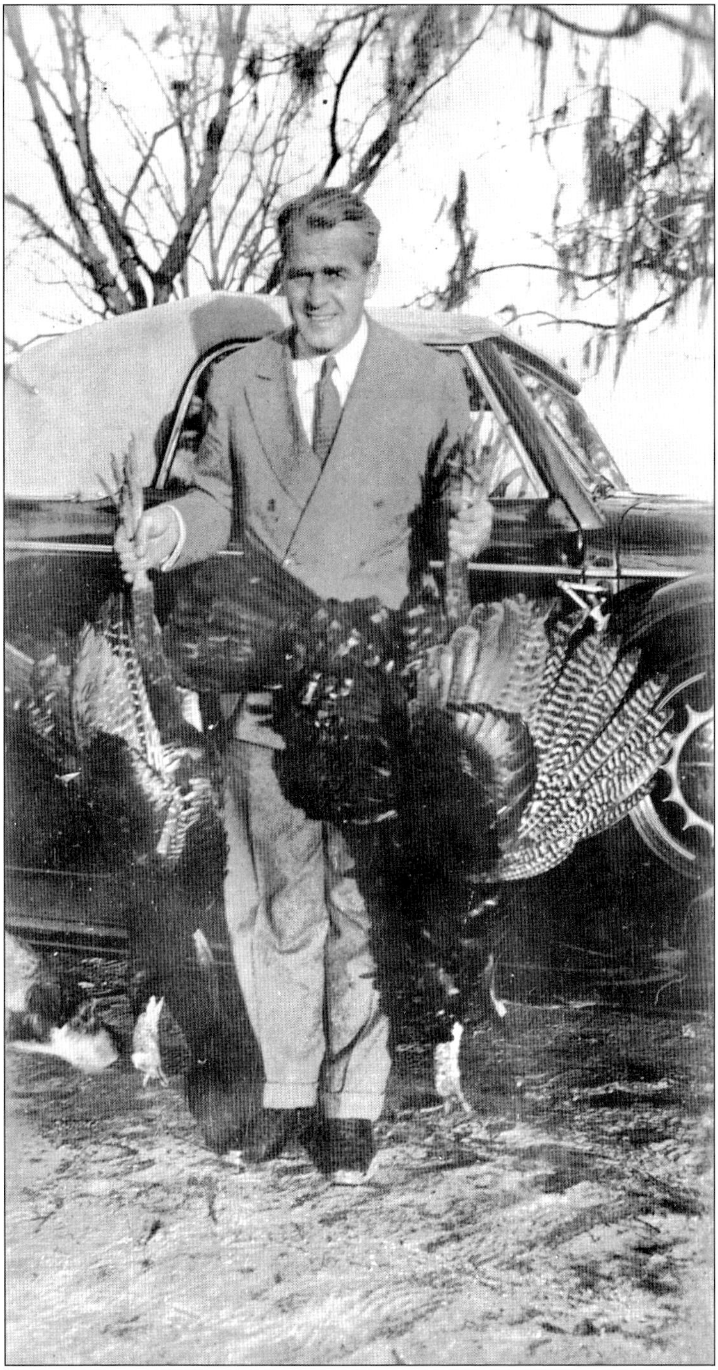

Hunting was a favorite activity at the plantation. Thomas Stone (shown here with turkeys) described that, "We have had practically no shooting or hunting since Christmas. It is too hot for the dogs, and the birds are away in the deep woods. . . . During the autumn we did not hunt deer much, and only three buck were killed on Boone Hall all year, of which I shot one, which was my first. In consequence, I was well blooded by Ephie Seabrook, who did his job with obvious enjoyment." (Courtesy of the South Carolina Historical Society.)

Ellen Stone was born in May 1936. Flora Stone, Thomas Stone's mother, wrote about her granddaughter, Ellen, on March 5, 1937, "I must tell you how charming little Ellen is. She is a darling piece of pink and white femininity, very sweet looking, with fair hair and lovely skin. Her room is just as pink and white as she is, and everything Alex has for her is the very prettiest you can find." Thomas Stone is shown here holding his daughter, Ellen. (Courtesy of the South Carolina Historical Society.)

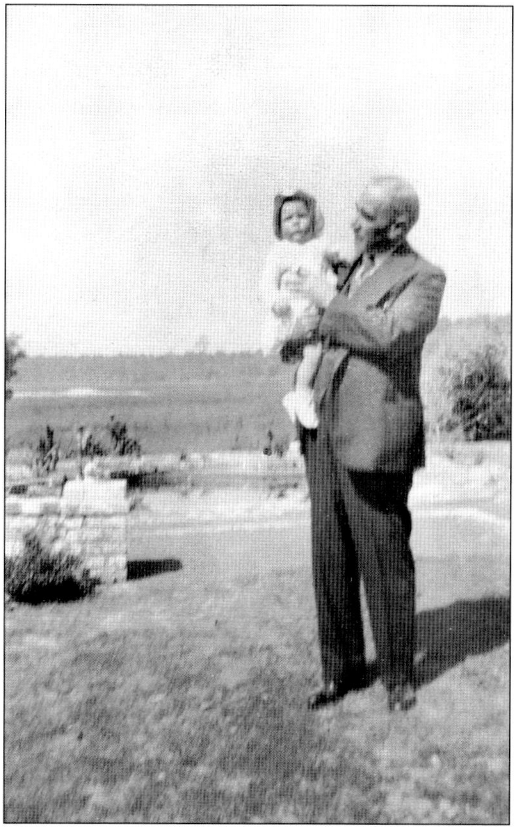

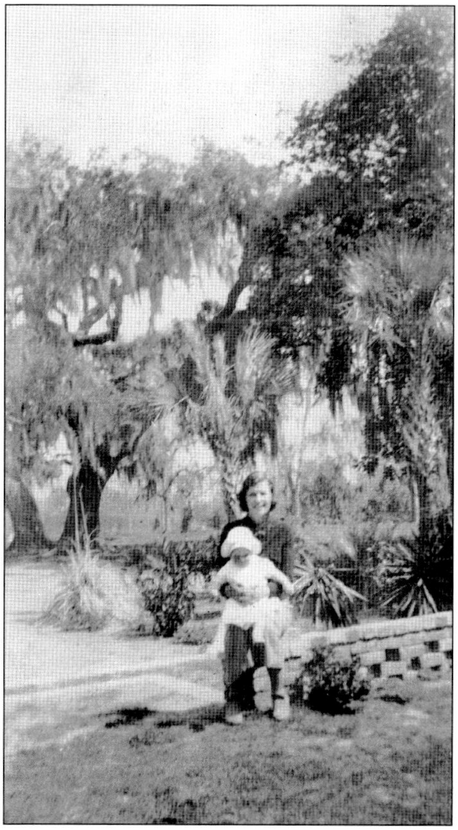

Thomas Stone described in his scrapbook on May 21, 1938, "Ellen's birthday celebration took place last night. There were about 200 people in attendance—too many! Despite the presence of about 50 to 100 total strangers . . . the party was a success. The Jenkins band arrived around 6:00 p.m. We danced and dined and as usual, we had to send away for more food! I sent the band back around 8:15 p.m., and the party fizzled out right away." Alexandra Stone is shown here holding her daughter, Ellen. (Courtesy of the South Carolina Historical Society.)

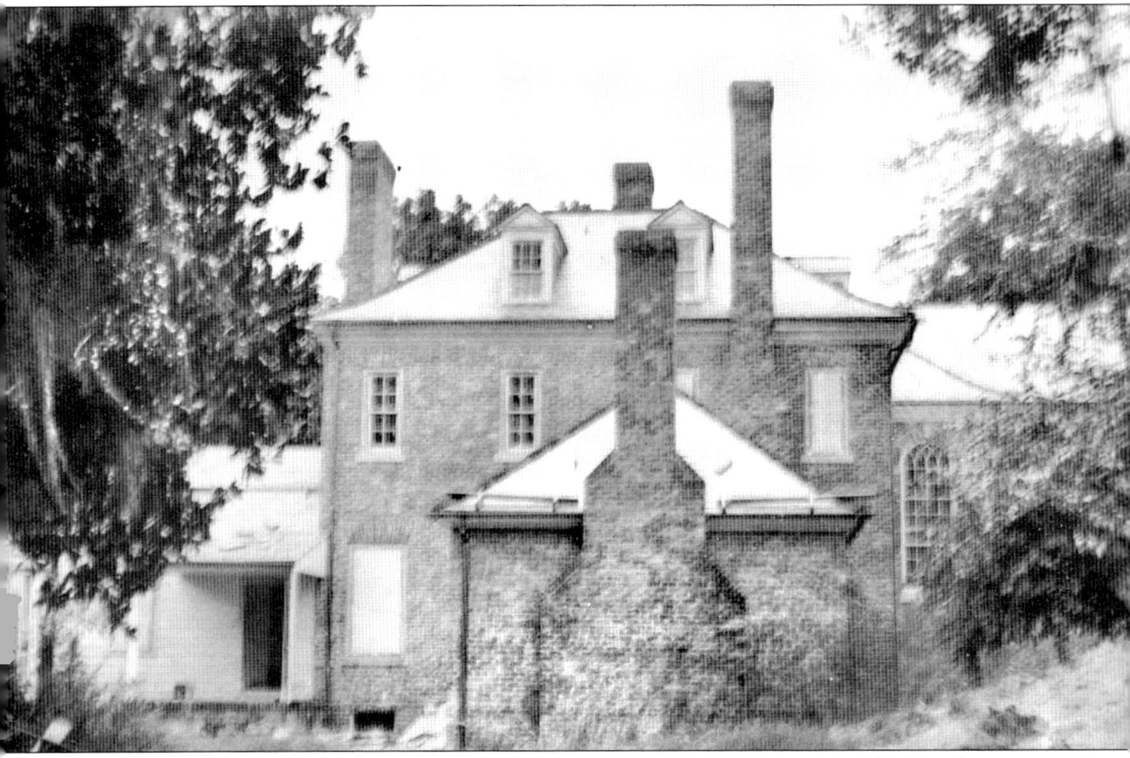

The Stones entertained frequently. Thomas Stone wrote on February 12, 1937, "At this season of the year Alex dreads her morning mail, because practically the whole Eastern Seaboard moves South. We have a big week-end for Washington's birthday. . . . It would be so much better if they could spread themselves over a longer period of time, instead of all arriving at once. Next week and the week-end, however, will be a very good test to see how elastic the house is." (Courtesy of the South Carolina Historical Society.)

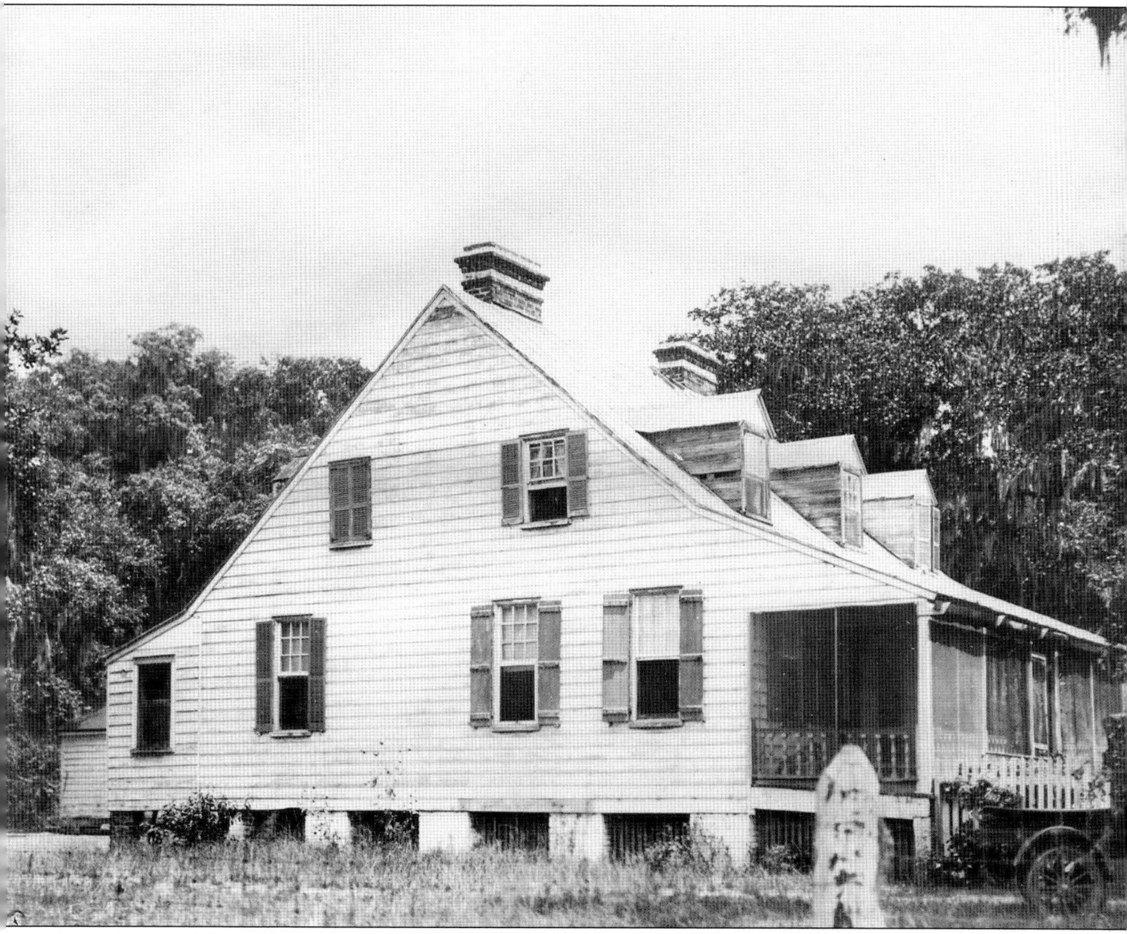

Anna Ewing, Alexandra Stone's mother, purchased a plantation across the street from Boone Hall called Snee Farm. Snee Farm was originally owned by the Pinckney family and was home to one of the signers of the Constitution, Charles Pinckney. Thomas Stone became responsible for the upkeep and agricultural production of both plantations. After the Stones sold Boone Hall, the family still visited Snee Farm often. (Courtesy of the South Carolina Historical Society.)

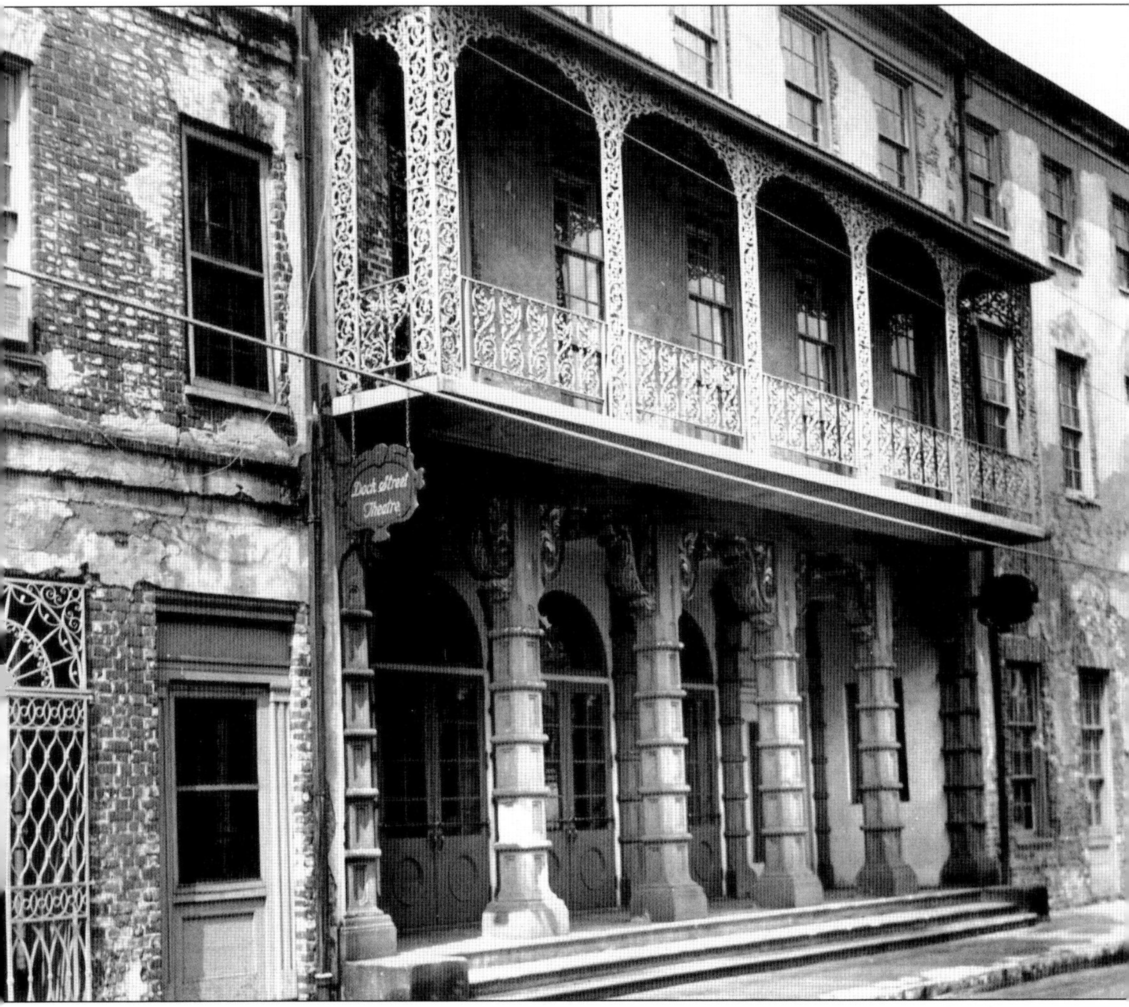

Thomas Stone became active in the Charleston community. He was a member of the Plantation Society and also worked with a committee on the Dock Street Theatre. In the 1930s, the building was restored by the City of Charleston as a Works Progress Administration project. During this project, a large section was constructed containing a stage and auditorium characteristic of the 18th century. (Courtesy of the Charleston County Public Library.)

The Stones entertained many famous people, including DuBose Heyward, who was the coauthor of the non-musical play adapted from his novel, which became the foundation of George Gershwin's opera *Porgy and Bess*. *Porgy and Bess* tells the story of Porgy, a crippled black man living in the slums of Charleston called Catfish Row (pictured here). (Courtesy of the Library of Congress.)

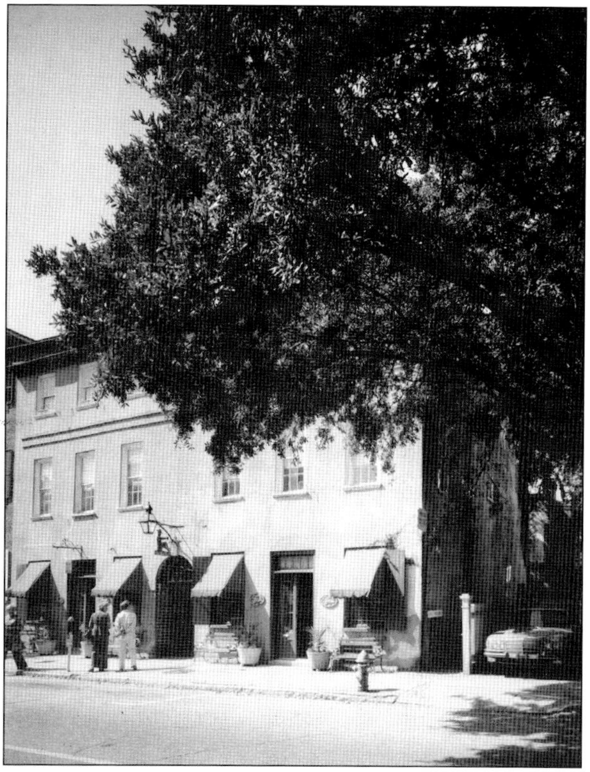

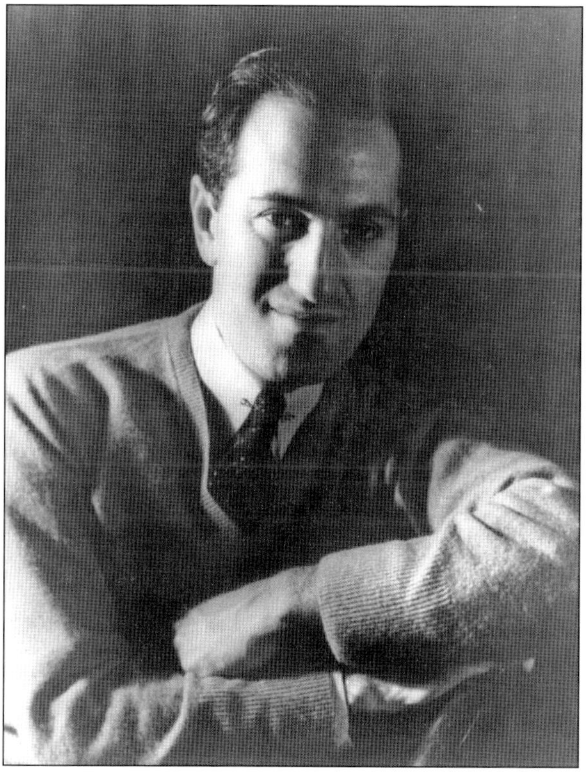

The Stones also entertained the composer of the opera, George Gershwin. Gershwin wrote most of his works in collaboration with his elder brother, lyricist Ira Gershwin. George Gershwin composed songs both for Broadway and for the classical concert hall, including the popular pieces "I Got Rhythm" and *Rhapsody in Blue*. (Courtesy of the Library of Congress.)

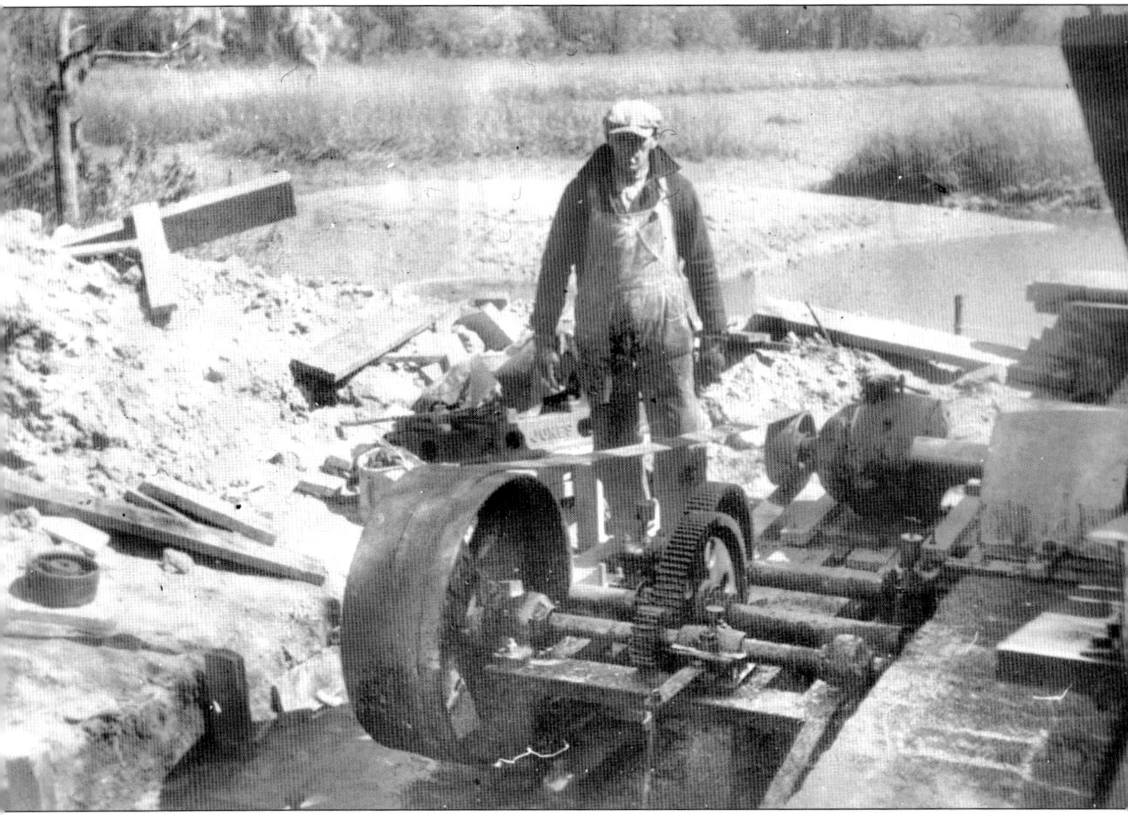

Thomas Stone's brainchild was the Passamaquoddy, a hydroelectric plant situated on the creek so that the tide would run it and the plant would supply the entire plantation with power. Before installing the plant, Stone spent considerable time making sure the tide was strong enough for the system to work properly, measuring the tide every 15 minutes for 12 hours. (Courtesy of the South Carolina Historical Society.)

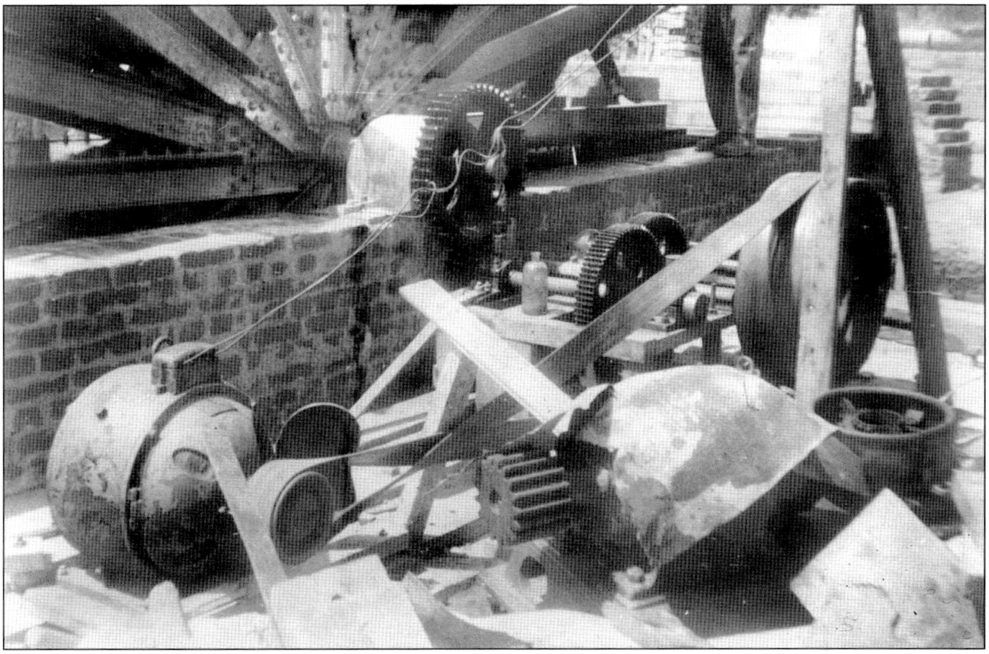

The hydroelectric plant took some trial and error, and proved not to be quite enough power during low tides when additional systems such as the beer refrigeration system were added. Stone found that the installation of a 2.5-kilowatt Delco plant was required to help the wheel when the tides were not strong enough. (Courtesy of the South Carolina Historical Society.)

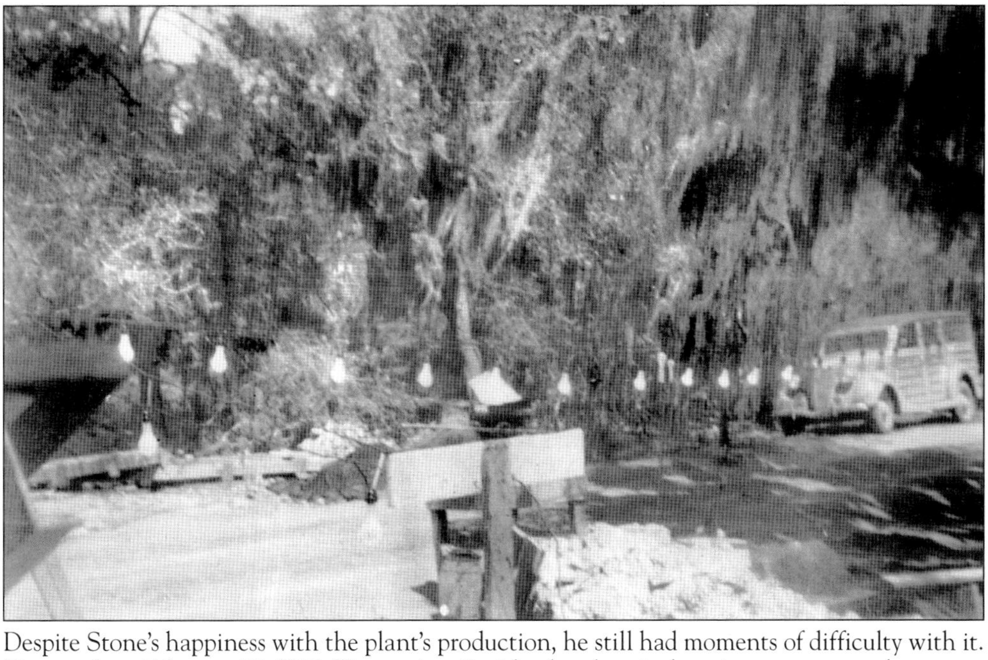

Despite Stone's happiness with the plant's production, he still had moments of difficulty with it. He noted on February 27, 1937, "Every time Smith, the electrical engineer, gets anywhere near the water wheel and fusses with it, it never works as well after he leaves. It seems to have to recover from his manipulations, and the period of convalescence is anywhere from three days to ten days." (Courtesy of the South Carolina Historical Society.)

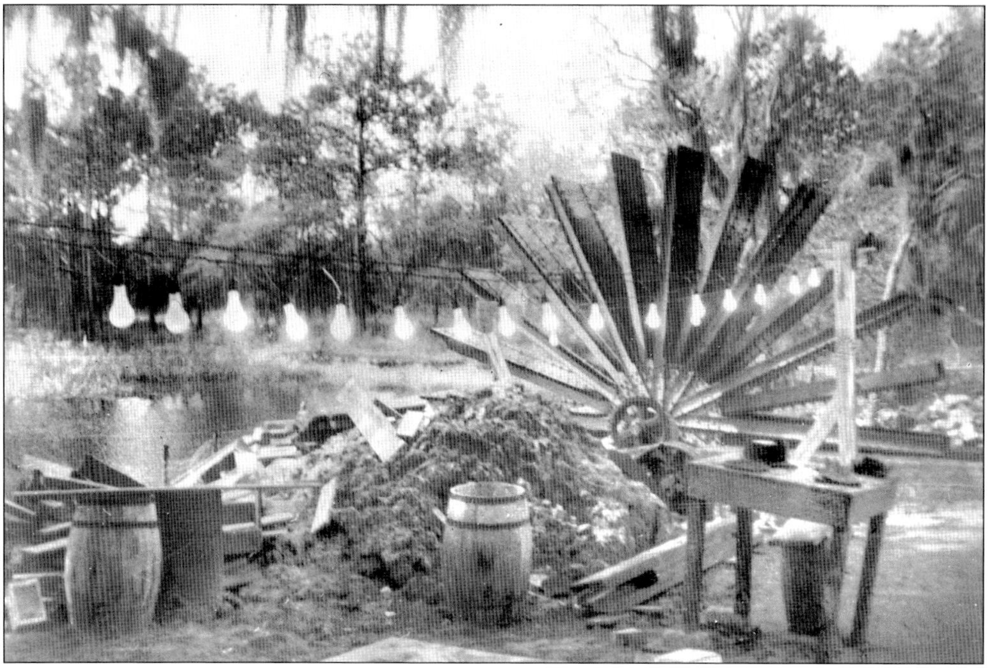

Thomas Stone was thrilled at the success of his plans: "Yesterday, March 10, we lighted the electric lights for 10 minutes with tide power. We have beaten Passamaquoddy! As far as we know, this is the first time ever that such a thing has been done.. It runs like a charm and we may not have to put in a second one." (Courtesy of the South Carolina Historical Society.)

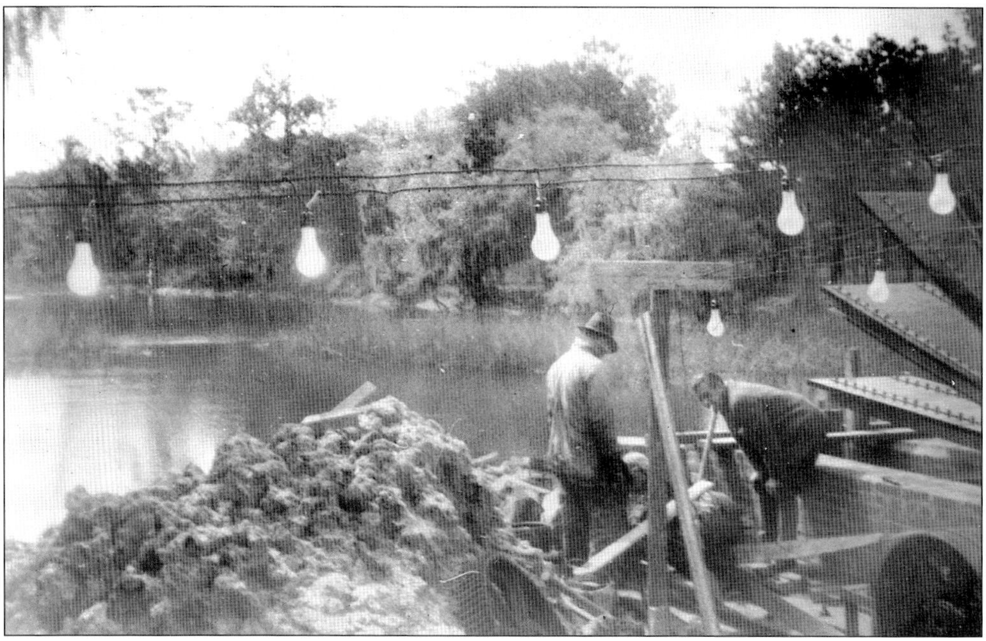

The power wheel was able to provide 600 to 650 kilowatt-hours per month, which Stone estimated to be a little more than half the requirements for the plantation. He decided to test it out for the summer to see if he needed to add an additional wheel in the fall. (Courtesy of the South Carolina Historical Society.)

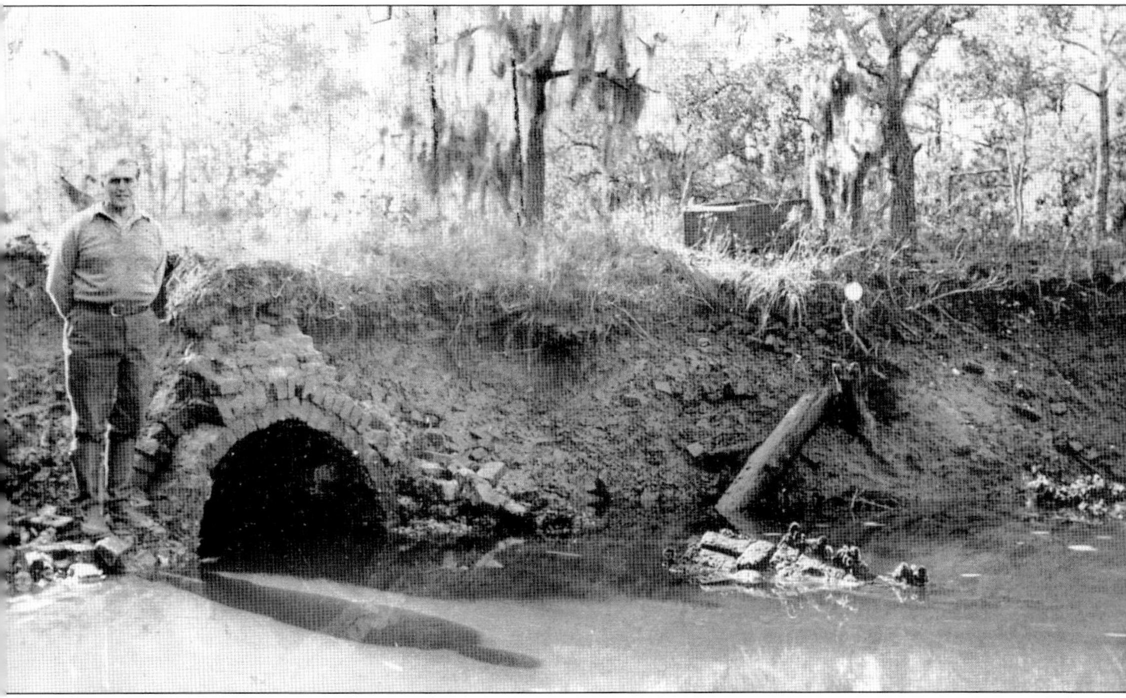

Every house, the barn, and the water pump had a meter that was read monthly. Because of a nine-acre lake on the property that was filled through a culvert from the tide of the Wampancheone Creek, Boone Hall was ideal for this type of electrical operation. Thomas Stone is shown here next to the culvert. (Courtesy of the South Carolina Historical Society.)

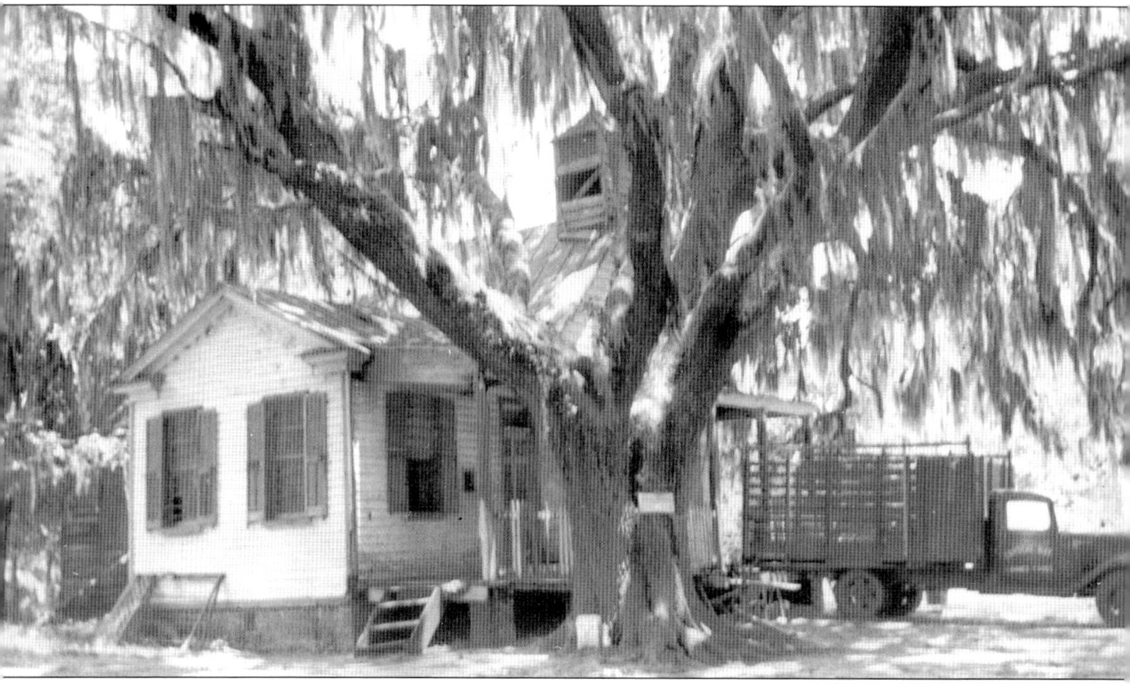

Other buildings served a variety of purposes over the years. Some have housed office space or were homes for employees. Buildings also consisted of laundry facilities, storage, and servants' quarters. The cotton gin often served as guest quarters for the Stones. This structure, built in 1892, once served as a snack shop and currently serves the hospitality center, housing restrooms and informational displays. (Courtesy of the South Carolina Historical Society.)

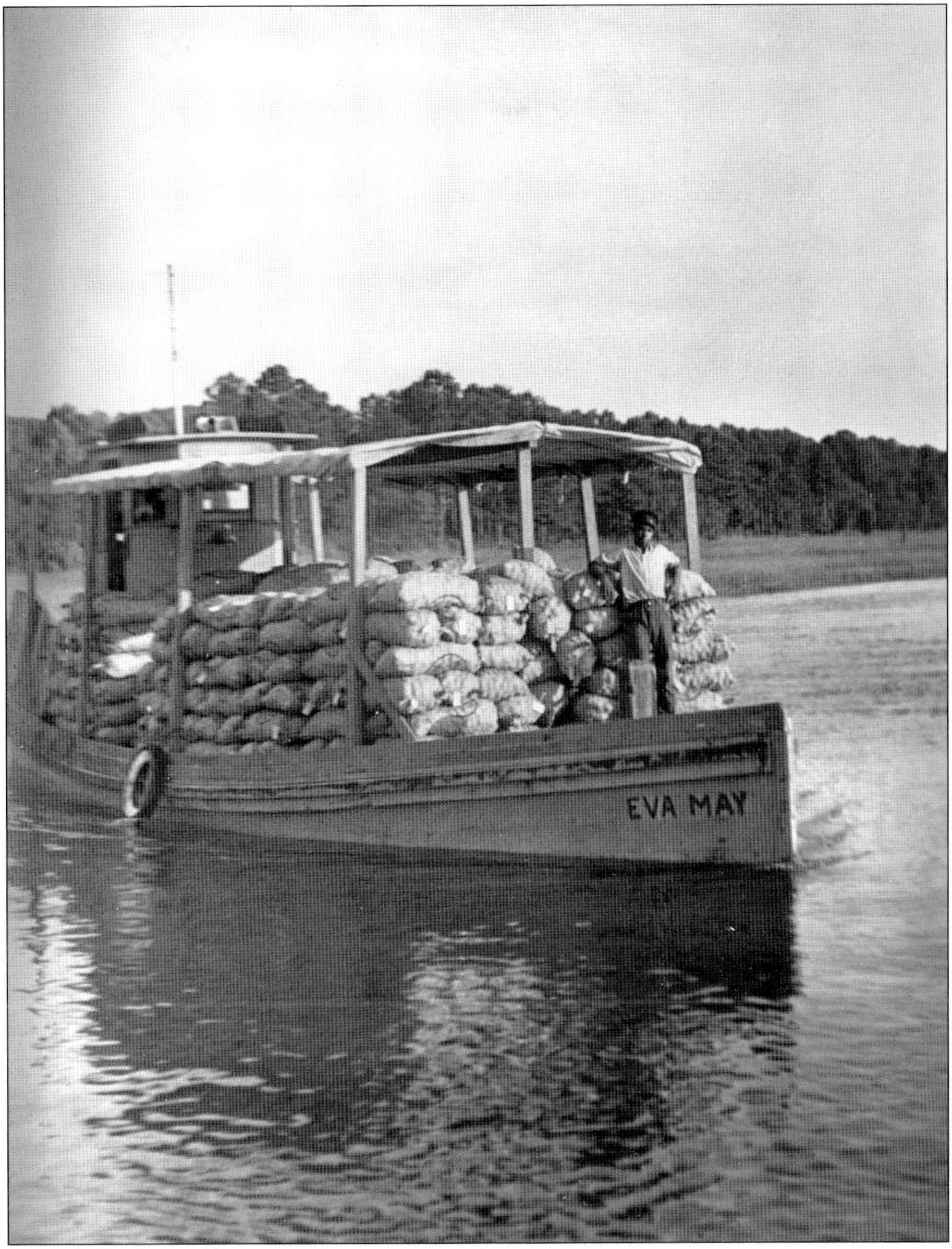

The Stones continued to take advantage of boating, one of the most important forms of transportation for early Boone Hall residents, especially in carrying the crops to town. They purchased a vessel called the *Wampancheone* and often used it for leisure with their friends and neighbors. They recreated the same social network as those previously living at Boone Hall probably had. (Courtesy of the South Carolina Historical Society.)

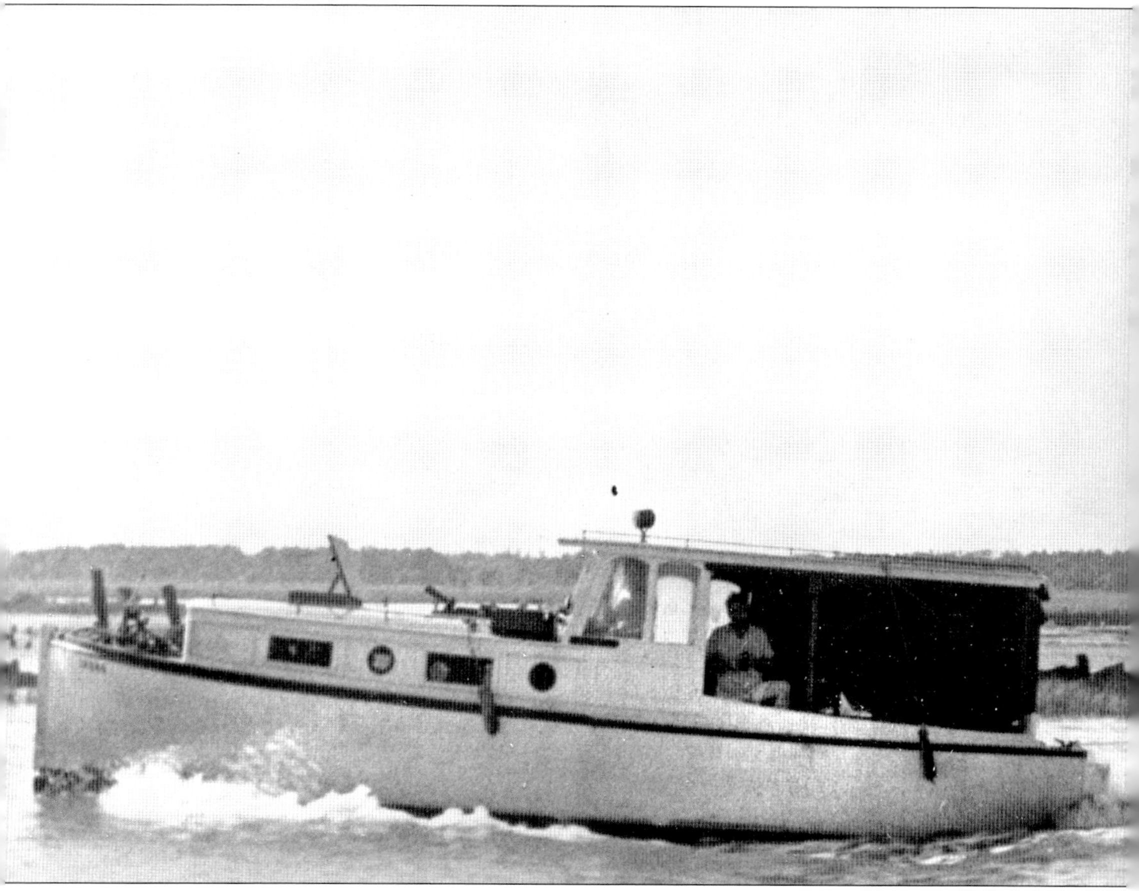

Thomas Stone included descriptions of some of his trips on the boat on May 25, 1937. "Last Thursday we spent our first night on the 'Wampancheone'. We left about 6:30 and crossed the Wando into Beresford Creek, where we cast anchor. . . . The LeGendres came over on Saturday morning and we sailed to Medway where we spent the night. Sunday we sailed up the Cooper as far as Mulberry Castle and called on the Kittredges at Dean Hall on the way." (Courtesy of the South Carolina Historical Society.)

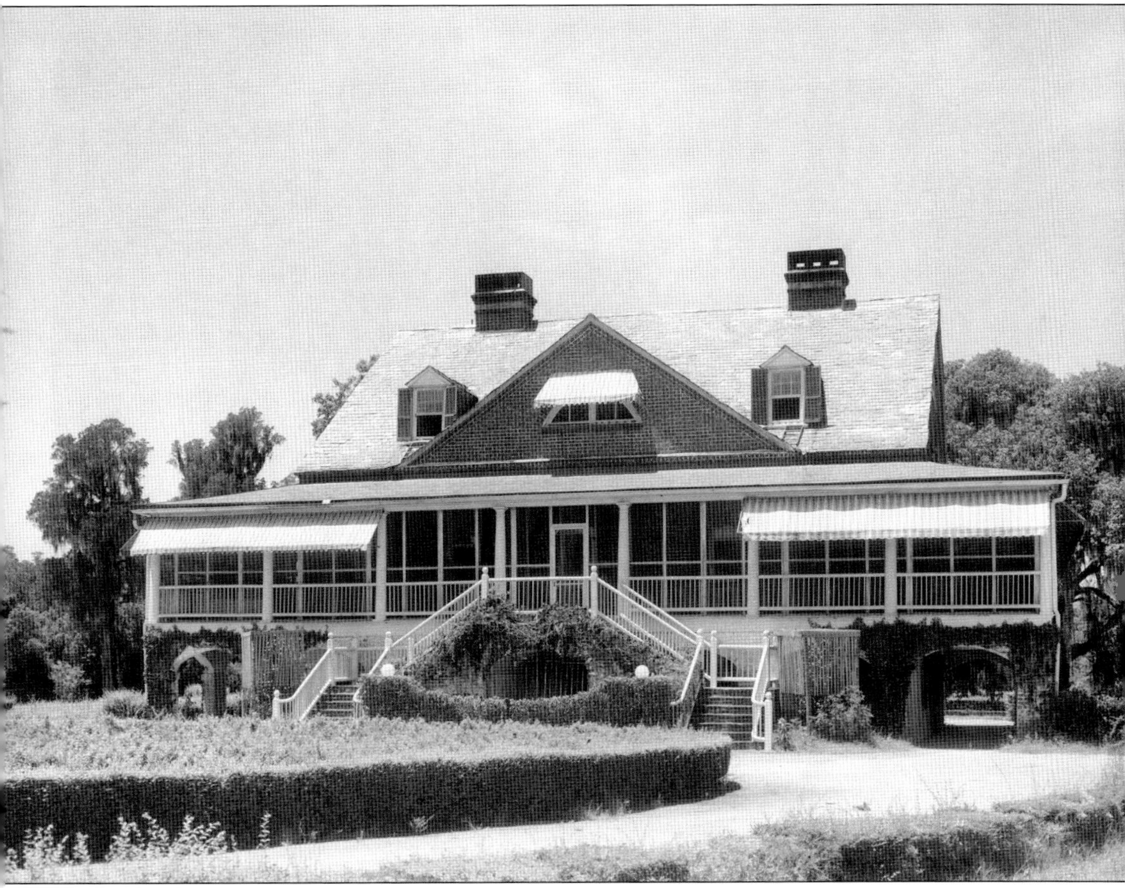

Dean Hall, one of the homes Stone mentions in his river travels, is pictured here. The Stones had many acquaintances prior to moving to Charleston, as many of the plantation owners were also Northerners. It was common during the early 20th century for Northerners to purchase plantation homes as second residences. (Courtesy of the Library of Congress.)

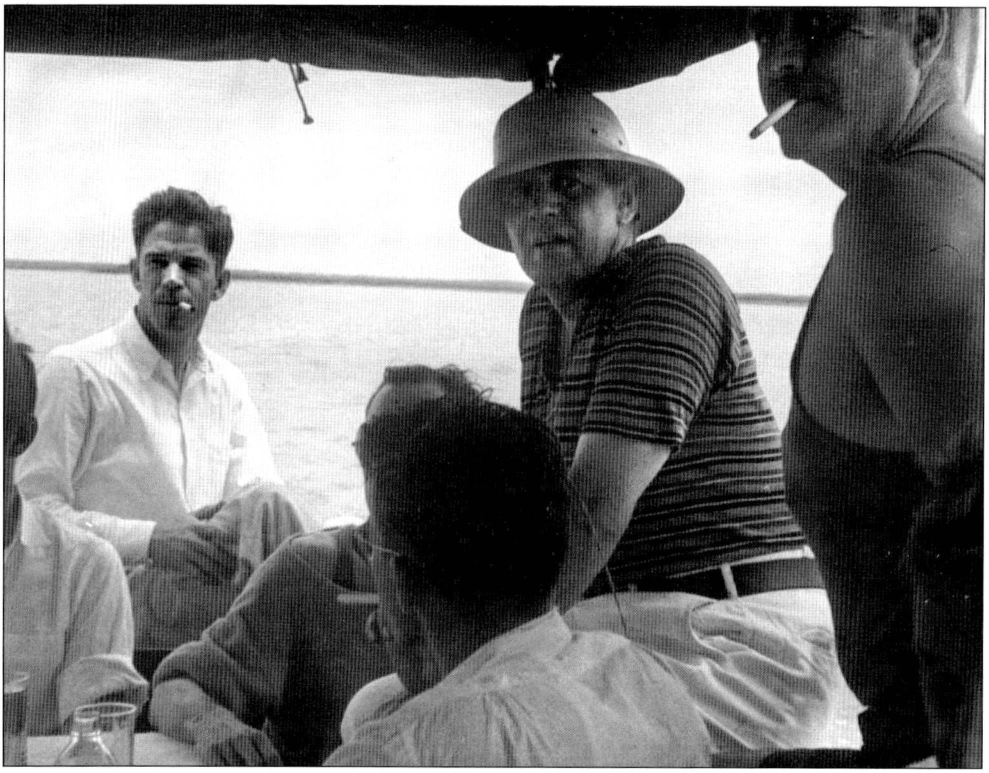

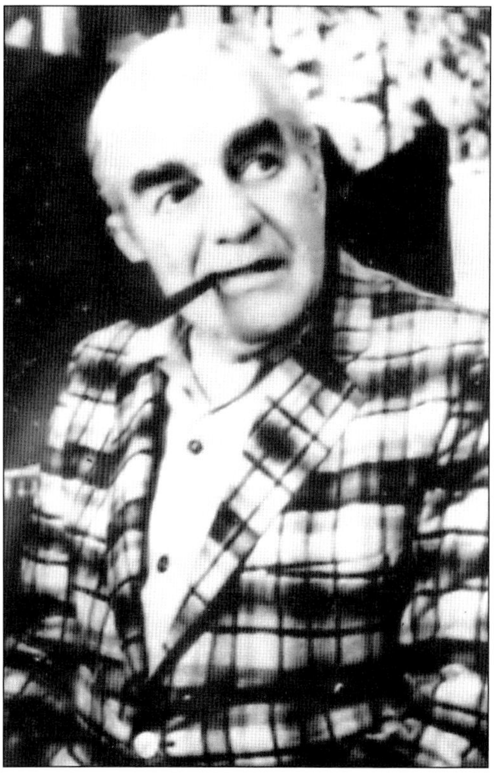

The boat helped provide entertainment for the Stones, as Thomas noted on June 9, 1937. "The yacht club cruise to Price's Inlet was a roaring success. . . . There were 14 or 15 boats and 65 or 70 people. A rather large majority of the crews of the various boats were at least two sheets to the wind by the time they arrived at Price's—and they remained in that condition throughout the weekend." (Courtesy of the South Carolina Historical Society.)

Later in his life, Thomas Stone retired from his diplomatic work and was employed in international relations for the International Nickel Corporation. Toward the end of his life, Stone retired to France, where he lived in a beautiful 14th-century farmhouse belonging to his third wife, Emily. He is buried in Recloses, France, about 30 miles outside of Paris. (Courtesy of Ellen Stone Devine.)

Four

FARMING

Farming was not as easy as the Stones originally thought. There were daily battles with weather, insects, and labor. The Stones were definitely learning as the years passed. The main crops planted by the Stones were tomatoes, cabbages, and potatoes. Thomas Stone was fortunate in his first year to have a seasoned farmer, William Seabrook, overseeing the operation. Seabrook was a vital resource for Stone, and he certainly played an important role in getting the plantation up and running. Stone's entries include many hilarious looks at farming as well as what makes farming such a precarious occupation. Through it all, the Stones and their employees managed to weather everything that could be thrown their way.

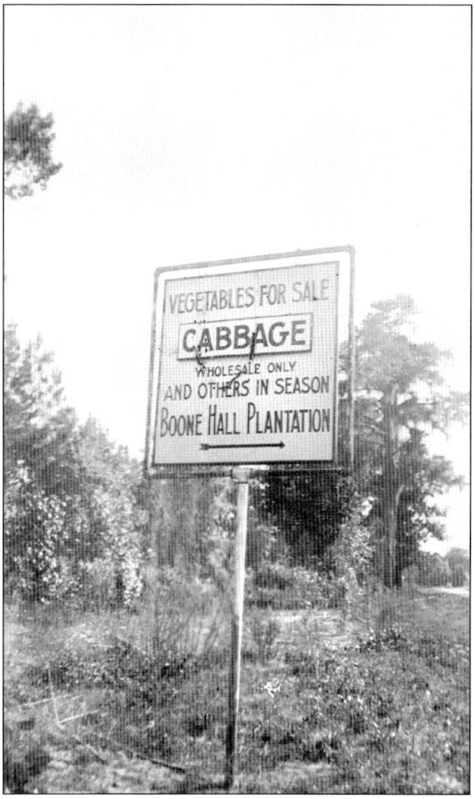

Cabbage was not Thomas Stone's favorite crop, as he observed on January 27, 1937: "Miserable things—cabbages. They make a dirty pack, and look more like six-day-old Cole slaw than anything else, even before they leave the plantation. What they look like in Baltimore or New York, the Lord only knows." (Courtesy of the South Carolina Historical Society.)

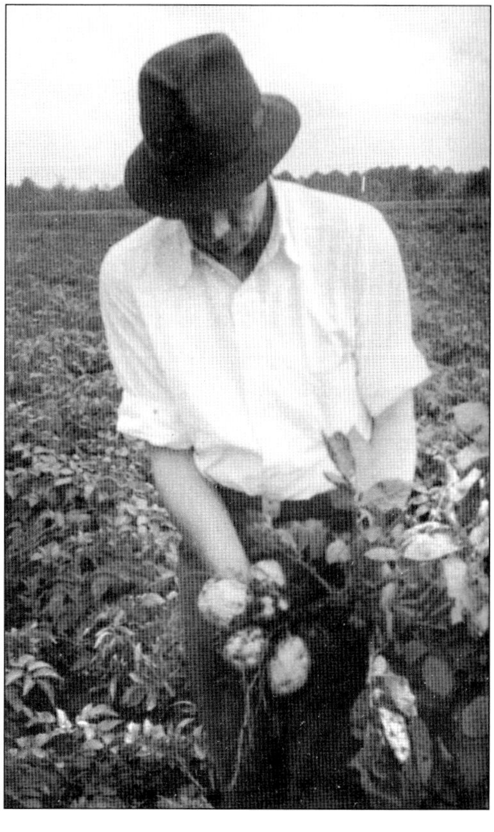

Stone began seeing the difficulty that farmers experienced amidst adverse weather conditions but eventually did enjoy his first sale. "We had a frost on April 4 which rather seriously burned our potatoes. What with loss from this and loss from rot we shall make a much smaller crop than we anticipated. . . . They are small yet, but delicious. We sold our first this morning—2 dozen heads to a negro for $1.00." (Courtesy of the South Carolina Historical Society.)

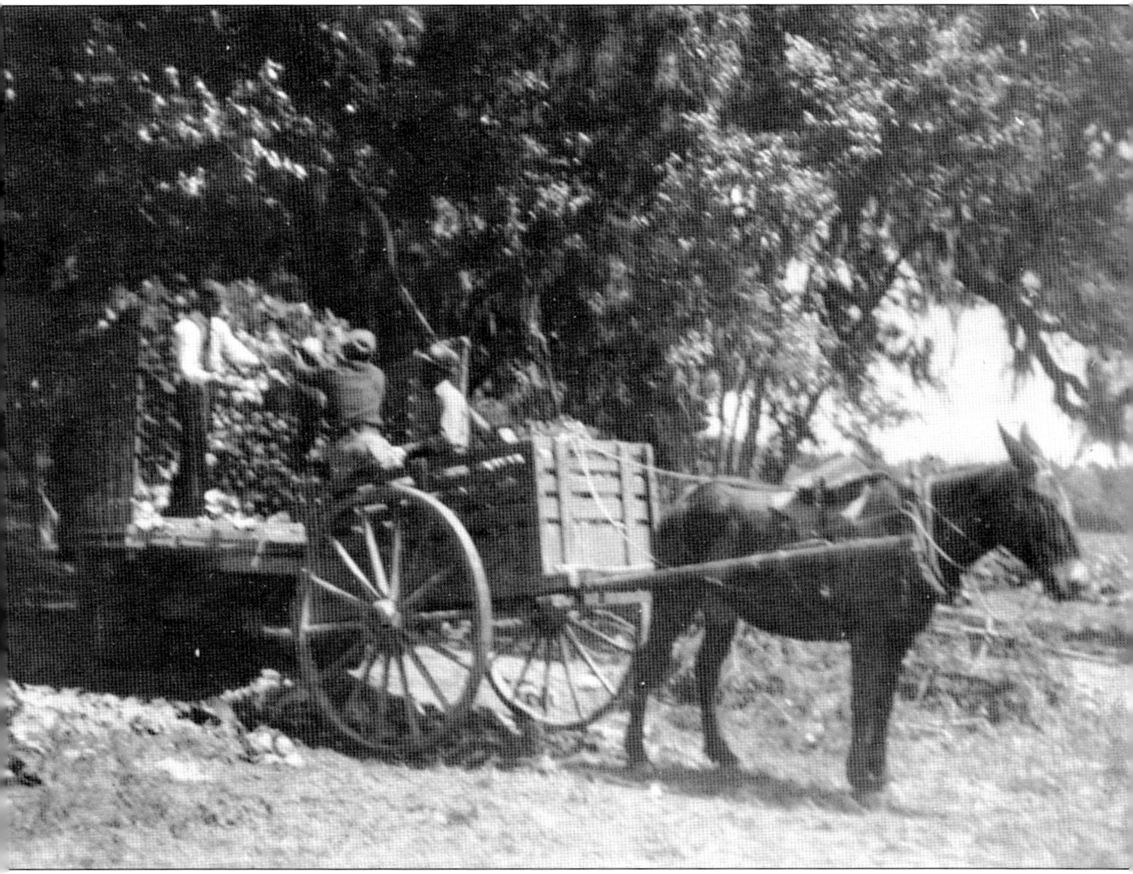

New issues arose as the Boone Hall brands hit the market. If the cabbage was not cut and sold quickly enough, it became wormy, and there were reports of many farmers plowing under the rest of their crops. Timing is everything when getting the product out onto the market. Charlie Schroeder often second-guessed whether or not it was better to get the crops out as soon as possible or wait until later in the market with better product. (Courtesy of the South Carolina Historical Society.)

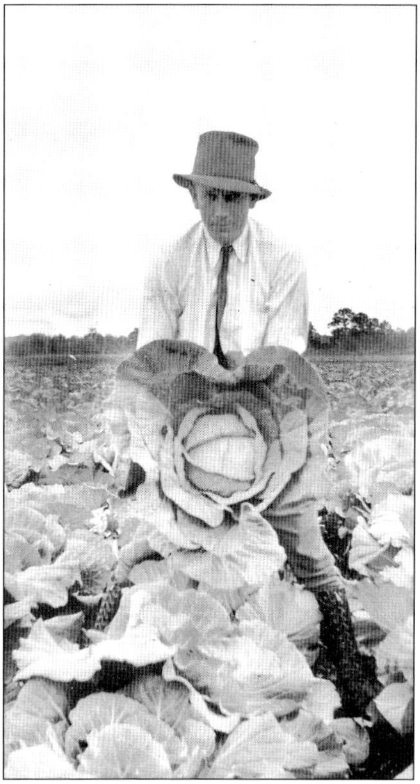

It became a challenge to figure out which city to ship the cabbage to and which markets would be the most profitable. Several cities were chosen for the Boone Hall brand, such as Baltimore, Maryland; Springfield and Cleveland, Ohio; and Boston, Massachusetts. Markets were also harder when they are inundated with product, and Charlie Schroeder often waited until the markets were cleared to get better prices. (Courtesy of the South Carolina Historical Society.)

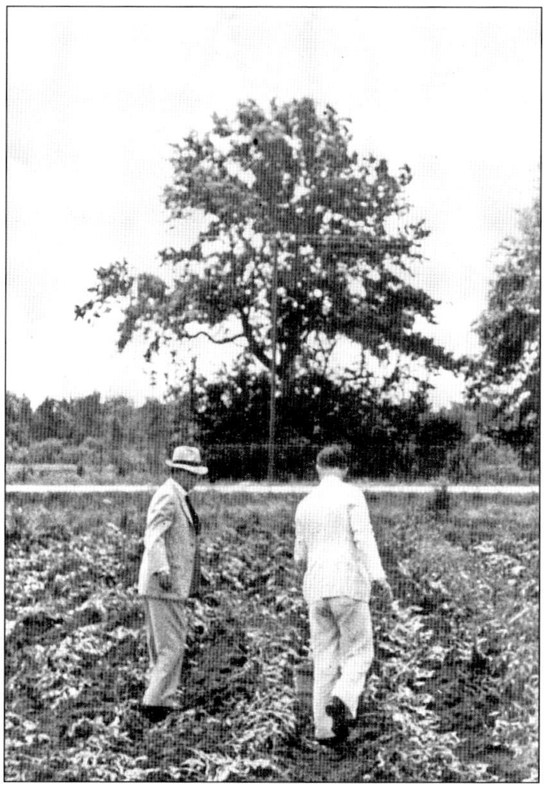

Farming took an enormous investment in money and labor, as Thomas Stone discovered. On February 10, 1937, fertilizer was placed just on the potato fields, equaling almost 700 bags in the Savannah fields. One bag equals 200 pounds of fertilizer, which works out to 2,800 pounds per acre. (Courtesy of the South Carolina Historical Society.)

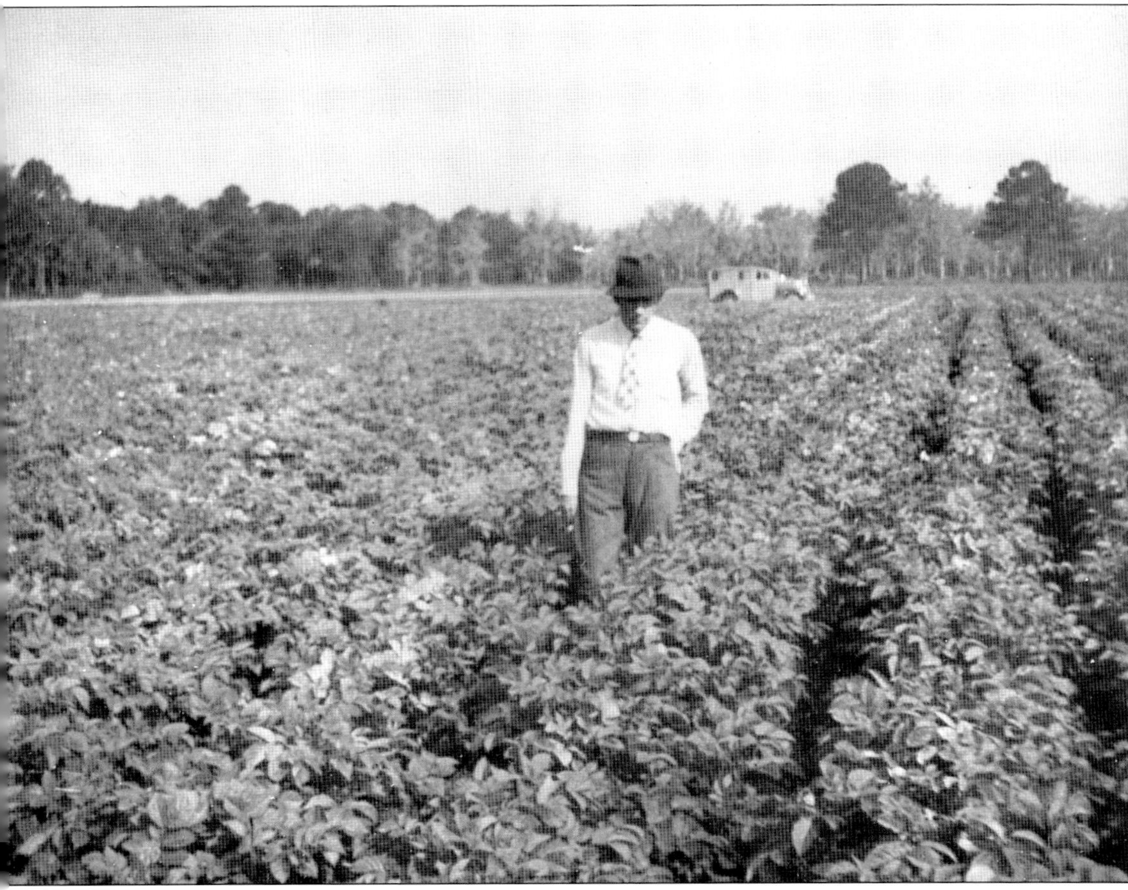

Thomas Stone became more familiar with the types of potatoes and more knowledgeable about their growth. He wrote on March 9, 1937, "The seems to be a slow starter, for while Cobblers next to them in the same field and planted at the same me have now sprouts two inches or more long, with a well established root system, the Chippewah sprouts are not more than one inch long, with the root system just beginning to put out." (Courtesy of the South Carolina Historical Society.)

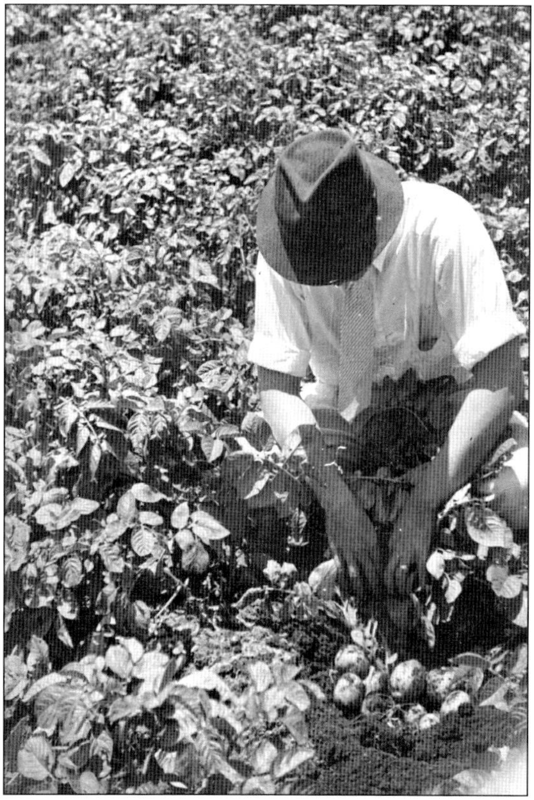

Thomas Stone commented on how difficult farming is on June 4, 1937: "By the grace of God! What a year to become a farmer! . . . This past winter proved to be the coldest one in 25 years. During spring . . . we had enough rain to drown. . . . The potato harvest proved very poor . . . and only a very strong market price exchange has saved us. Cabbages are wonderful but we had no use for them. . . . Tomatoes will be good if . . . we have enough water!" (Courtesy of the South Carolina Historical Society.)

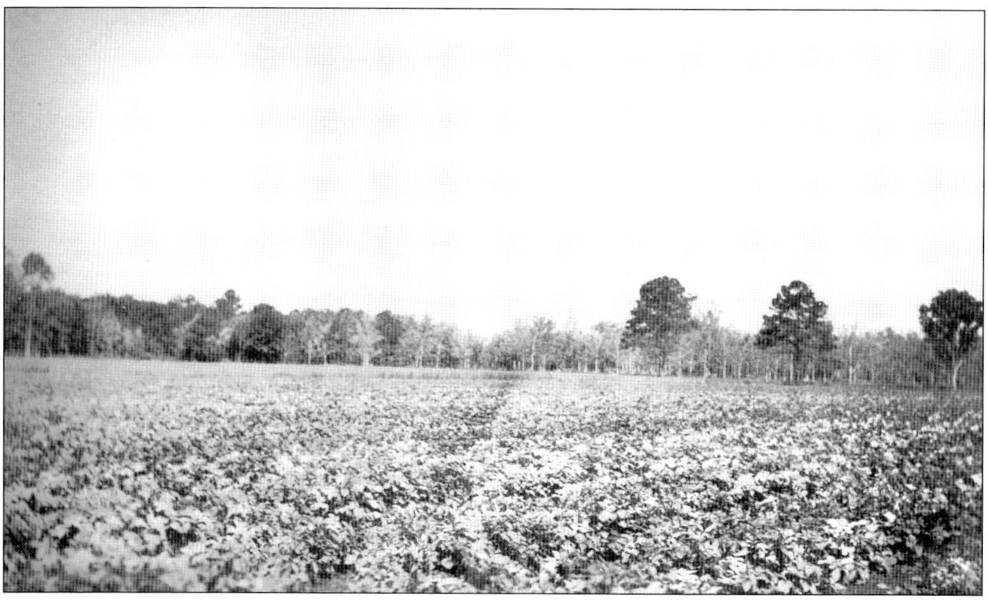

Weather plays a large part in the success of a farm, as Stone commented again and again: "The frost on Sunday night last which knocked our potatoes to the ground, and second, the cabbage market on Monday morning going down to rock bottom. Our tomato plants, which are up about an inch in most hills, were scarcely touched, strange to say beans and cucumbers which were up were almost completely wiped out." (Courtesy of the South Carolina Historical Society.)

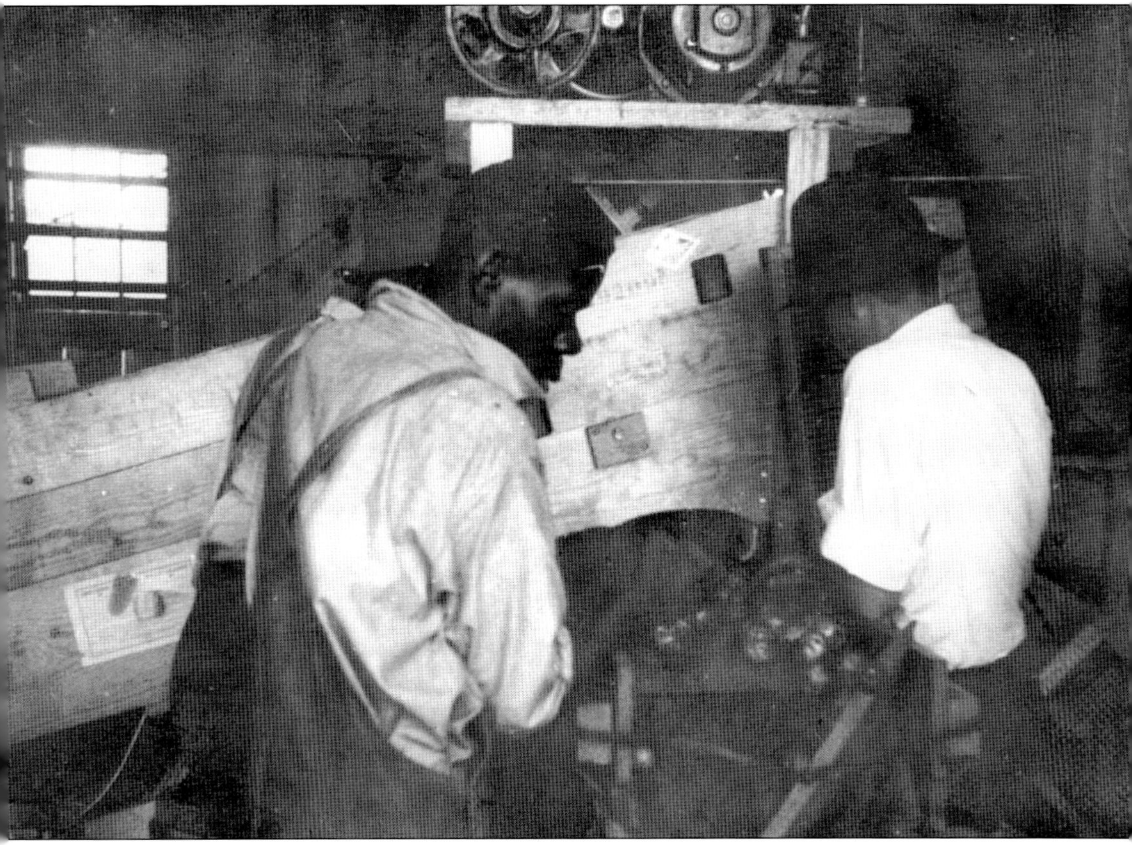

In the second year, the plantation took on a more mechanized air. A new motorized potato grader was installed in mid-May 1937. Stone commented that it looked extremely efficient. Grading the potatoes was extremely important in determining the price one would receive. (Courtesy of the South Carolina Historical Society.)

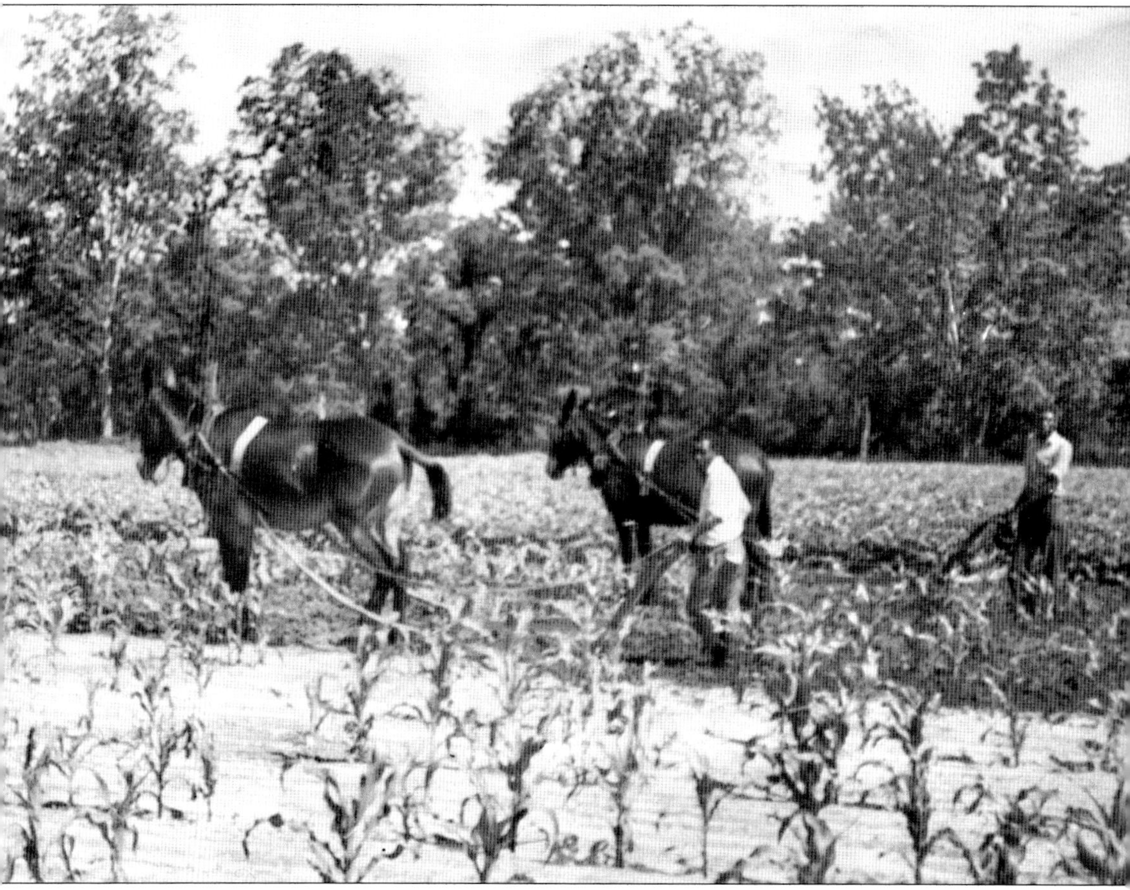

Not only was weather an issue, but bugs presented problems as well. Leaf-legged plant bugs eat the Chippewa potatoes. These bugs suck the chlorophyll from the tips of the stems and cause the new-growth leaves to wilt and die off. Small boys were sent out to pick them off. Potato bugs, blight, and rhyzotomia, a soil-borne fungus, were also cited as problems. (Courtesy of the South Carolina Historical Society.)

Thomas Stone also started planting other crops in his second year as a farmer, learning about plants that improved the soil or were excellent cover crops. Peas, beans, *crotalaria*, and soybeans were used for this purpose. Cover crops were used in areas that were badly in need of fertilizing. (Courtesy of the South Carolina Historical Society.)

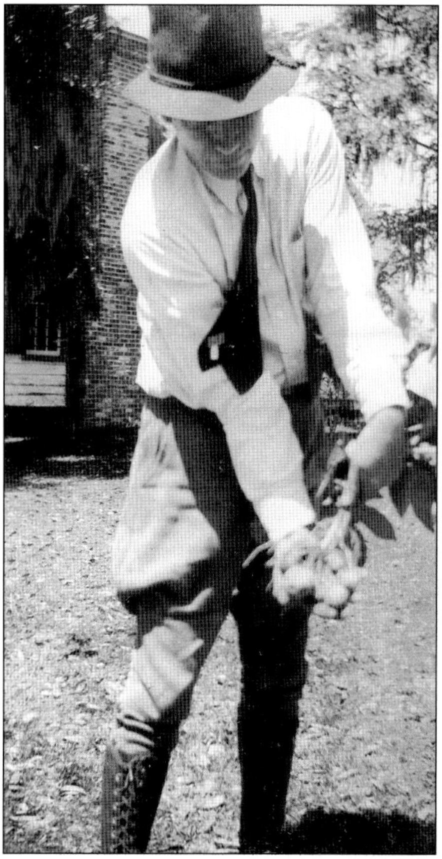

Boone Hall brands become successful with their first entry into the potato market, as Charlie Schroeder reported in a May 26, 1936, letter: " 'Boone Hall Brand' has them all talking. Would have a heavy demand for them but for the high prices which tends to turn the demand to smaller sizes. Hope he is not kidding me, but personally think we have one of the best packs." (Courtesy of the South Carolina Historical Society.)

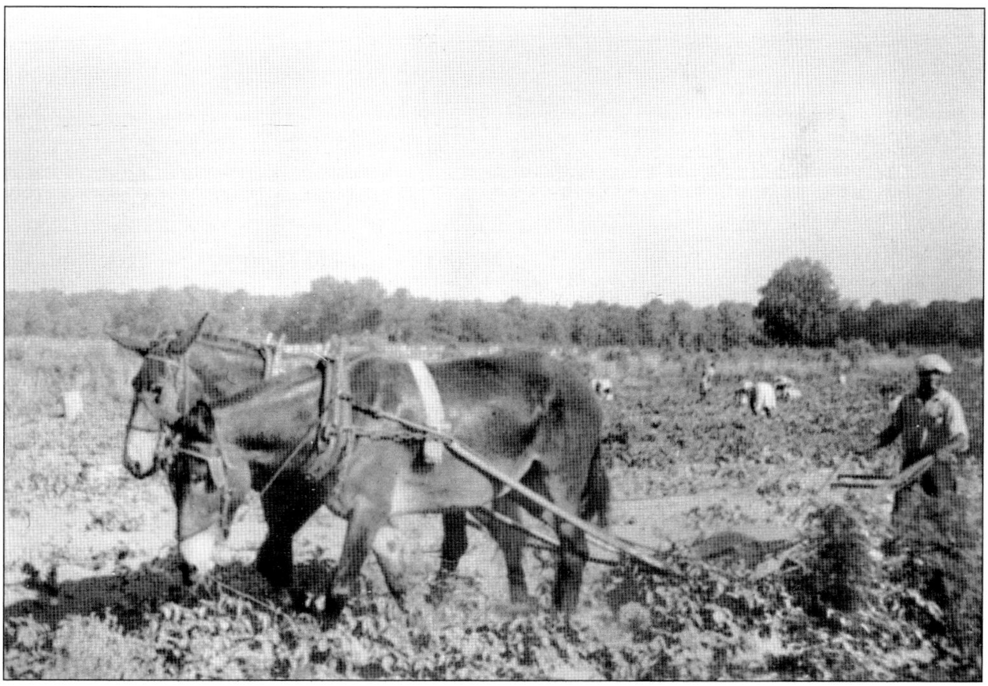

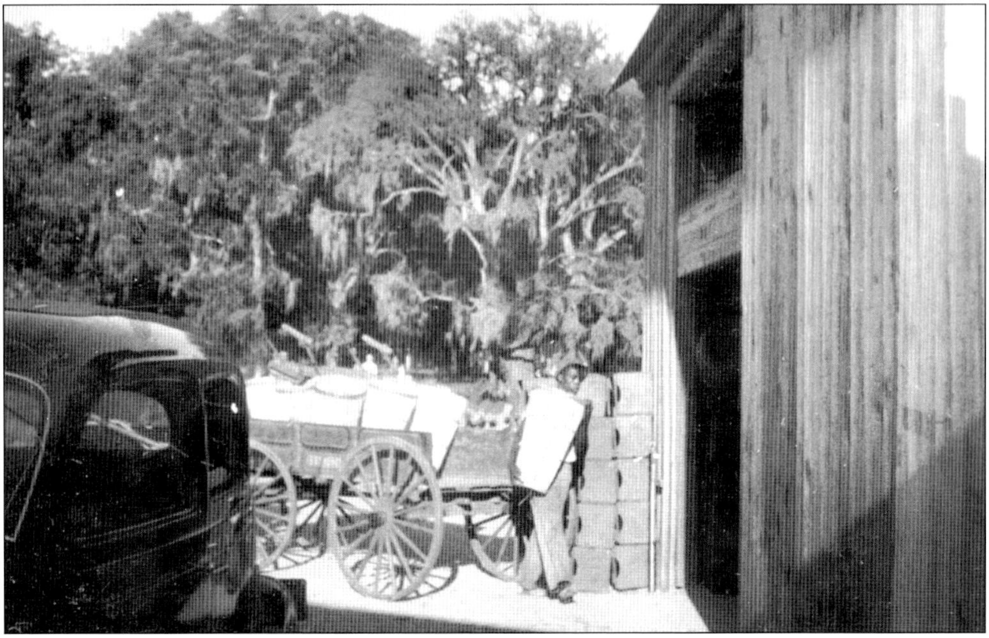

Despite their enthusiasm and high hopes, the potatoes were not as profitable as hoped. Charlie Schroeder reported that he was disappointed with Boone Hall's yields of 30 barrels an acre shipped and that they appeared to be under the county average of 50 barrels. Despite the disappointment, the net profit was estimated at $2,884. (Courtesy of the South Carolina Historical Society.)

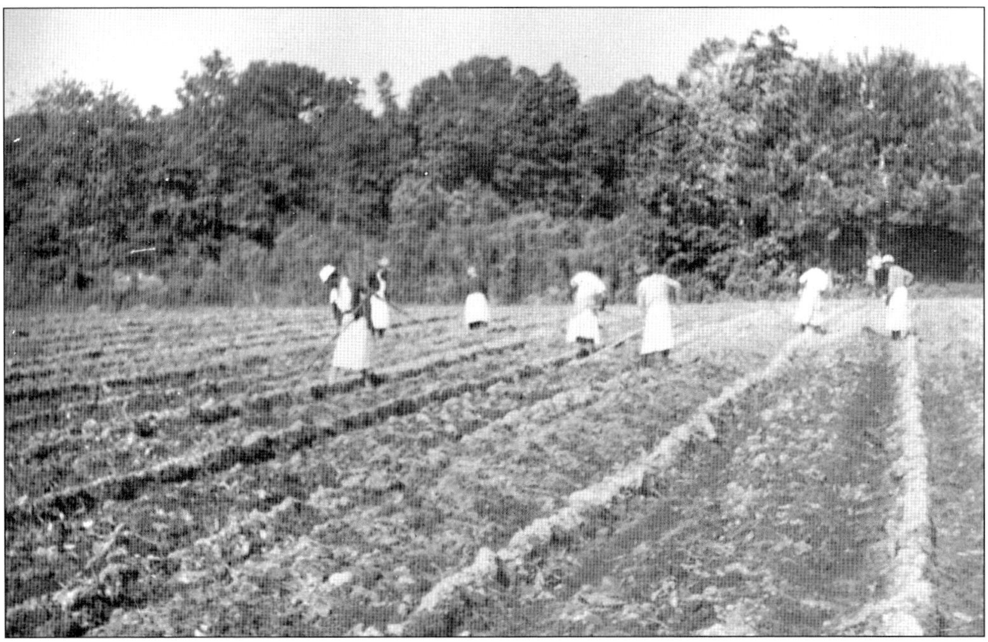

Schroeder was also learning and tried to glean as much as he could from the plantation manager, William Seabrook. According to Schroeder, "You know we have been expecting 8,000 to 10,000 lugs. I am told not to worry. I do not know just what an acre of tomatoes is supposed to pack out so as a result have to rely upon what I am told. I am keeping my eyes open and watching everything closely." (Courtesy of the South Carolina Historical Society.)

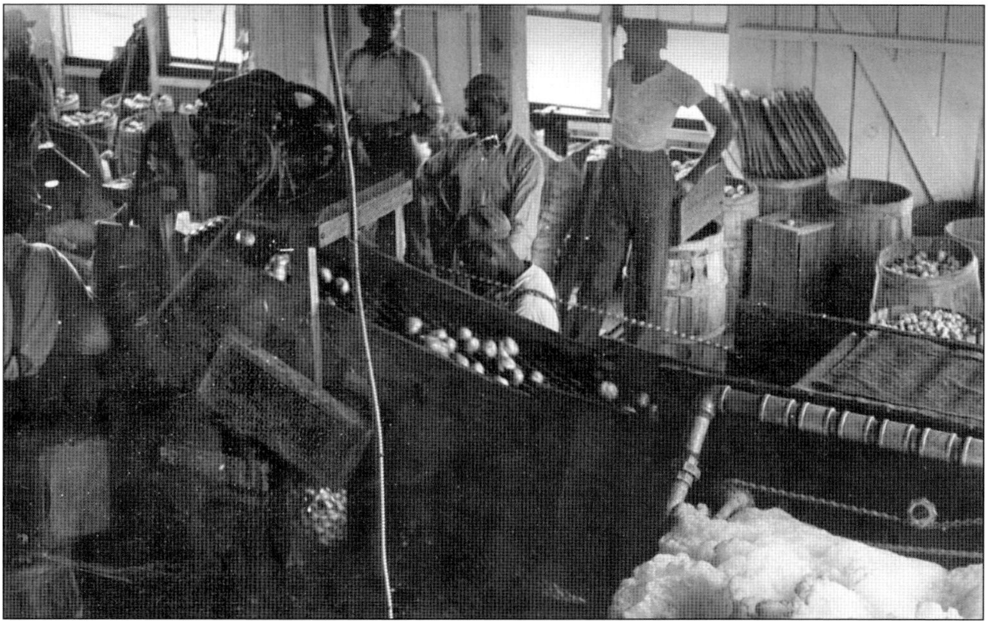

Packing the tomatoes became a concern, as Schroeder reported on June 2, 1936: "We are very strict with our packing and it has been going along nicely, only had one complaint. . . . The complaint was that we were . . . packing large tomatoes in the bottom of the lugs and finishing off the top with smaller ones. This practice is all right as far as tomatoes were concerned, yet on the other hand it does not leave a good impression with some buyers." (Courtesy of the South Carolina Historical Society.)

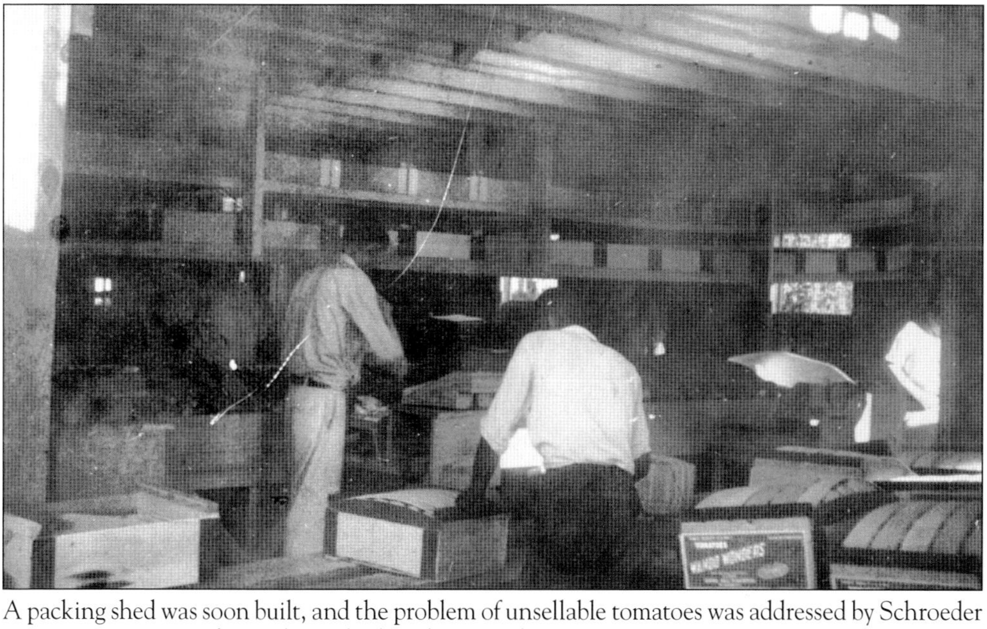

A packing shed was soon built, and the problem of unsellable tomatoes was addressed by Schroeder on June 10, 1936: "The packing shed is about ready. Spent the entire day at Beaufort with Mr. Seabrook and Wise. . . . The crop down there is rather ordinary poor shape due to lack of rain. . . . I want to go to Georgetown and contact the canning plant there so as to be prepared to have an outlet for ripes in the event we want it." (Courtesy of the South Carolina Historical Society.)

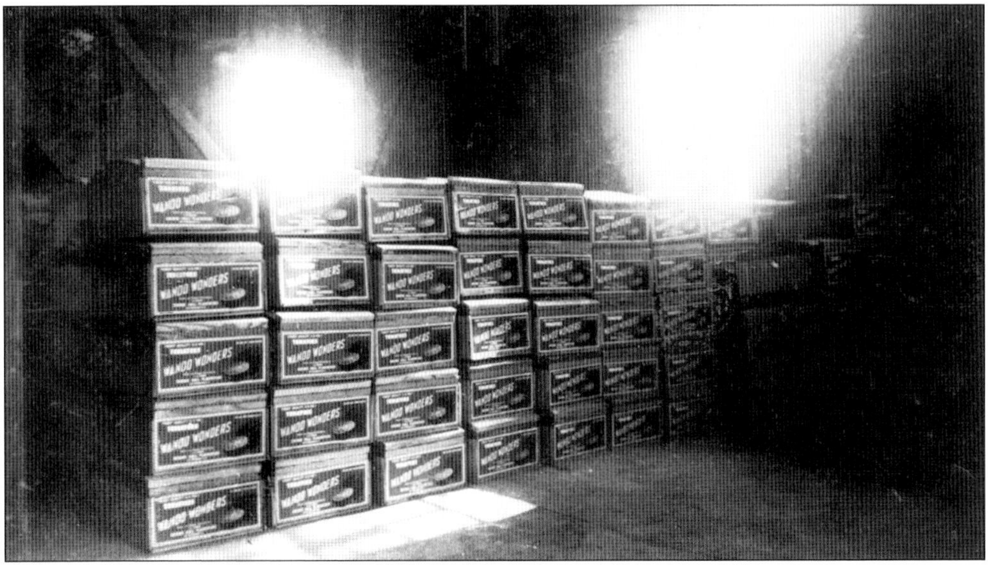

Charlie Schroeder made a great effort to ensure that Boone Hall tomatoes were high quality, as he wrote on June 24, 1936: "I am striving to get our crop into as many markets as it is possible price permitting for I am very anxious for the trade to know Boone Hall quality which can only be seen when so distributed. . . . I have been told by cash buyers that we certainly were shipping beautiful stock and we have been paid some very nice compliments." (Courtesy of the South Carolina Historical Society.)

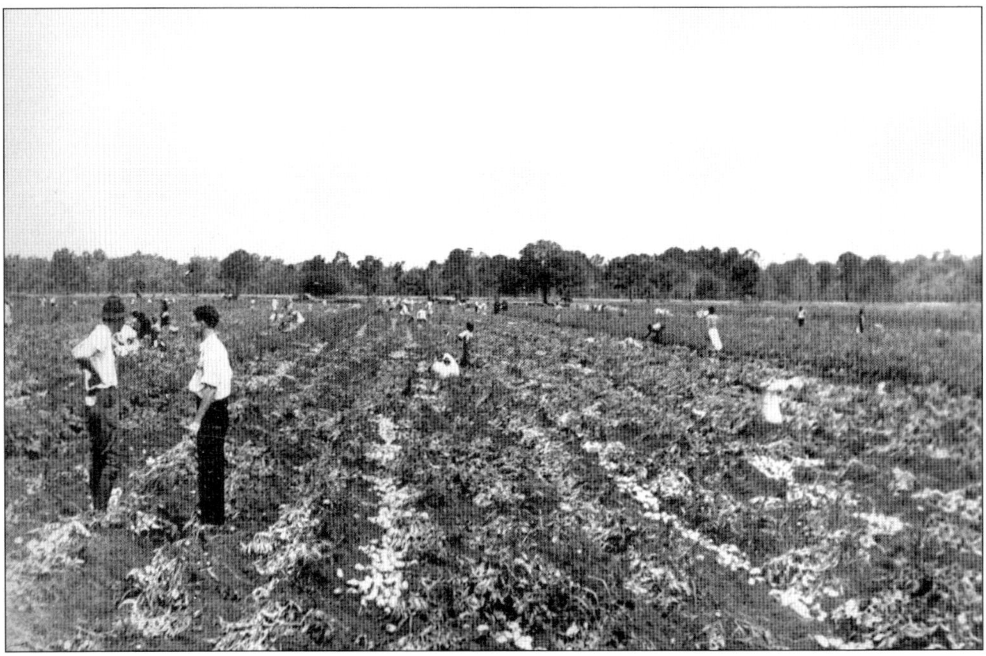

Grading often affected pricing, Schroeder noted on July 1, 1936: "Shipped one car yesterday to Albany, New York, have orders for two more which I would like very much to get off today, also have an order for 450 lugs via truck for Roanoke, Virginia. This sold ones 1.25 two's $1.00 and three's 70 cents on two orders and 75 cents on other two." (Courtesy of the South Carolina Historical Society.)

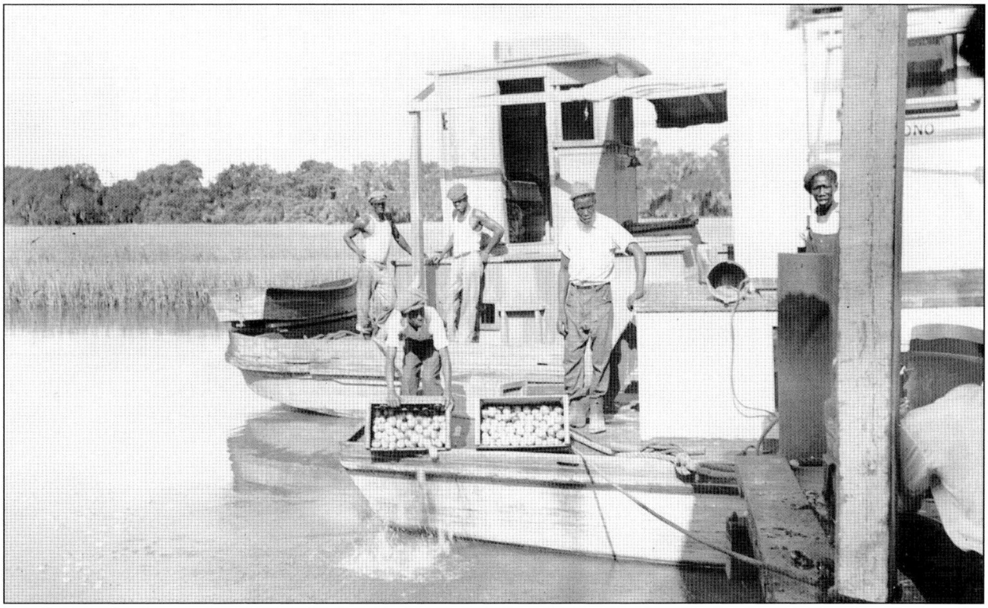

Schroeder reported buyers' growing interest in Boone Hall's product on July 13, 1936: "Miles was delighted with our grade and pack and . . . asked that we give him the exclusive right to our tomato pack next season. . . . I am not so sure that I would care to do this—still this is just the attitude I am trying to work up in various markets regarding our brands—get them all asking for our products." (Courtesy of the South Carolina Historical Society.)

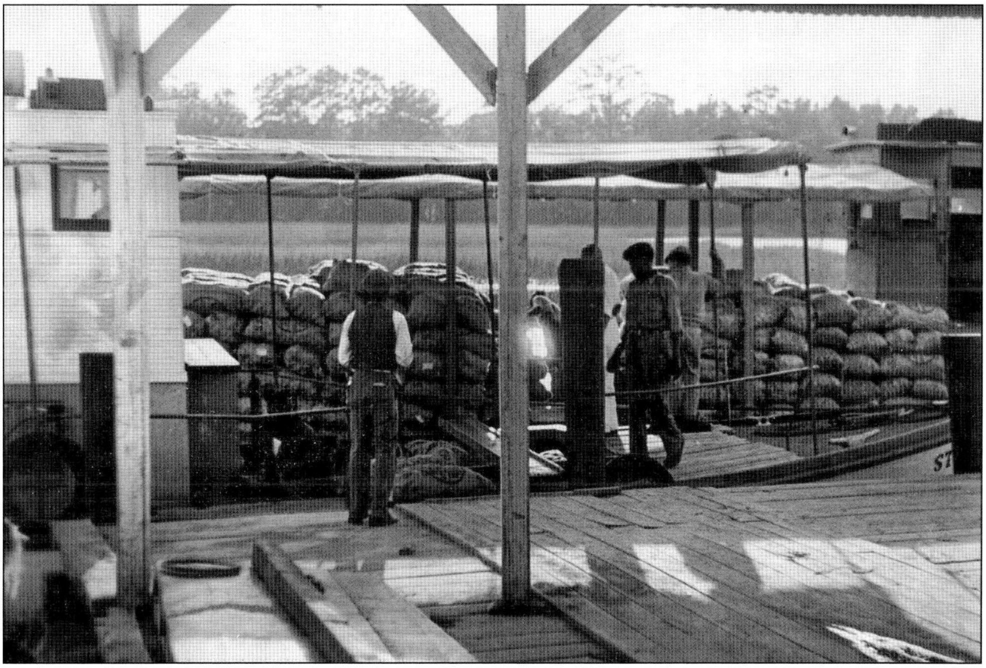

"We have persuaded the Southern Railway to build us a 25' dock at the Boone Hall landing, the construction of which will probably start next week. We shall then construct a warehouse on the landing, which will be most useful," Thomas Stone wrote on January 27, 1936. (Courtesy of the South Carolina Historical Society.)

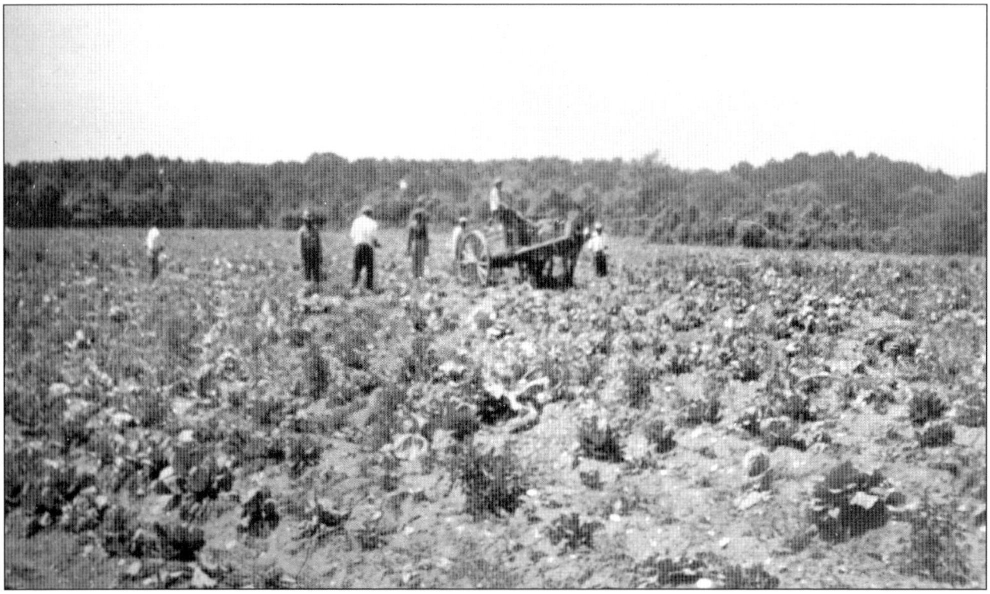

Women were paid less than men while working in the field. Three men were tasked with sweeping corn for $3 for the week, while 19 women were paid $1.40 each for hoeing and thinning, a combined $26.60 for the week. The total payroll for the week of May 23, 1940, was $169.61. (Courtesy of the South Carolina Historical Society.)

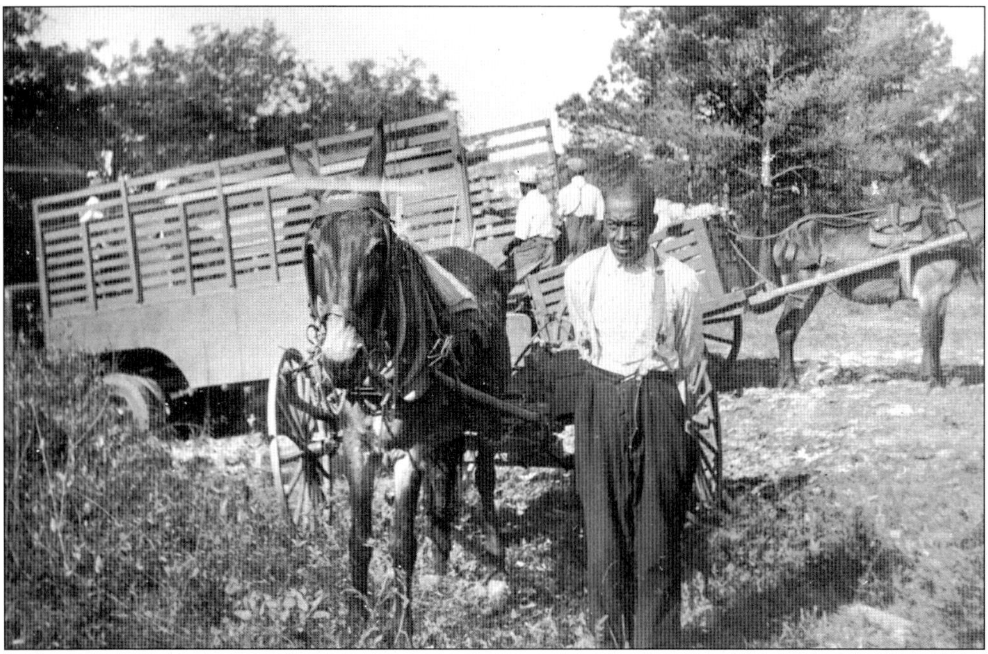

Farm machinery and work animals often caused problems for the plantation, as William Seabrook reported on September 24, 1938: "We naturally was very much upset over the death of a favorite animal, but did everything possible only to have her pass out. We questioned the Doctor closely trying to get a slant on what could have possibly made her sick . . . only to be told it was a condition that frequently occurs and over which there is no control." (Courtesy of the South Carolina Historical Society.)

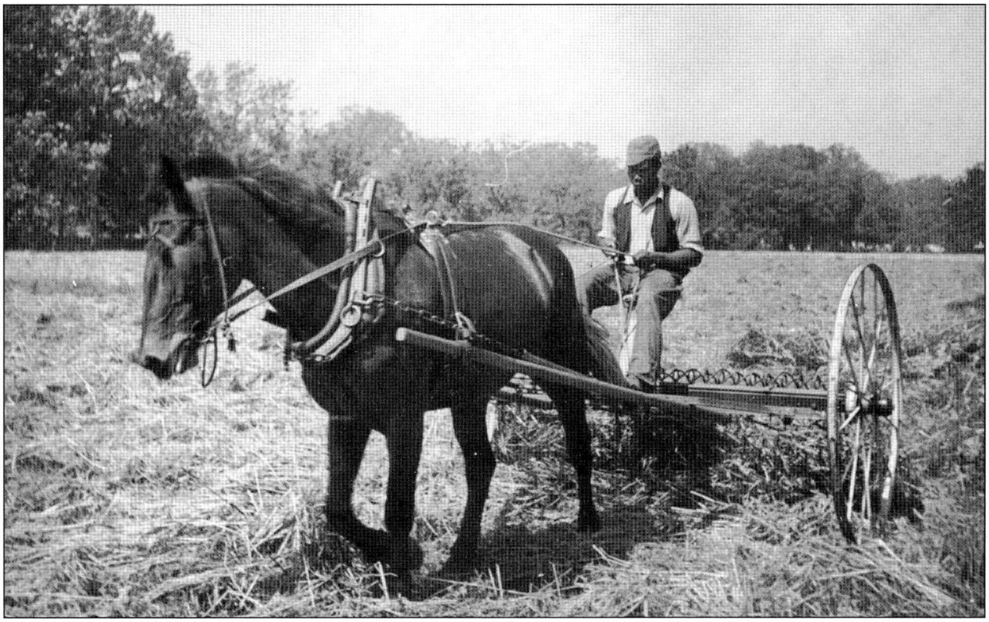

Labor could be fickle, as Seabrook reported on September 30, 1938: "The Wando river bridge work has taken on quite a few of the good young men about us, including even Morgan and Frankie. They are paying common negro laborers $2.00 per day. Most of the other young negroes are on WPA projects. I have Slim on the Case and I am trying to break in John Foreman on the Deere." (Courtesy of the South Carolina Historical Society.)

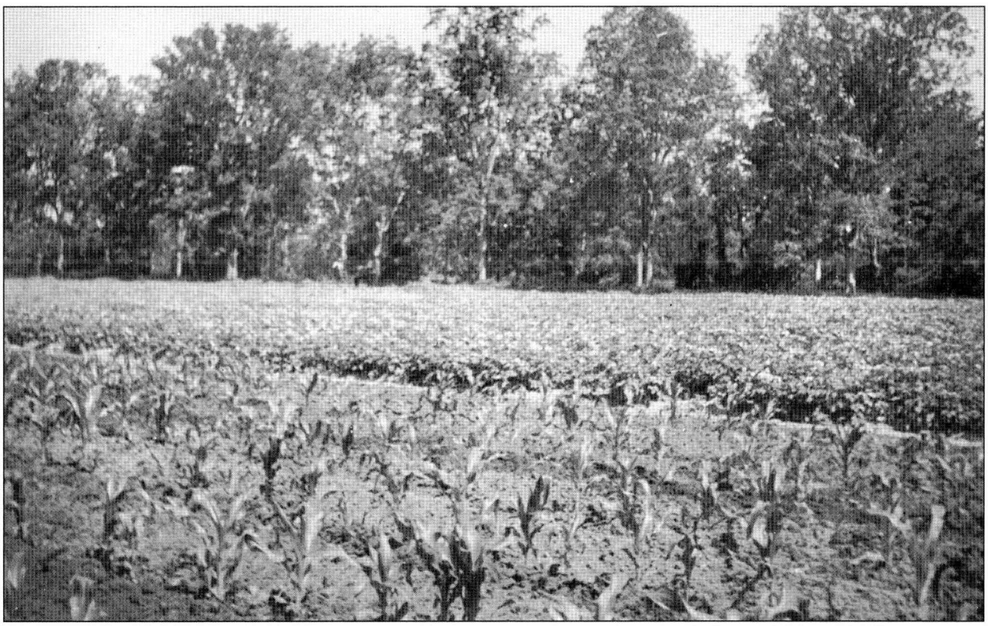

Want of rain, as well as horrific storms, were also a worry, as Thomas Stone described on September 30, 1938, "We had terrible rains lasting through the night and all day Thursday, the blow came entirely unexpected, much like hail storm with not as much warning. Charleston is really a wreck with half of the Seaboard's pier gone also. Last count was 29 lives and several hundred injured." (Courtesy of the South Carolina Historical Society.)

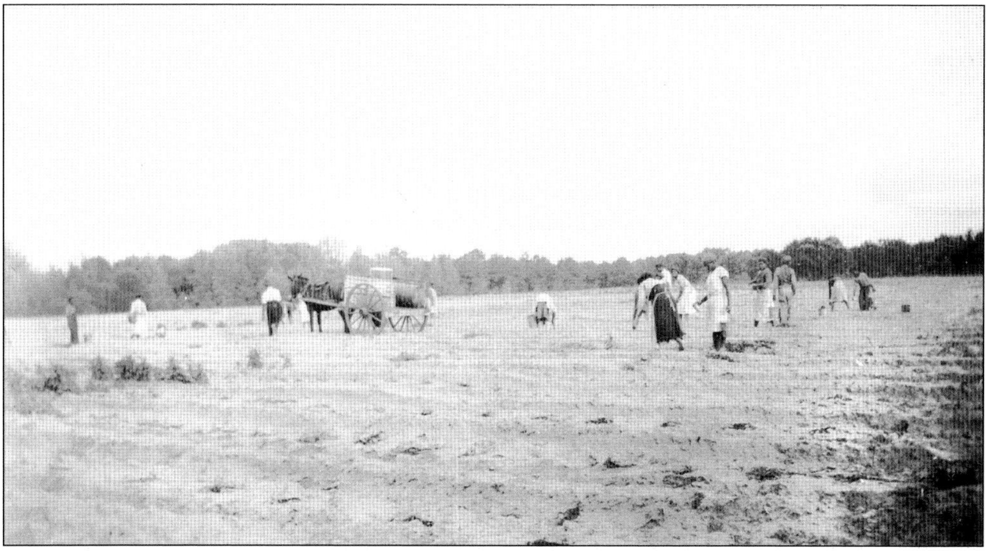

It was not that easy to resolve the drought issues. Sprinklers were not a convenience in the 1930s, so large farms and plantations had to manually supply the crops with water. This photograph shows women in the field supplying tomatoes in a drought with a water cart. (Courtesy of the South Carolina Historical Society.)

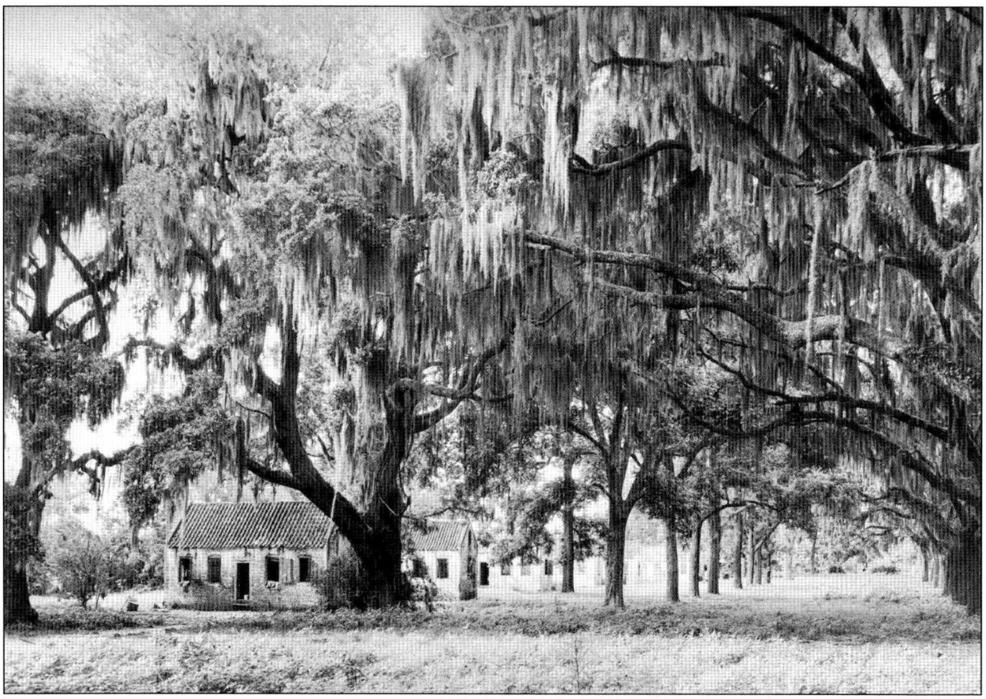

Wildlife was also a common problem on the plantation, as Charlie Schroeder reported on May 4, 1936: "Killed three or four more snakes since you left, they are bad. Friday night . . . Bill Seabrook started home ahead of Mr. Seabrook and myself, when suddenly Bill yelled to me to bring a stick, whereupon I flashed the lights of the station wagon upon him and ran the car down to amidship of the cotton gin, and Mr. Seabrook cut in half with a cabbage knife." (Courtesy of the South Carolina Historical Society.)

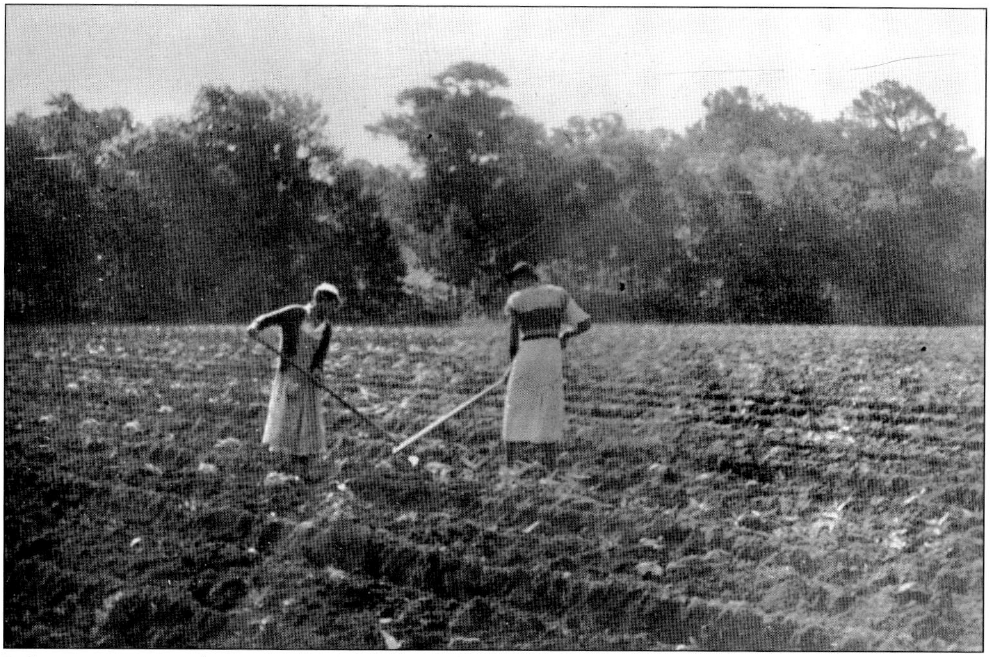

Labor issues popped up often in the scrapbook, providing an interesting look into the economy of the surrounding countryside. At one point, 15 women and about the same number of boys walked out, demanding higher pay. Thomas Stone found the culprits were fellow farmers a Mr. Rich, a Mr. Bradham, and a Mr. Mellichamp, who were paying their workers 70¢ a day. Boone Hall had to follow suit and was soon back in business. (Courtesy of the South Carolina Historical Society.)

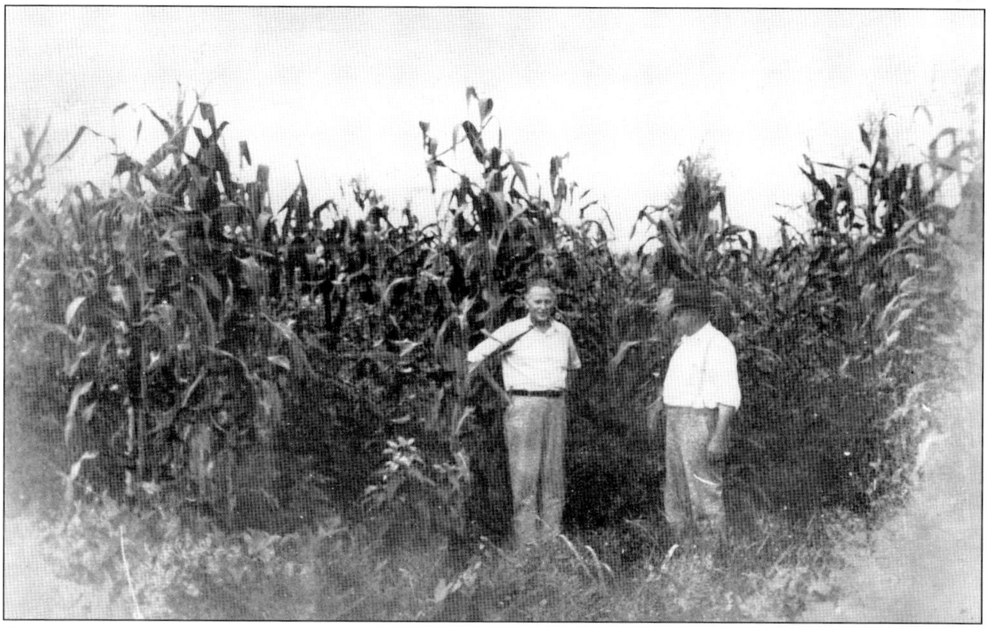

Seasonal workers were not the only labor issues that Boone Hall faced. Several entries were made into the journal regarding workers leaving due to rain and the difficulty of keeping them employed all the time on inside work. William Seabrook also complained of employees coming in late or leaving early for various reasons. (Courtesy of the South Carolina Historical Society.)

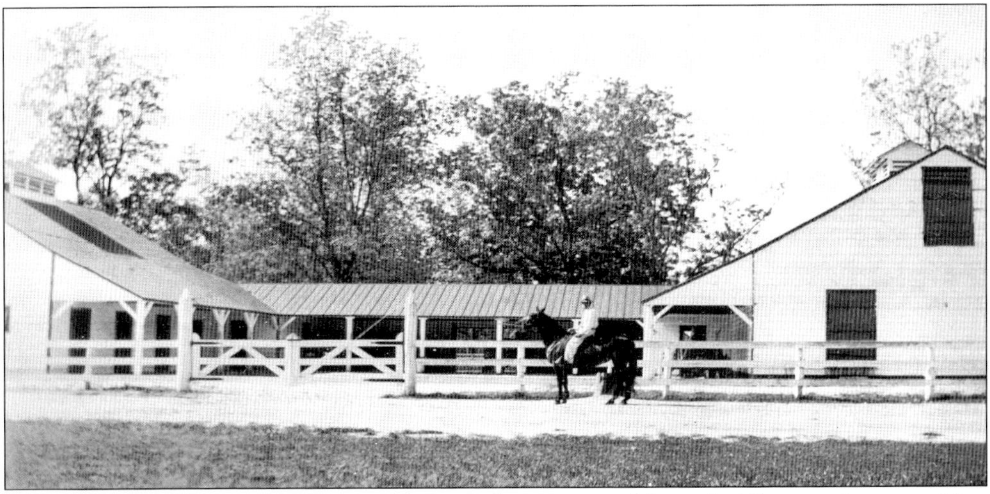

The animals on the plantation could cause their own problems for Thomas Stone and his employees. Snakes were often mentioned found out in the fields, as Charlie Schroeder described on August 31, 1937: "Kinsey killed a small alligator in the creek today which we sent to Mr. Matthews, the taxidermist, to be mounted. On Palmetto a few days ago Joe White killed a very large rattlesnake with thirteen rattles." (Courtesy of the South Carolina Historical Society.)

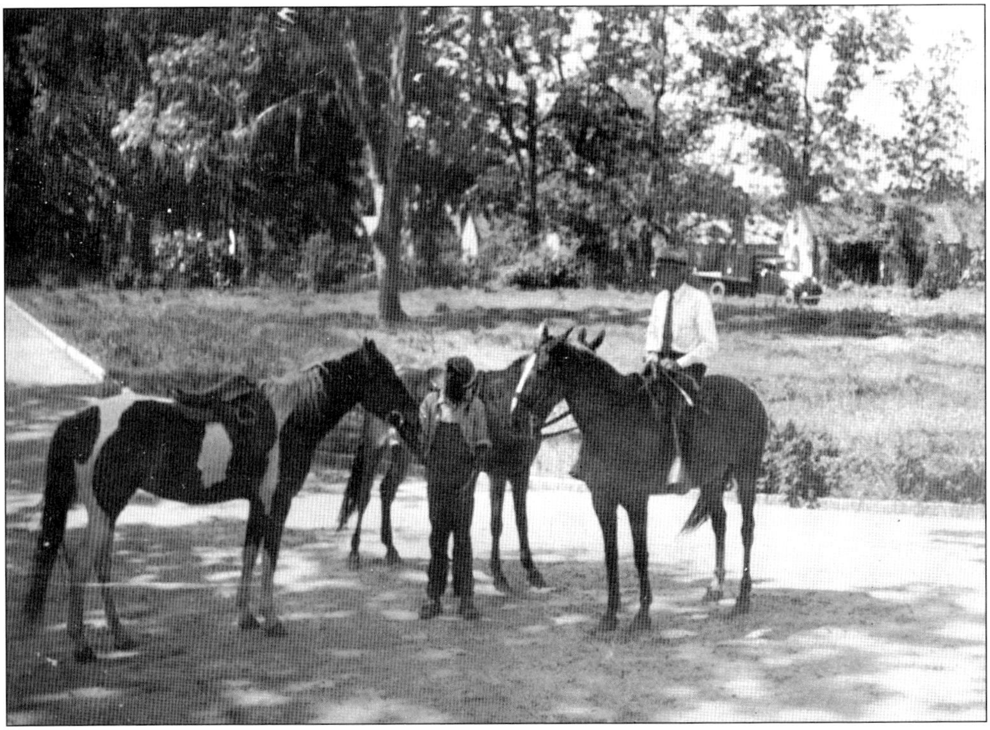

The animals could also offer some comic relief, as Stone reported in his scrapbook on February 18, 1936. "Schroder is a great horseman. He took Virginia out this morning but could not handle her so he came back for Pet. At Peter Brown's house he dismounted and tied her to a tree. She promptly broke her bridle and came home like a streak! Seabrook Sr. simply said that one had to make allowances for a city boy trying to learn country tricks! I wonder what he thinks of me trying to be a farmer!" (Courtesy of the South Carolina Historical Society.)

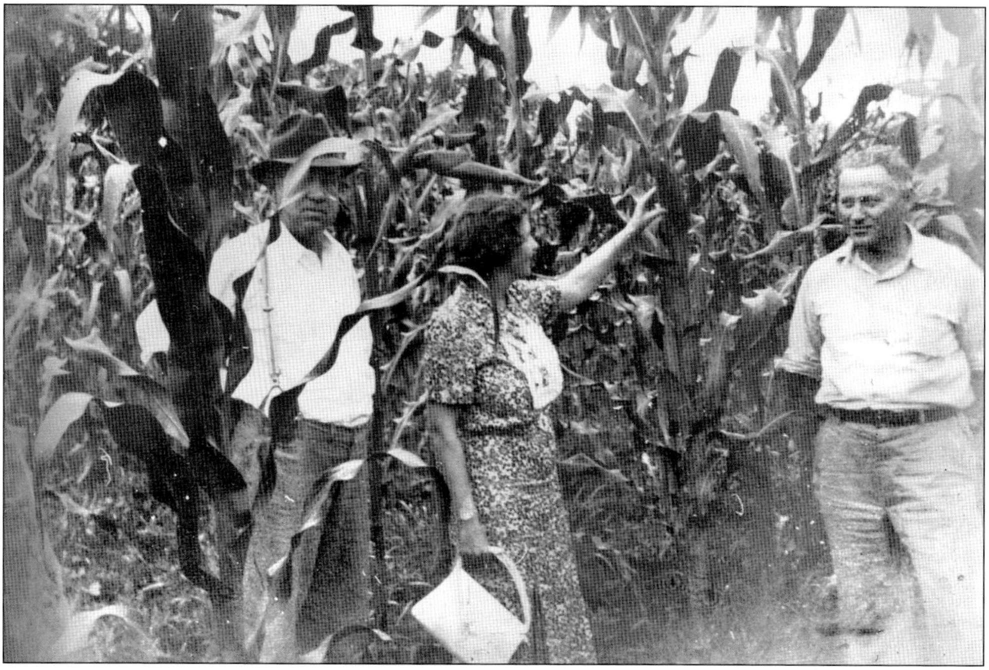

Thomas Stone noted the passing of William Seabrook (left) on January 26, 1937. "He was not only one of the finest gentlemen that it has been my privilege to know, but in addition he was one of those instinctive farmers who are perhaps rarer than men of equal ability in any other profession." (Courtesy of the South Carolina Historical Society.)

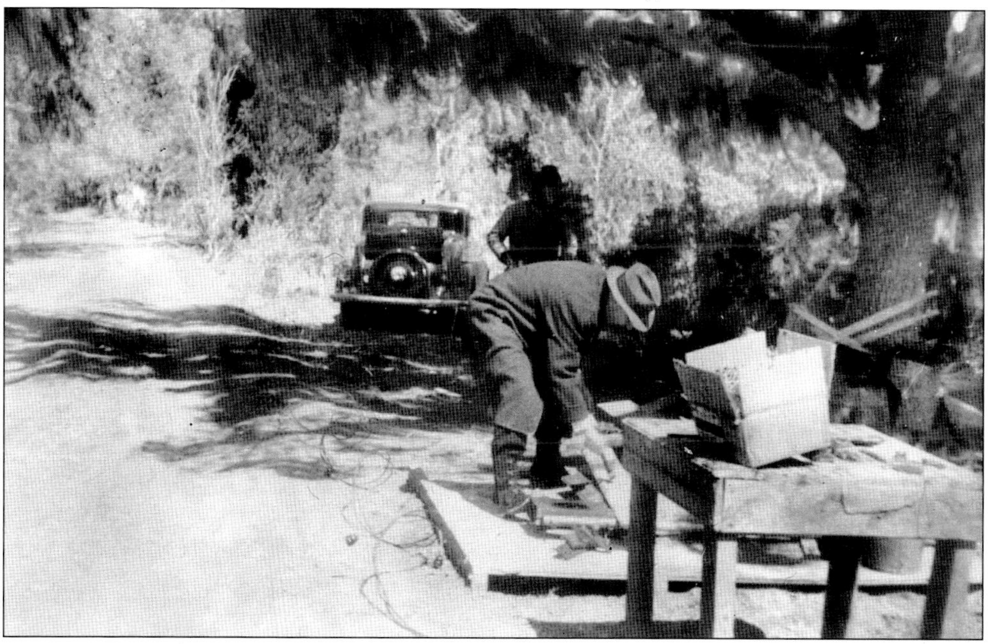

One interesting thing about Thomas Stone's scrapbook was his use of French periodically in his writing. Whenever he did not want his employees to read his entries about them, he would write in French. Obviously, he was discussing them and their inability to get along. (Courtesy of the South Carolina Historical Society.)

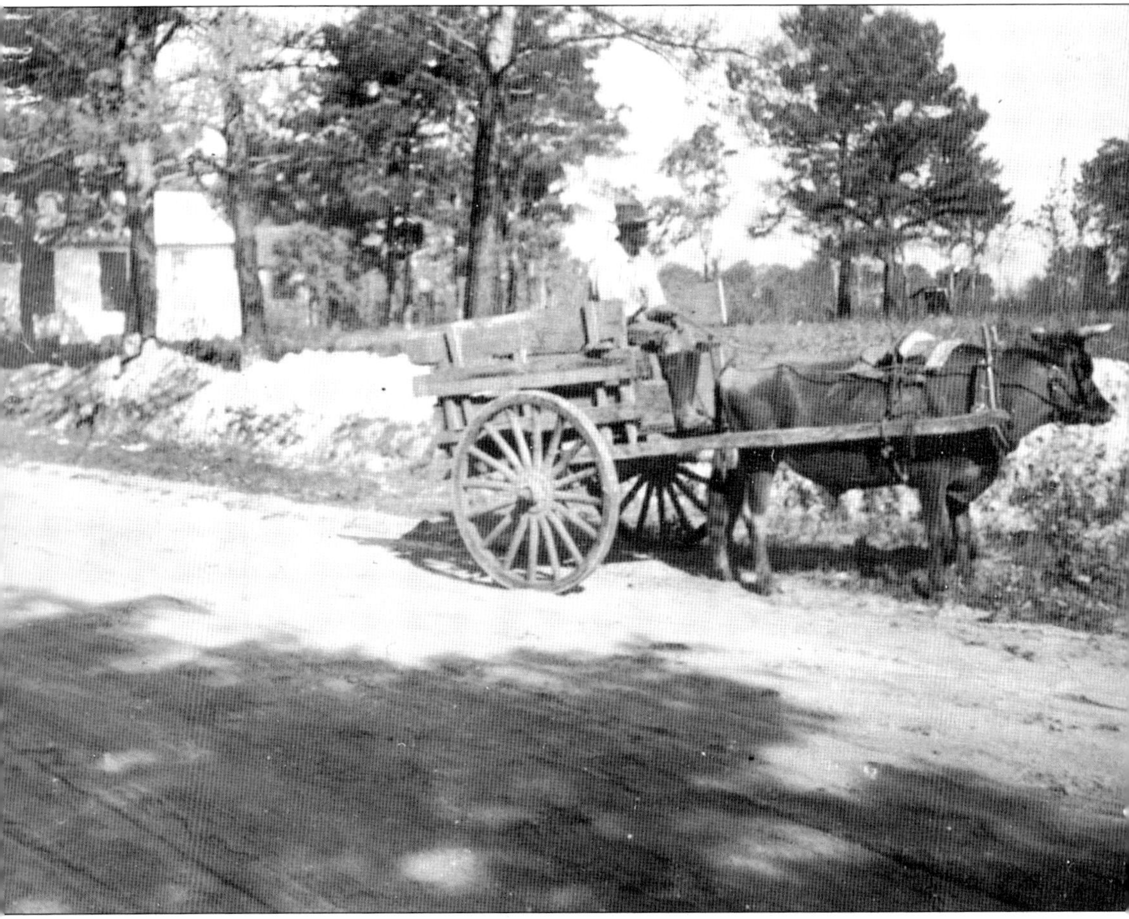

Weekly payroll distribution sheets included men and women working in the house and grounds at Boone Hall and Snee Farm for as little as $5 a day or as much as $11. The week of May 23, 1940, includes five workers at Boone Hall making a combined total of $43 and four workers at Snee Farm for a total of $31 for the week. One worker, Cecelia Brown, was paid $1 a day for working in the Snee Farm mansion. (Courtesy of the South Carolina Historical Society.)

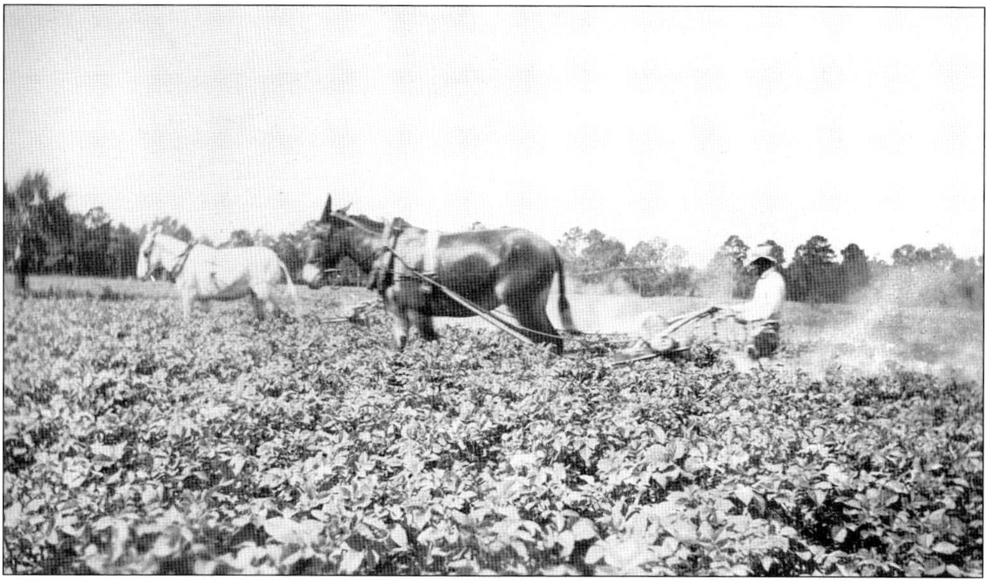

Other plantation occupations included working with the team for $6 a week and working feed and cover crops, raking, stacking, and baling hay for on average of $5 a week. One young lad named Dan Washington was paid $1.50 to be the water boy. Boone Hall paid a total of 18 workers $96.11 for the week of March 15, 1940. (Courtesy of the South Carolina Historical Society.)

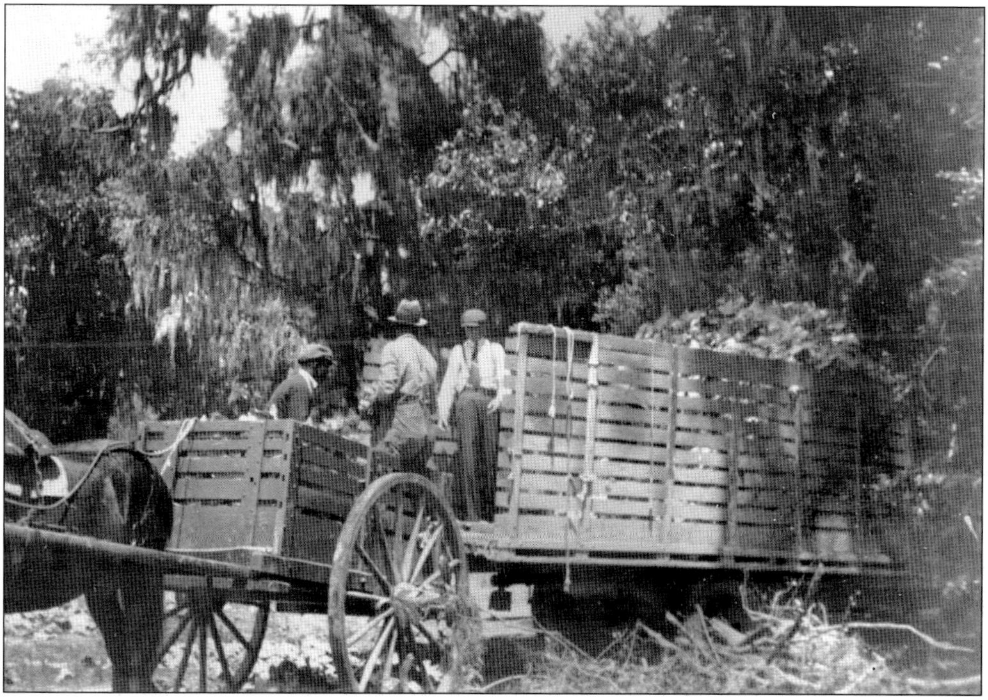

The pecan groves were one of the main reasons the Stones were initially interested in the area, and they were included in the plans for cultivation. Thomas Stone noted that "Dr. Moore & Mr. Jenkins from Clemson came over to-day to look at the pecan groves. They advise thinning and fertilizing and judge the expense involved to be a good investment. They accepted Ash Pringle's (also here) suggestion of bone meal." (Courtesy of the South Carolina Historical Society.)

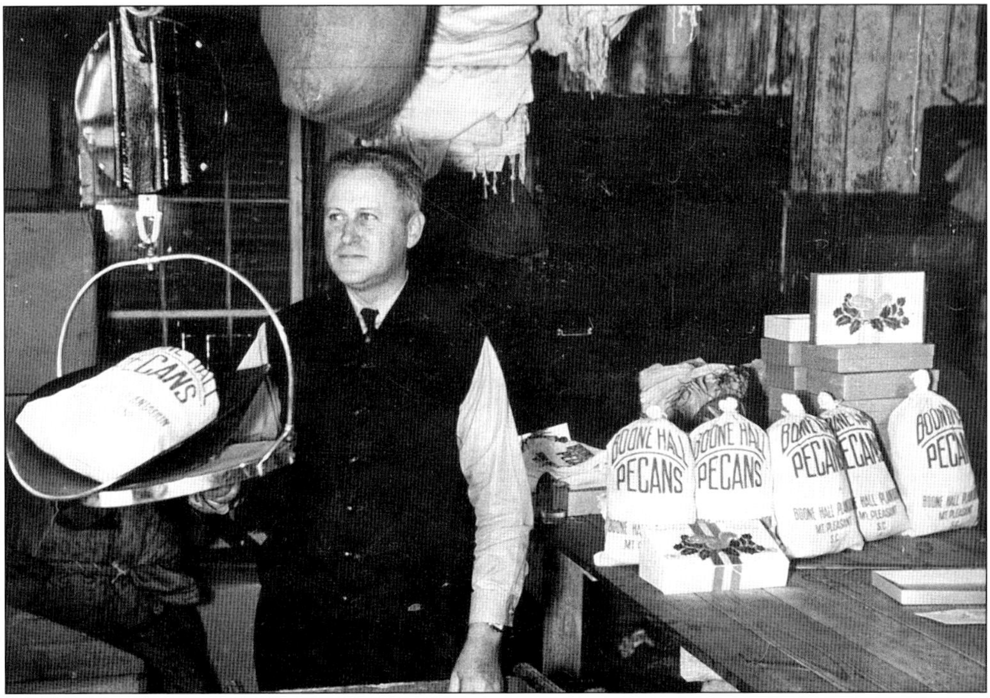

Charlie Schroeder is pictured here with Boone Hall pecans. Selling the pecans turned out to be a different challenge, and Schroeder tried selling them in packages to local hotels and businesses. One idea that worked was selling them in gift packages at Christmas time. (Courtesy of the South Carolina Historical Society.)

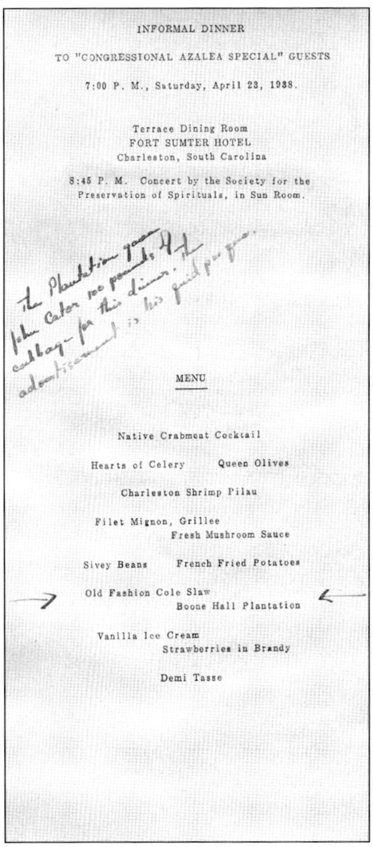

INFORMAL DINNER

TO "CONGRESSIONAL AZALEA SPECIAL" GUESTS

7:00 P. M., Saturday, April 23, 1938.

Terrace Dining Room
FORT SUMTER HOTEL
Charleston, South Carolina

8:45 P. M. Concert by the Society for the Preservation of Spirituals, in Sun Room.

The Plantation gave John Cator 100 pounds of cabbage for this dinner. The advertisement is his quid pro quo.

MENU

Native Crabmeat Cocktail

Hearts of Celery Queen Olives

Charleston Shrimp Pilau

Filet Mignon, Grillee
Fresh Mushroom Sauce

Sivey Beans French Fried Potatoes

Old Fashion Cole Slaw
Boone Hall Plantation

Vanilla Ice Cream
Strawberries in Brandy

Demi Tasse

Boone Hall was also very creative in selling its products locally and in garnering as much marketing from the produce as possible. This menu mentions its cole slaw coming from Boone Hall Plantation. This was another inventive way to sell the much-despised cabbage crop. (Courtesy of the South Carolina Historical Society.)

Five

THE LOCAL COMMUNITY

The surrounding community was a vital part of Boone Hall, not just a source of labor. Thomas Stone was often amused by the local folk, white and black, from the stories he included in his scrapbook. These glimpses, as well as payroll sheets and lists of plantation occupations, depict the rural life of the surrounding community and the residents of the still-standing slave cabins. These cabins have been left virtually unchanged since the days of slavery, and people continued to live in them well into the 1940s.

One of these residents was Martha Gaillard. Gaillard was born at Boone Hall Plantation in 1919 in Cabin No. 1, where she lived with her grandmother Serena, a former slave still residing on the plantation. Martha lived at Boone Hall until the 1930s and returned in the 1940s after her marriage. The following chapter includes excerpts of her recollections of life at the plantation. Her memories give an idea of the difficult life of the descendants of the plantation slaves and how they were able to carve out a life and community after slavery.

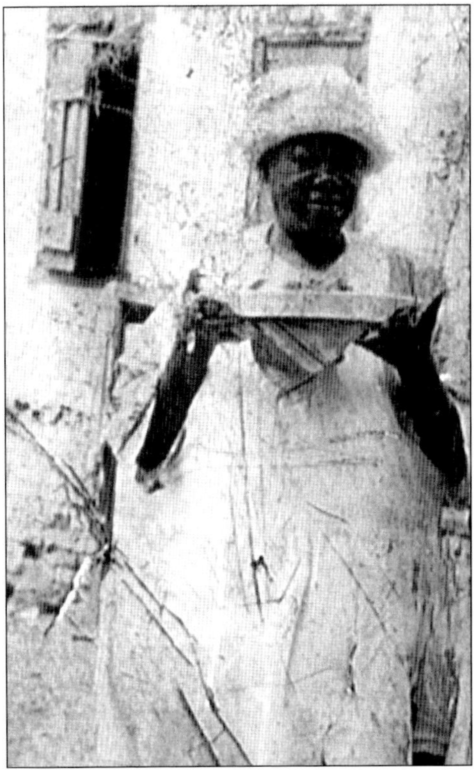

Serena (pictured here) was born in Virginia in 1864. She was brought to Boone Hall Plantation that same year and ended her days of slavery on the plantation. She continued to live at Boone Hall and became a well-known cook for the plantation. Her family also resided at the plantation and within the local community. (Courtesy of Boone Hall Plantation.)

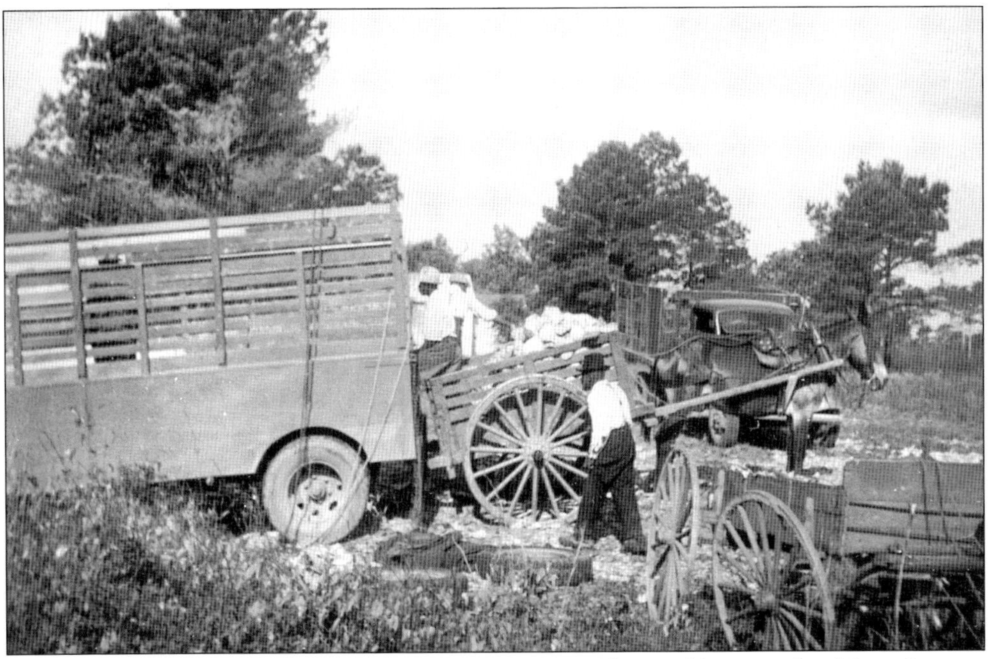

Martha Gaillard remembered picking pecans in winter. She would go to school from January through April and then pick cucumbers, tomatoes, squash, white potatoes, and sour beets; in the fall she picked beans, pecans, peas, and corn too. She was paid a penny a pound for what she picked. (Courtesy of the South Carolina Historical Society.)

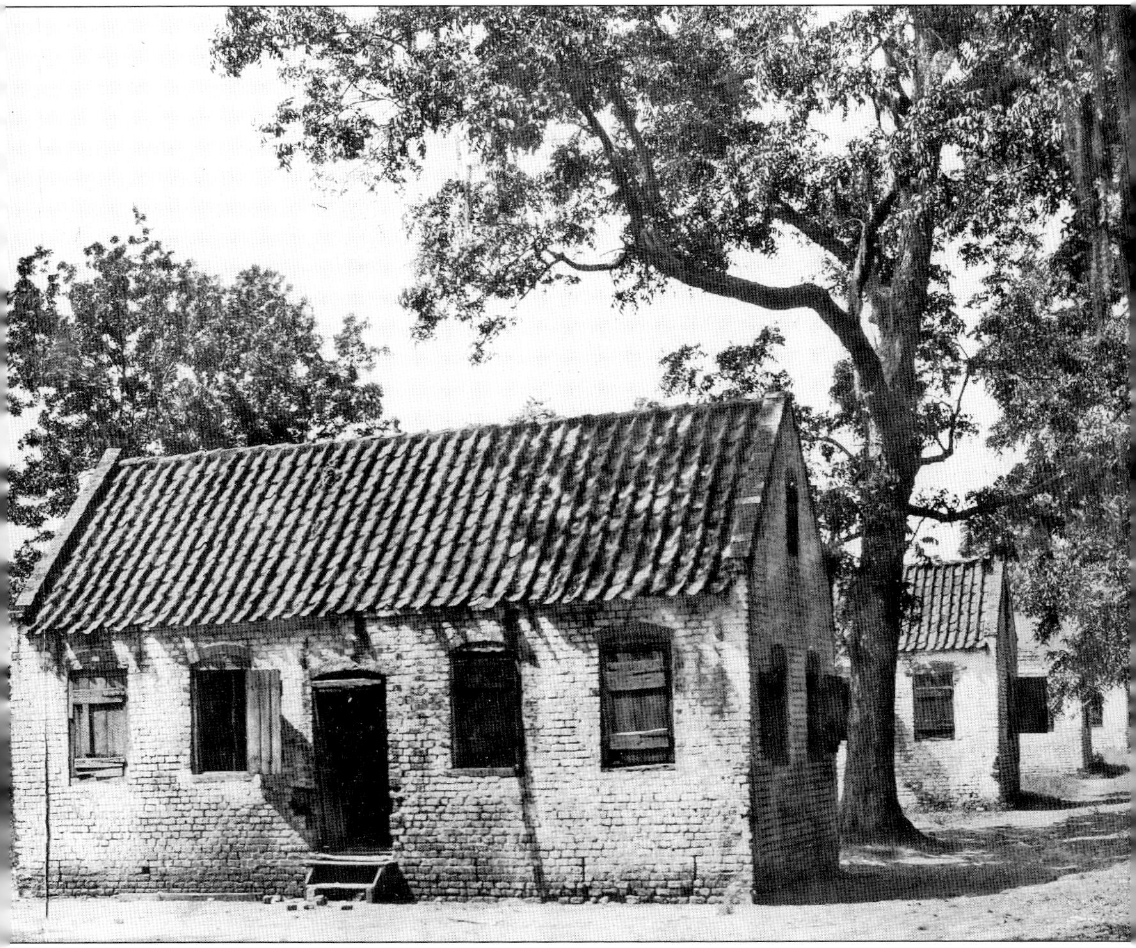

Gaillard lived with her grandmother in a three-room cabin that consisted of two bedrooms and a living room. Other cabins used the three rooms as a bedroom, a kitchen, and a living room. She remembered sleeping with her grandmother and getting up with her everyday at five o'clock to go to the kitchen and fix breakfast. (Courtesy of the South Carolina Historical Society.)

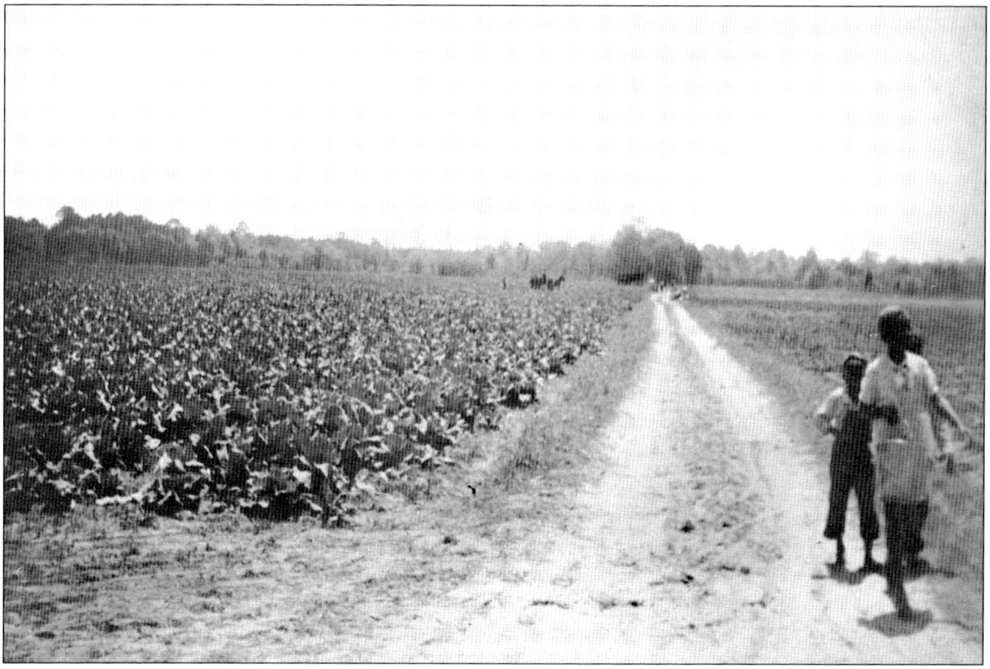

As a child, Martha Gaillard played ball and walked to the school down by Six Mile. The school was in a church. She commented that people used to know more about growing rice than school learning back then. The children often played near the plantation's gate and watched people drive up in their cars to see the plantation. Back during her residency, people paid an entrance fee of 25¢ to see the plantation. (Courtesy of the South Carolina Historical Society.)

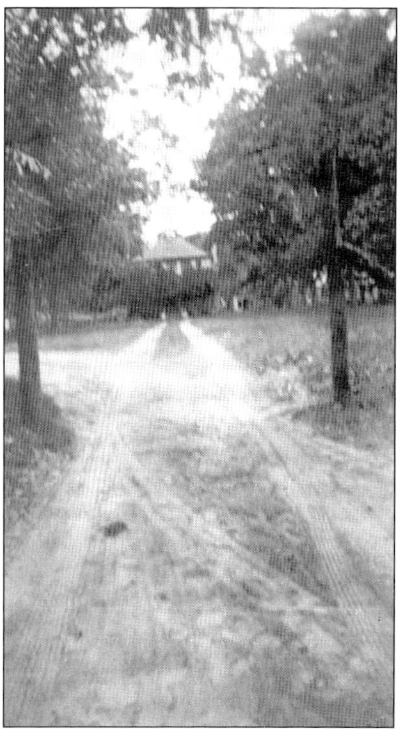

Gaillard remembered orange trees growing in the front yard of the main house. As children, they were not allowed to climb the trees and pick the oranges; however, they were much too tempting to Martha and her brother. They were caught several times climbing the trees and were chased out by the owners. (Courtesy of the South Carolina Historical Society.)

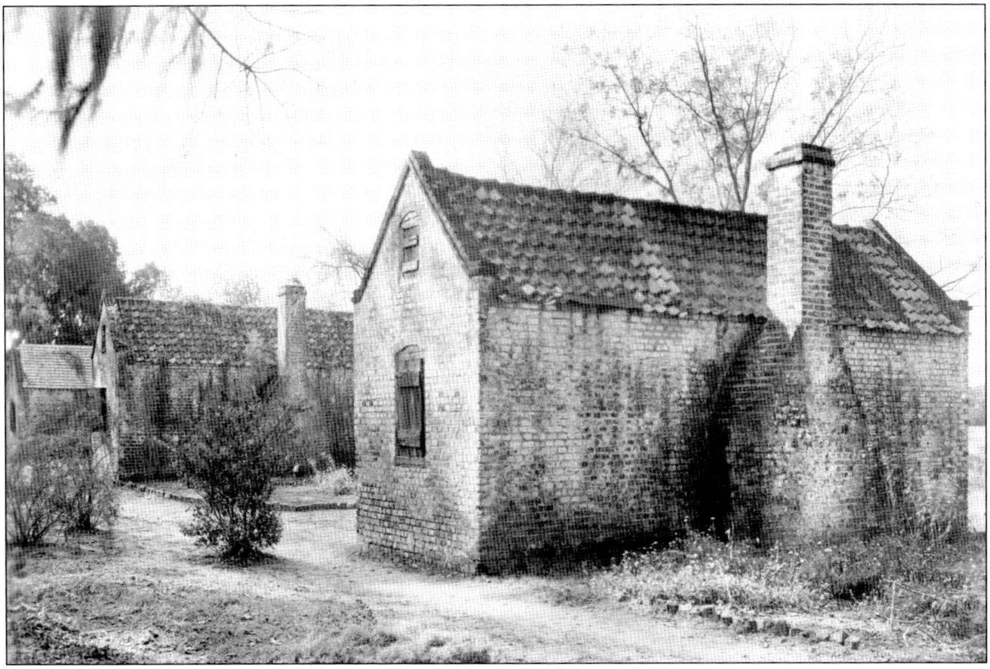

Gaillard lived on the plantation until 1925 and then again when she married in 1939. She was 18 when she married and remembered that her husband started courting her when she was 17. They would often go to dances that coincided with holidays like the Fourth of July, Easter, Labor Day, Thanksgiving, and Christmas. (Courtesy of the South Carolina Historical Society.)

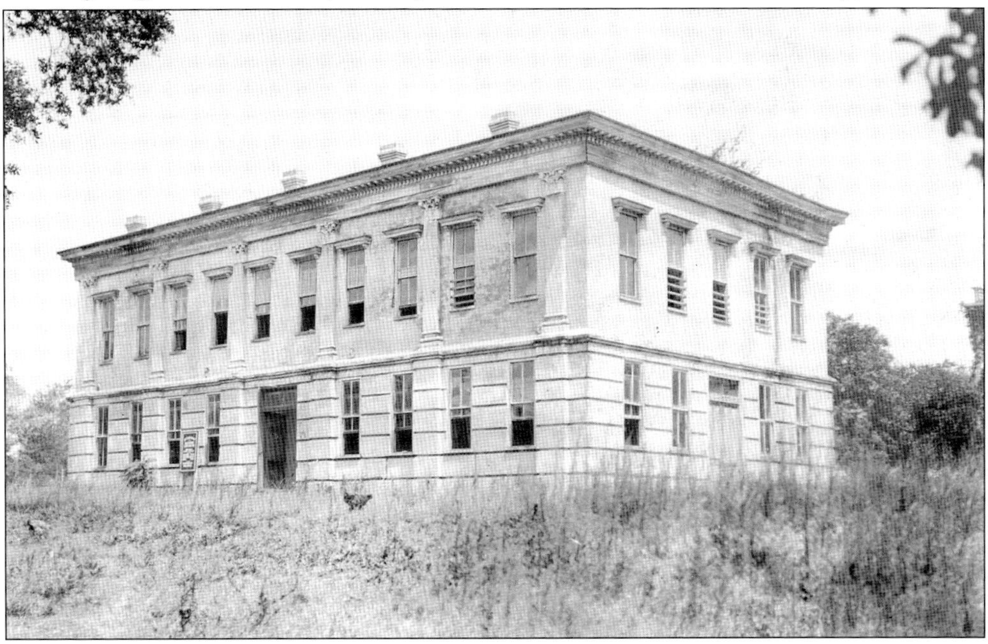

Gaillard recalled going into Mount Pleasant with a Miss Katie, a white lady on the plantation. They would go by car to the grocery store every Saturday, and it was a long drive from Boone Hall to the city of Mount Pleasant. Pictured here is the courthouse in Mount Pleasant on Pitt Street. (Courtesy of the South Carolina Historical Society.)

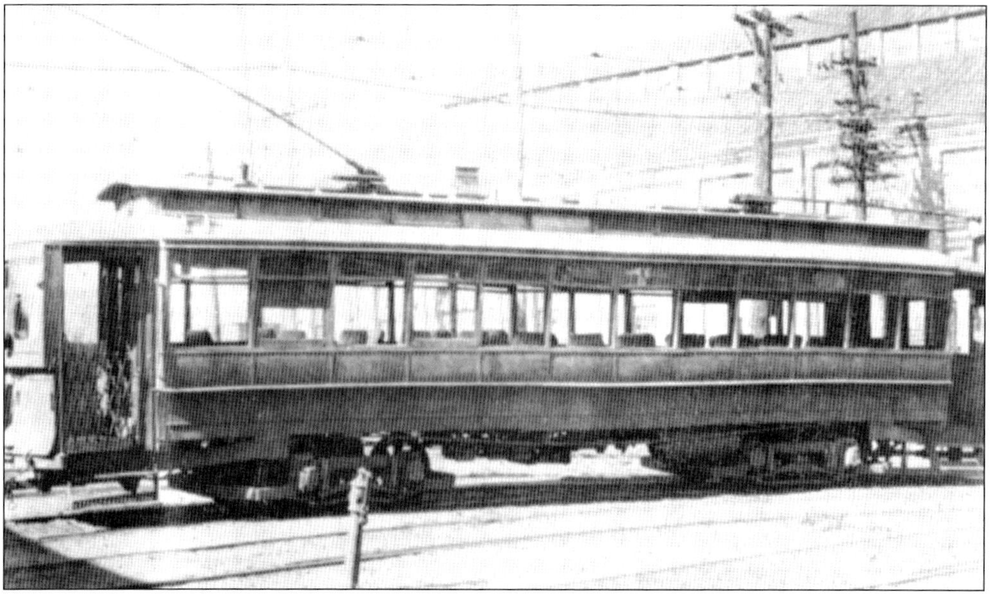

Martha Gaillard remembered going into the city of Charleston with her grandmother. She would ride the bus with her grandmother and remembered that it would come round East Battery Street and go up King Street. She said you could ride the bus for a dime and 15¢, but now it is $1. (Courtesy of the South Carolina Historical Society.)

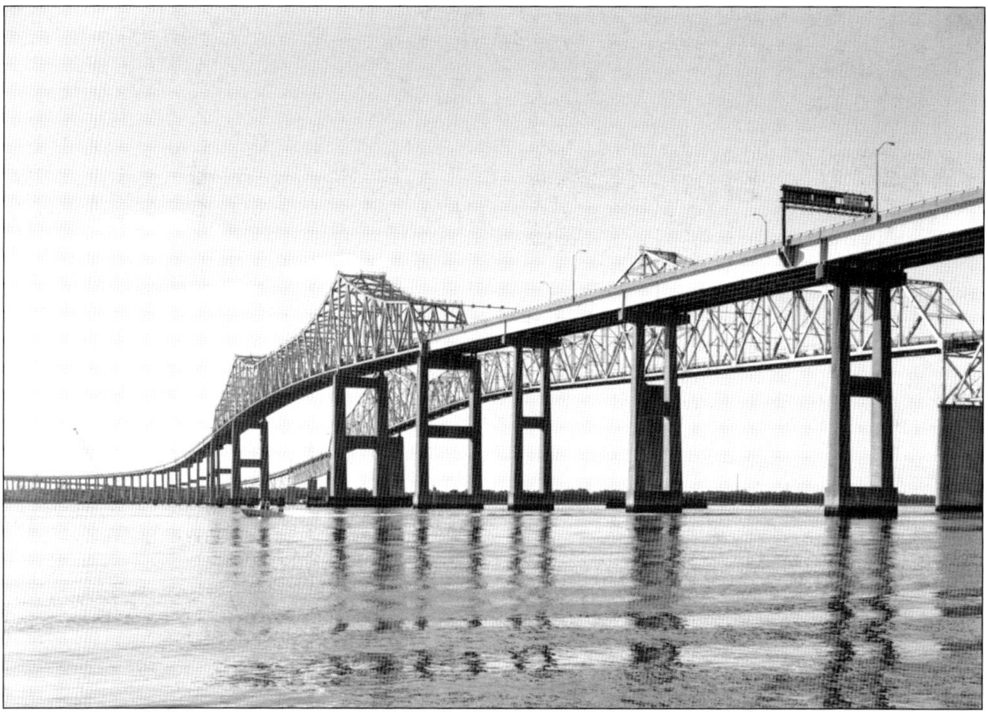

To get to Charleston from Mount Pleasant prior to 1929, one would take a ferry across the Cooper River. Finally, in 1929, the Cooper River Bridge was opened to motorists. The main span of the second cantilever was the 12th longest in the world. The total length of the structure was about 2.7 miles. (Courtesy of the Library of Congress.)

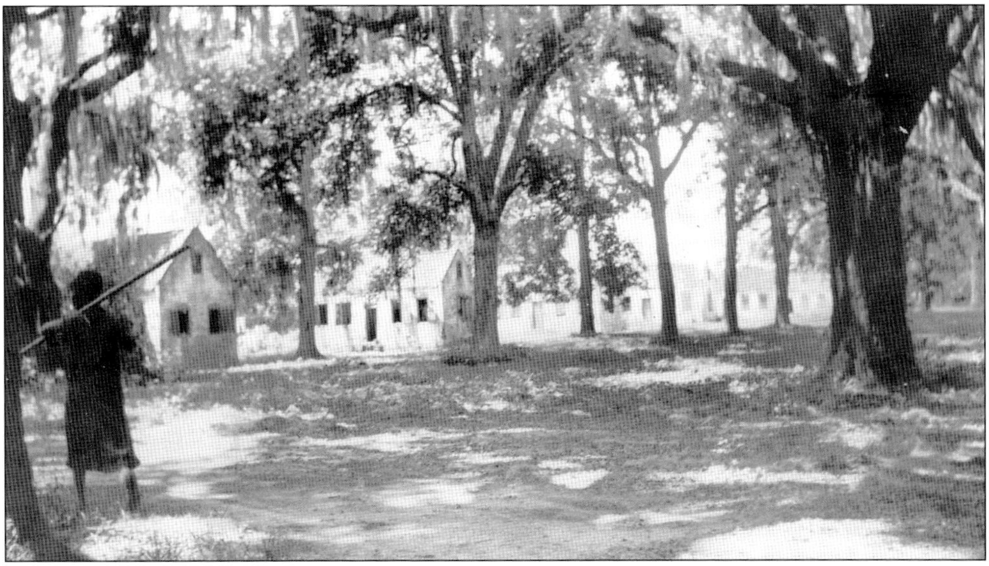

Holidays at the plantation, such as the Fourth of July, had a large turnout, according to Gaillard. They would walk down to Six Mile. Everyone with a horse had a flag up. Other holidays they celebrated were Christmas, New Year's, Easter, Mother's Day, May Day, and Labor Day. (Courtesy of the University of South Carolina.)

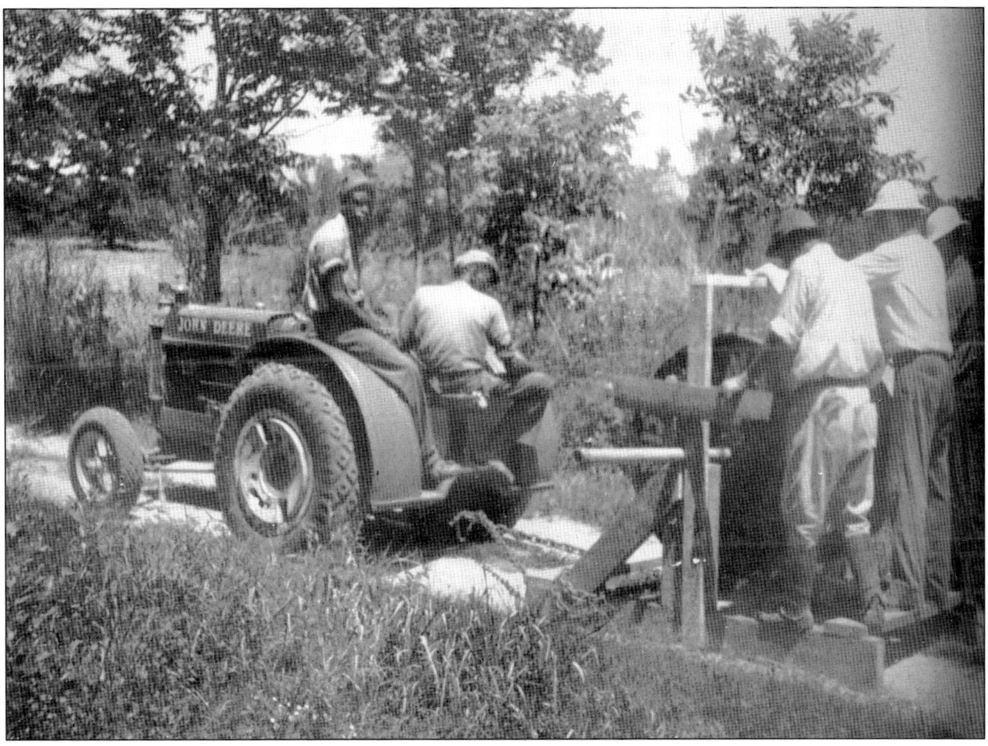

Gaillard reminisced about the farm work and farm life on the plantation. She remembered that they had cows. When her grandfather worked on the plantation, he made about 20¢ a week; when she got married in 1939, her husband made $7 a week and she made $3. (Courtesy of the South Carolina Historical Society.)

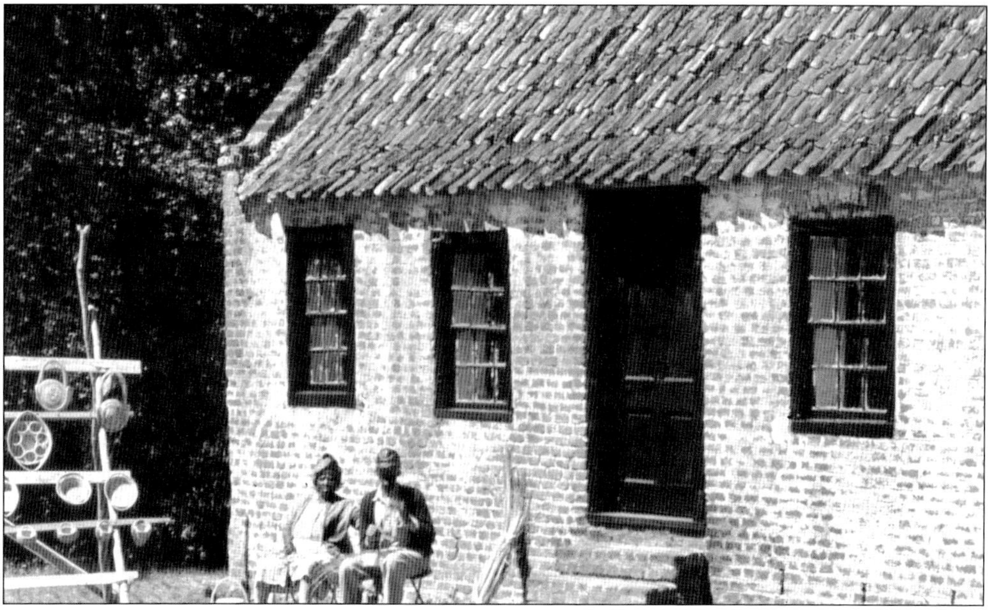

Sweetgrass baskets were also a part of plantation life. Martha Gaillard remembered selling the baskets for 25¢ for a 9-inch oval basket, 7-inch baskets for 15¢, 9-inch baskets for 25¢, bread trays for 25¢, wall pockets for 15¢ and 10¢, and wastebaskets for $1.50. She compared the prices to today, saying that now basket makers can get $100 or more for a wastebasket. (Courtesy of Boone Hall Plantation.)

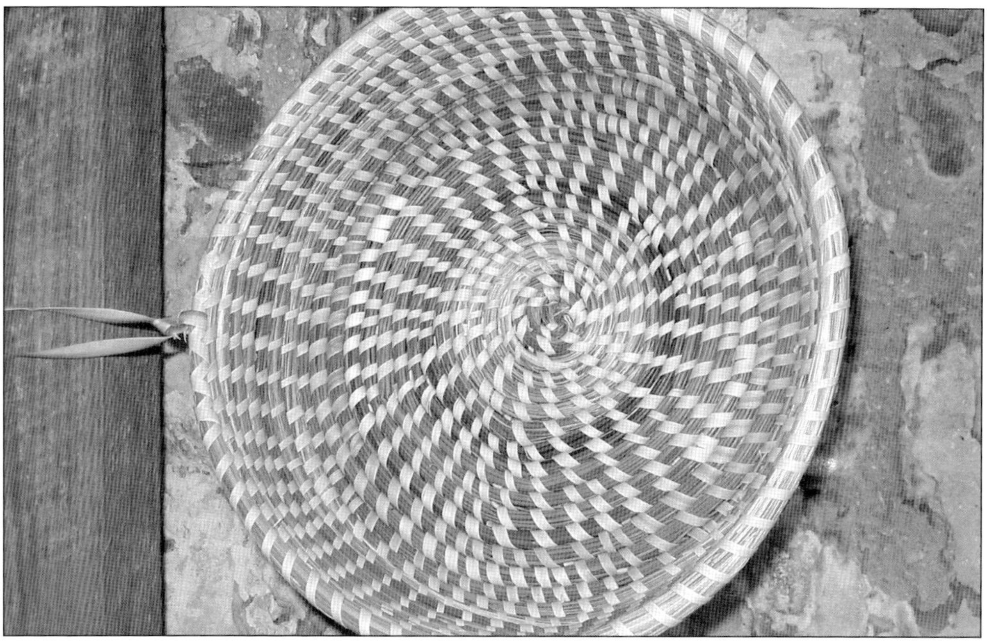

Sweetgrass basket making was brought to the Charleston area by slaves who came from West Africa, where it was a traditional art form passed from generation to generation. The basket makers still line the roadside in Mount Pleasant, selling their baskets to passing motorists. Boone Hall also enjoys the presence of local basket makers that teach guests about the rich heritage of the slaves and the Gullah culture. (Courtesy of Boone Hall Plantation.)

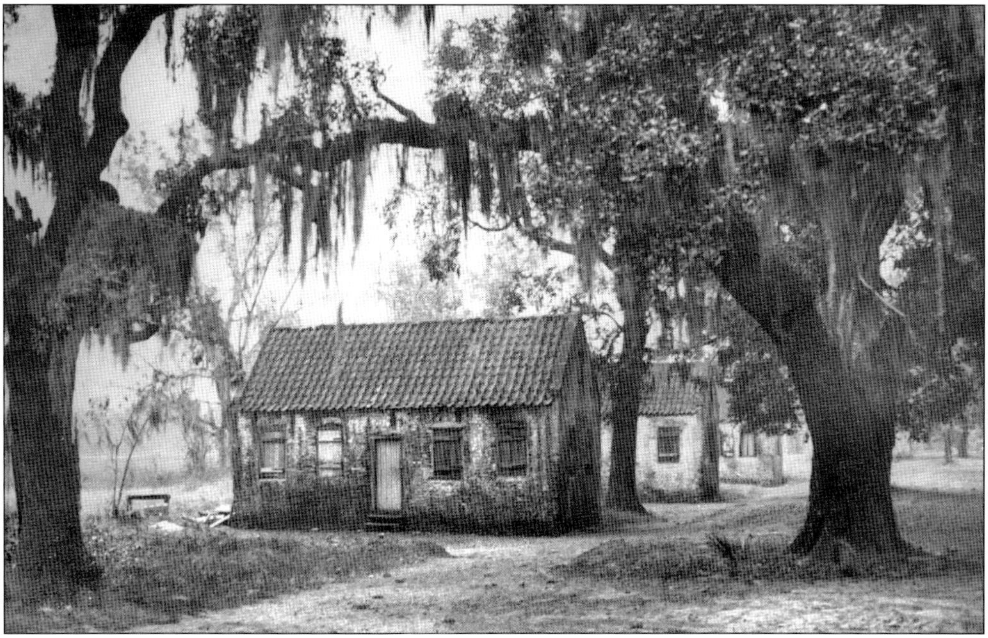

Residents of the plantation continued to take advantage of the convenient food source the creek provided them, not unlike the slaves before them, as William Seabrook commented on July 29, 1938. "Fishing and shrimping has become very popular among the residents of the street, and if they continue to visit the creek as often as they have in the past two weeks, our supply of sea food will soon be on the ebb." (Courtesy of the South Carolina Historical Society.)

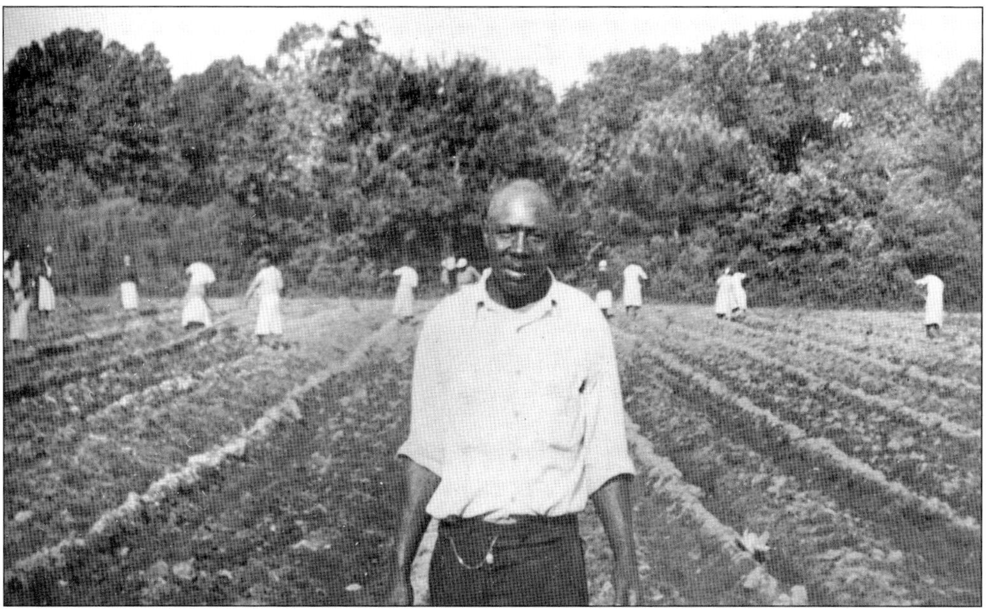

Thomas Stone was often entertained by the community and his workers, as noted in his scrapbook entries. In this entry from May 17, 1937, Stone said, " Old Ben Seabrook loves his little jok[illegible] During Easter week he came up to Bill saying 'Cap'n Bill, when is yo all payin' off this a week?' 'Friday as usual Ben', said Bill. 'No yain't, Cap'n Bill, no yain't. Christ done bin crucified in de banks bin close!" (Courtesy of the South Carolina Historical Society.)

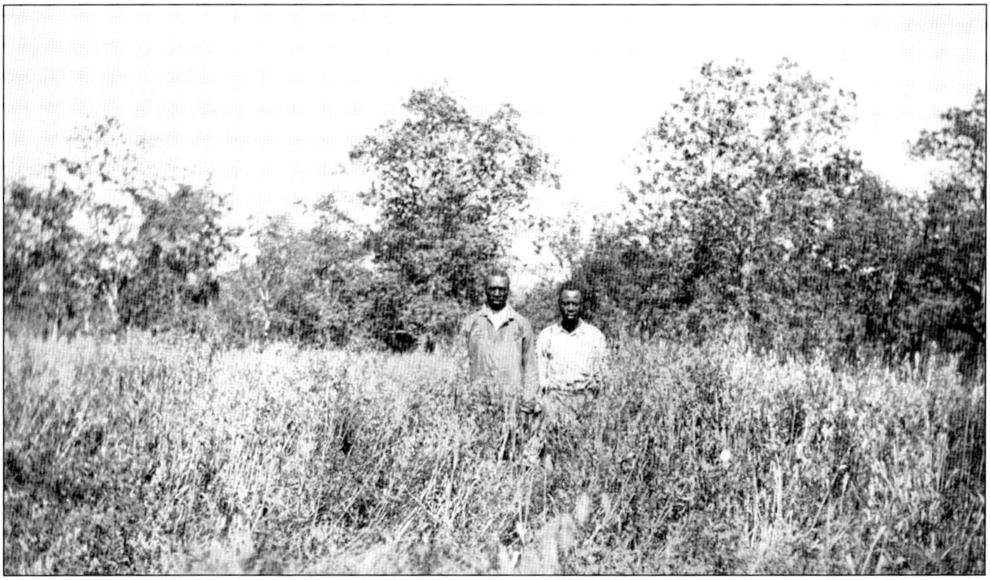

Thomas Stone had many entertaining comments about the surrounding community. "The baby's birthday party was a great success. We expected 50, prepared for 100, and had about 150. The mulatto rice, cake, ice cream, beer, soft drinks and candy disappeared . . . and the sparklers which we provided for the children were much enjoyed. Absolute perfection was only missed because of the rank smell from about 100 2 1/2 cent cigars being smoked furiously at the same time," Stone wrote on May 19, 1937. (Courtesy of the South Carolina Historical Society.)

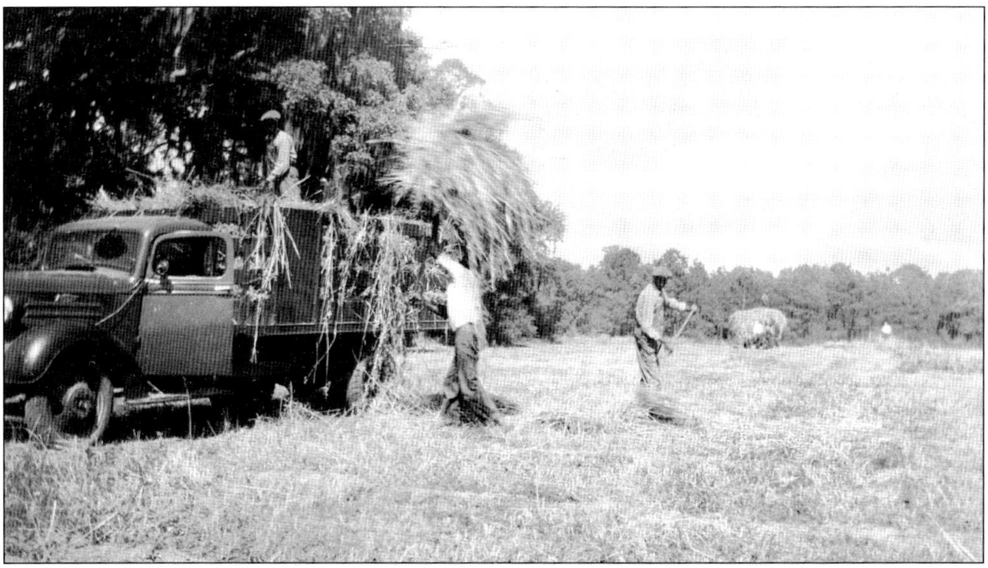

Another entertaining entry by Stone was on July 9, 1937: "I forgot to write in this journal about a minor 'Porgy' incident. Clarence Ellis . . . was being pursued by a furniture company for payment. He asked for a loan of $14 . . . then sent his wife . . . with the $14 to pay for the furniture and the next he heard from her was a postcard from New York! Clarence said he did not mind much losing the woman as he had a better one lined up anyway. But he was pretty sick about the $14." (Courtesy of the South Carolina Historical Society.)

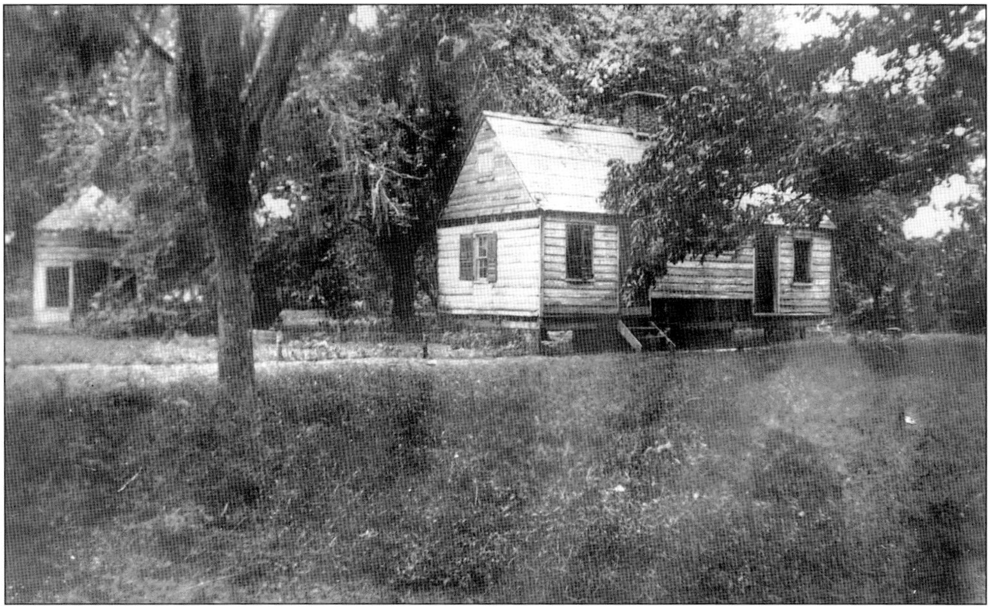

Many of the descendants of the former slaves continued to live on the plantation, as William Seabrook commented on July 20, 1937. "Grace has asked me to put a small addition on the back of her house and if possible a small brick flue for a stove in the room. They are crowded there in that small house only having two rooms and I hope that this idea of adding on for her will meet with your approval." (Courtesy of the South Carolina Historical Society.)

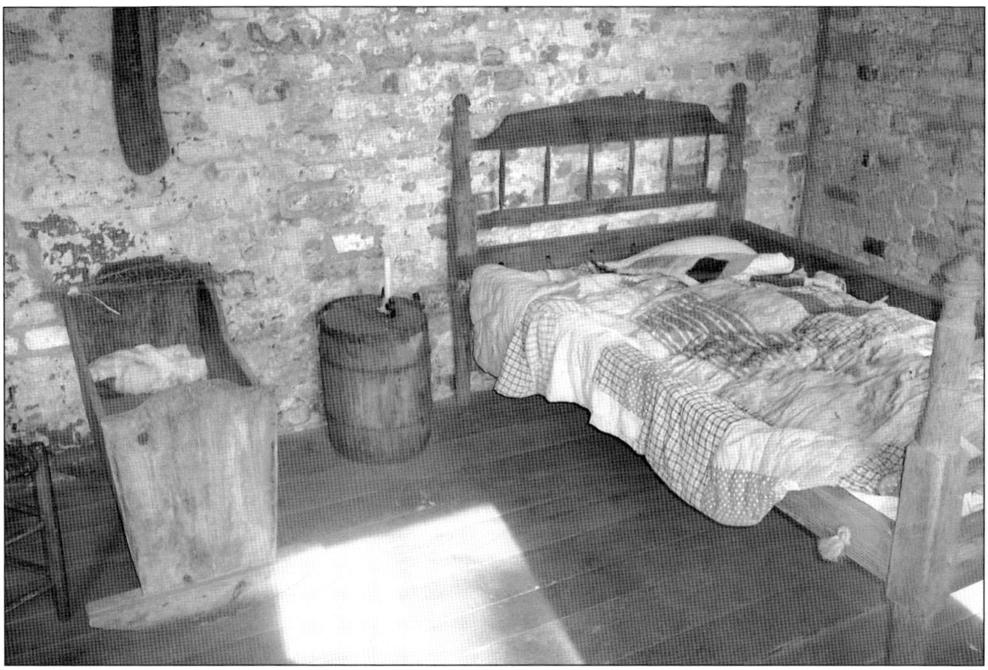

According to the slave cabin narration, all the cabins except Cabin No. 8 measured approximately 12 feet by 31 feet, or 372 square feet. The cabins were made of bricks that the business would not have been able to sell. Wooden slats were used to create a floor, and holes in the lower part of the walls were believed to have been used for ventilation. (Courtesy of Michelle Adams.)

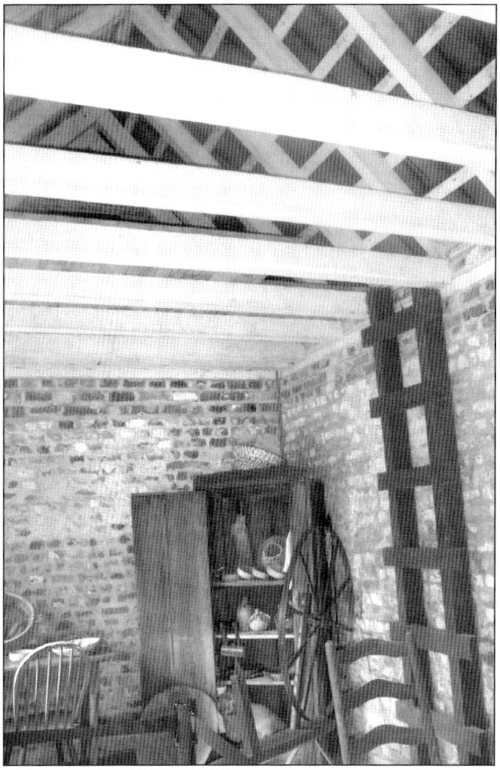

Lofts were created with wooden slats across the upper beams of the cabins and may have been used for storage as well as a sleeping area for small children, as two windows also exist on that floor. All the buildings have five windows, none on the west wall, except in Cabin No. 8, which measures 14 feet by 31 feet, or 434 square feet. Iron bars in the fireplaces were probably used to hang pots, and bricked hearths probably help stop the spread of fire from sparks. (Courtesy of Michelle Adams.)

Slaves were provided a few utensils, such as ceramic tableware, including bowls, plates, jugs, jars, and platters. Many lead sinkers used on fishing nets were found around the cabins as well, indicating that slaves probably provided the master's family as well as slave families with fish from the creek. Slaves often trapped animals and fished at night and on Sundays in order to supplement their diet. Many bones and seashells have also been found, giving evidence of the diet that the slaves had. (Courtesy of Michelle Adams.)

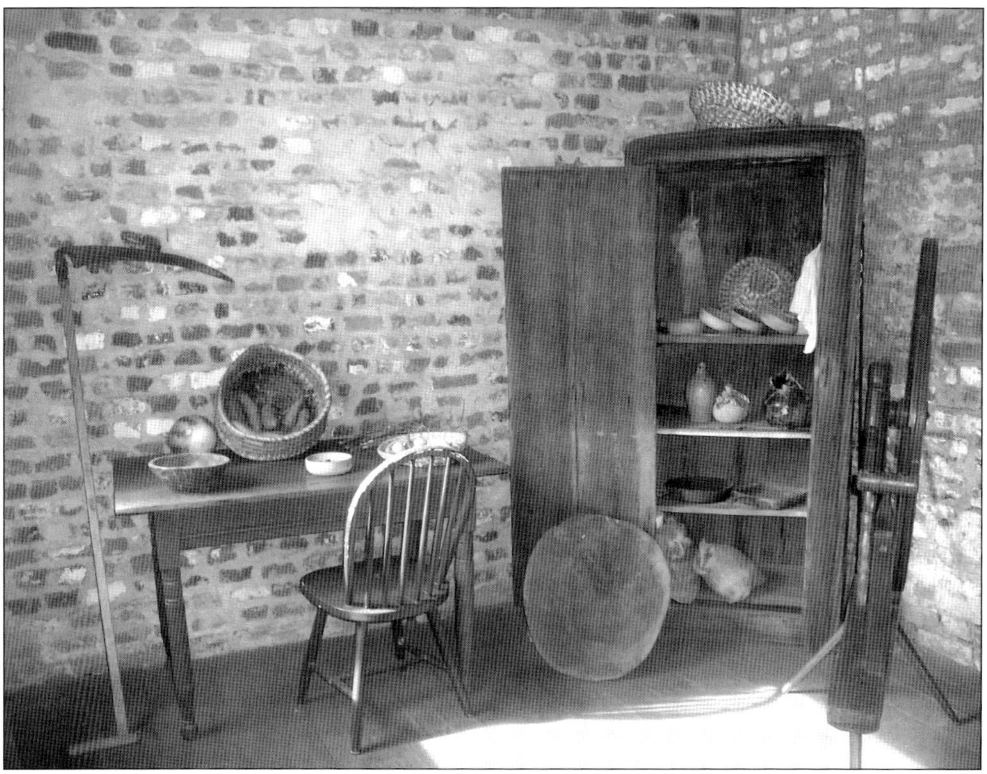

This interior shot of a slave cabin from Wormsloe, Isle of Hope, in Savannah, Georgia, shows the darkness of most slave cabins as well as the furnishings. Boone Hall's reproduction is closer in retelling the slaves' stories by including the basic needs of slaves and not much more. (Courtesy of the Library of Congress.)

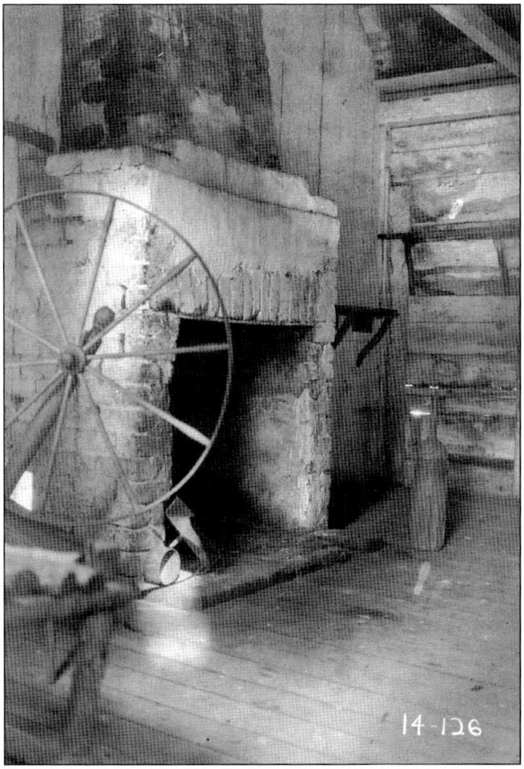

Fires in a windowless cabin must have created a challenge not only in the hot summers, but also in airing out the cabin. This was the only form of light on the inside of the cabin that the inhabitants had, although they would spend most of their time working and not needing light to read by. (Courtesy of the Library of Congress.)

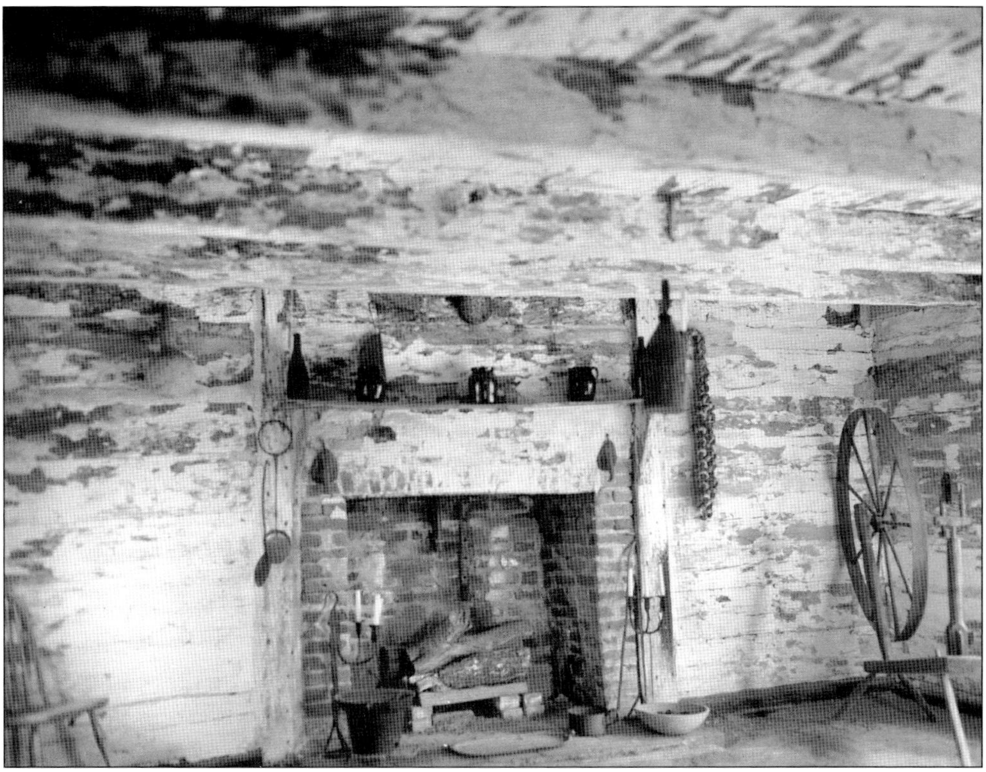

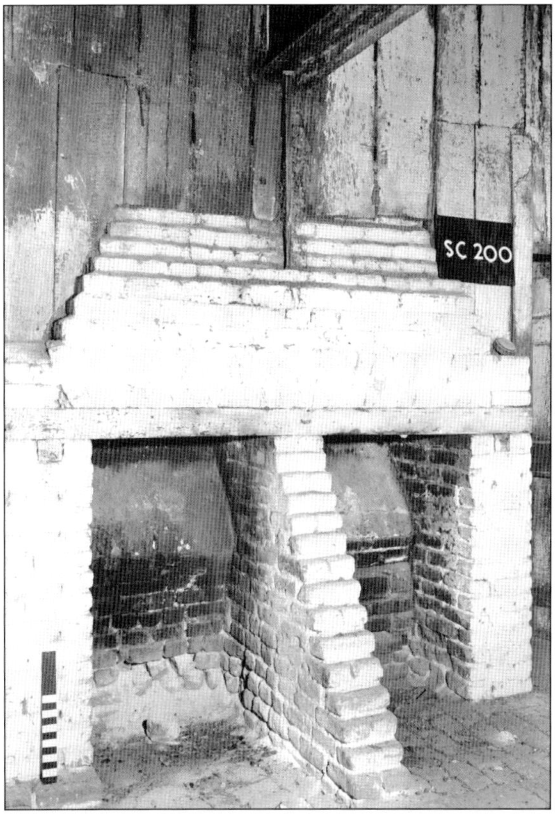

The interior of this slave cabin found in Hopsewee Plantation in Georgetown is indicative of the tradition of more than one family living in a single slave cabin. This cabin has a small divider, indicating that some effort was taken to provide separate living spaces for two families—probably most appreciated if the two families were not in fact related. (Courtesy of the Library of Congress.)

This interior shot of a slave cabin at Strawberry Hill Plantation in Greene County, Alabama, in 1936 depicts much of the same dark and bare residences as the other photographs. It also shows a current resident dressed in her Sunday best for the special visitor and photo opportunity. (Courtesy of the Library of Congress.)

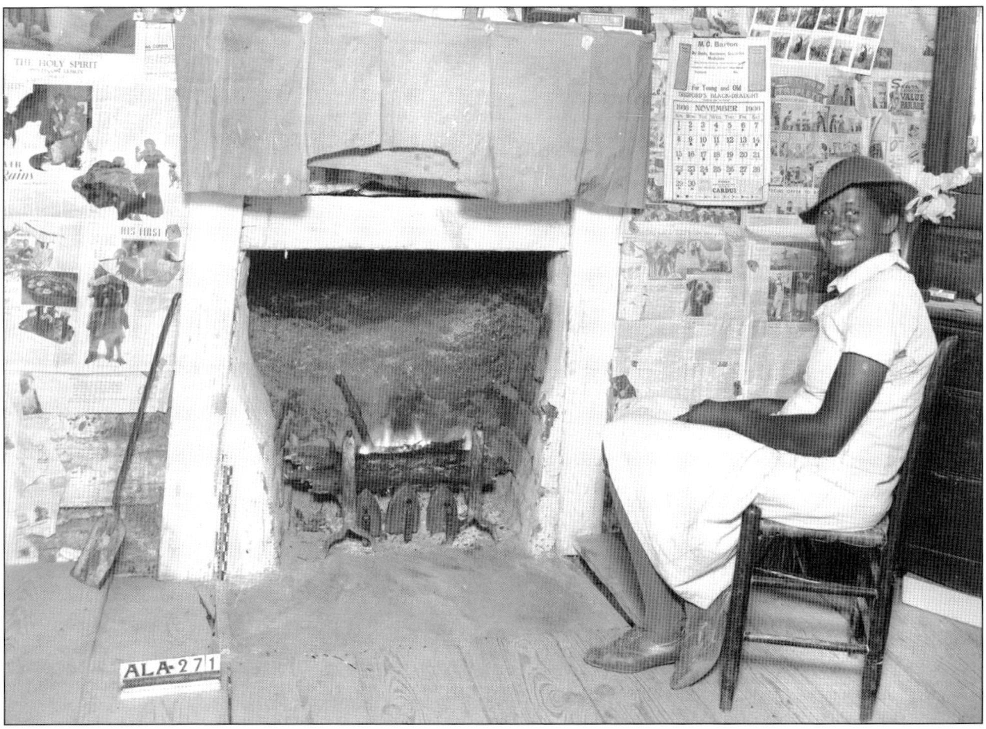

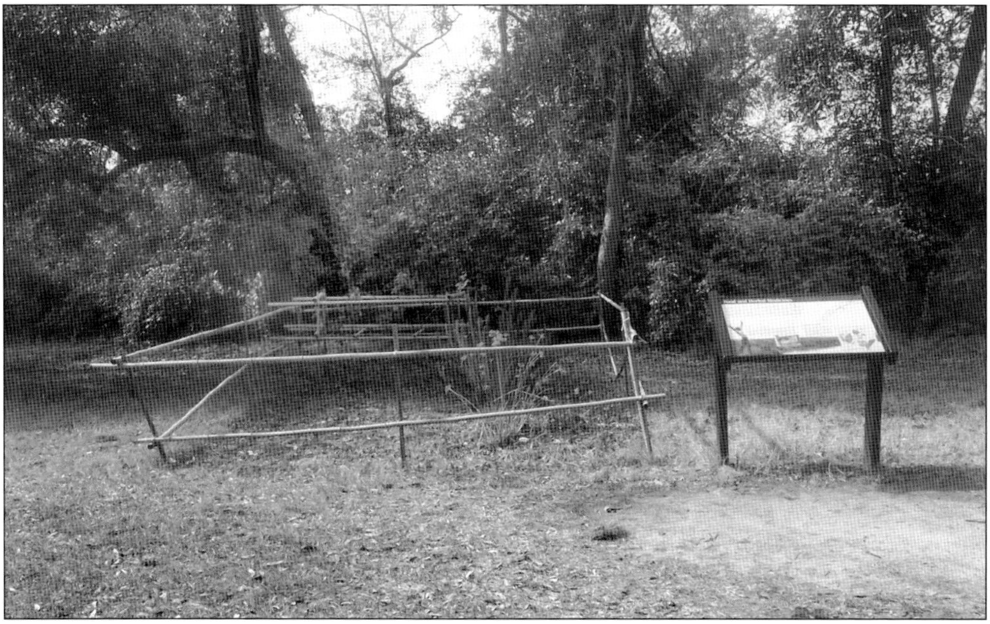
Slaves and those that continued to live on the plantation kept small gardens next to the cabins. Their diets, especially those of the slaves, were sparse and not rich in vitamins. Keeping a garden for fresh vegetables was an excellent way to supplement their diet. Slaves would often work in their gardens on Sunday, usually their only day off. (Courtesy of Michelle Adams.)

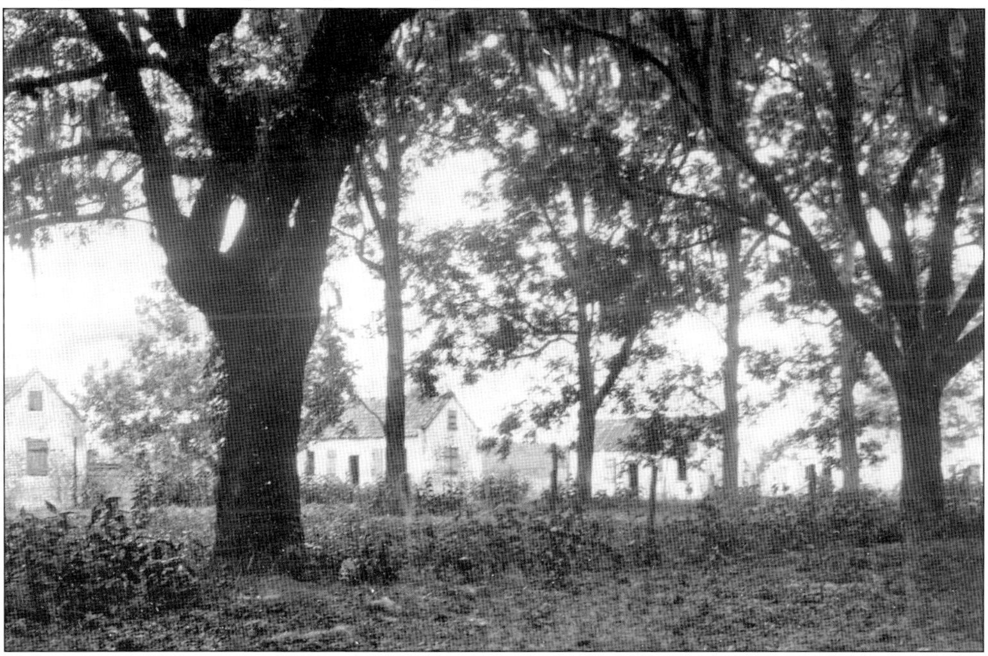
Boone Hall's cabins fit the average size in square footage but were nicer in quality because of the windows, brick walls, and wooden floors. The location of these cabins is found in front of the house; normally cabins are found behind the main house. It was common for cabins to be arranged in streets, as is seen at Boone Hall. The location of the other slave cabins, as well as their descriptions, is unknown. (Courtesy of the South Carolina Historical Society.)

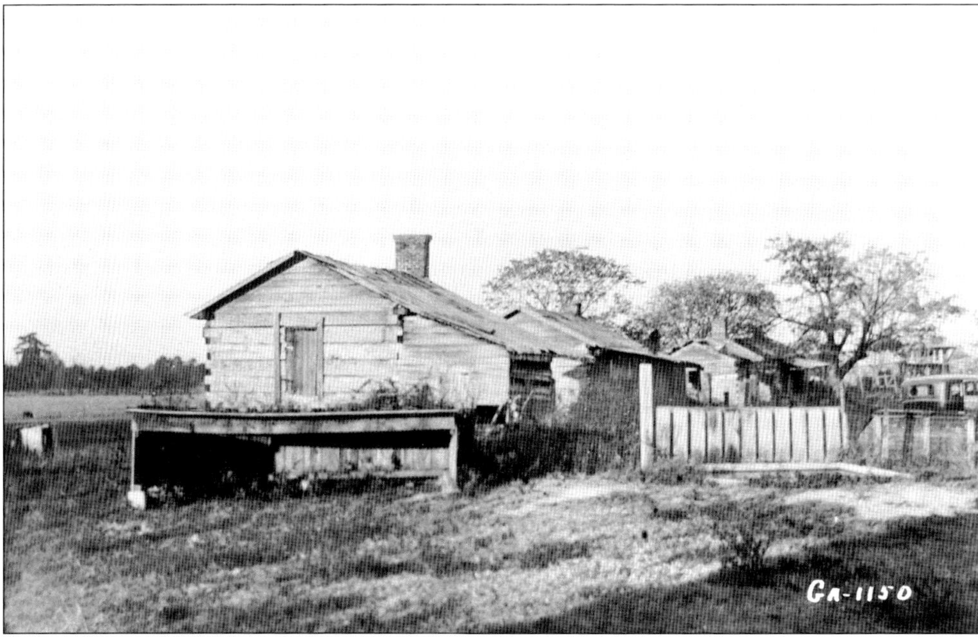

Slave cabins varied from plantation to plantation. The conditions that the slaves lived in relied heavily on the benevolence of the master. Many cabins were wooden with a dirt floor and no windows, such as these from Bass Place in Muscogee County, Georgia. Many cabins also housed two families and may or may not have had a wall to separate the two living spaces. Cabins made of brick were usually reserved for the house servants or skilled slaves. (Courtesy of the Library of Congress.)

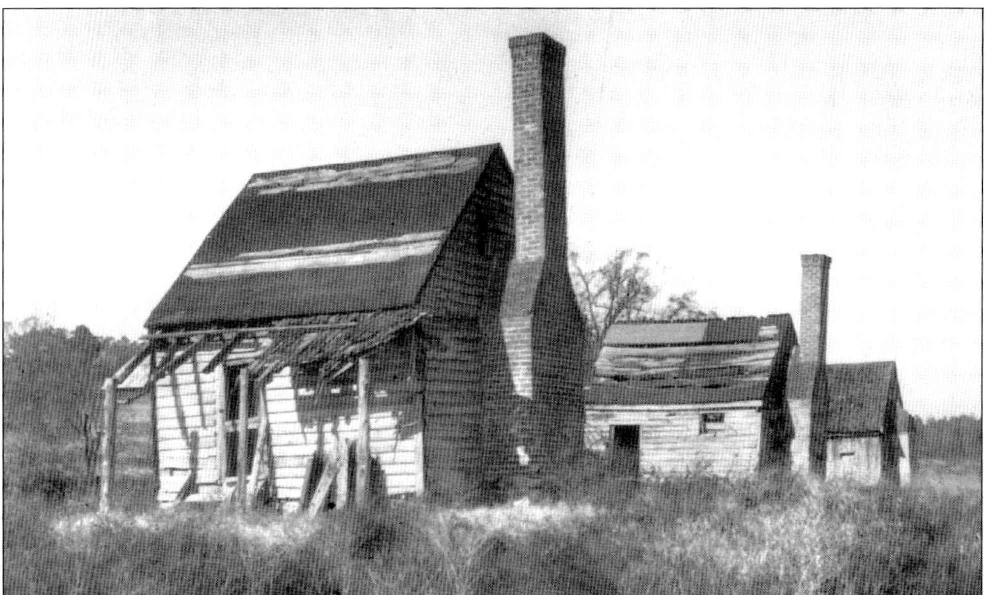

Many plantations had wooden cabins with few windows for light or ventilation. These cabins would probably be used for the field slaves, and often slave streets may be found in different locations around a plantation, possibly closer to the fields where the slaves would work. (Courtesy of the Library of Congress.)

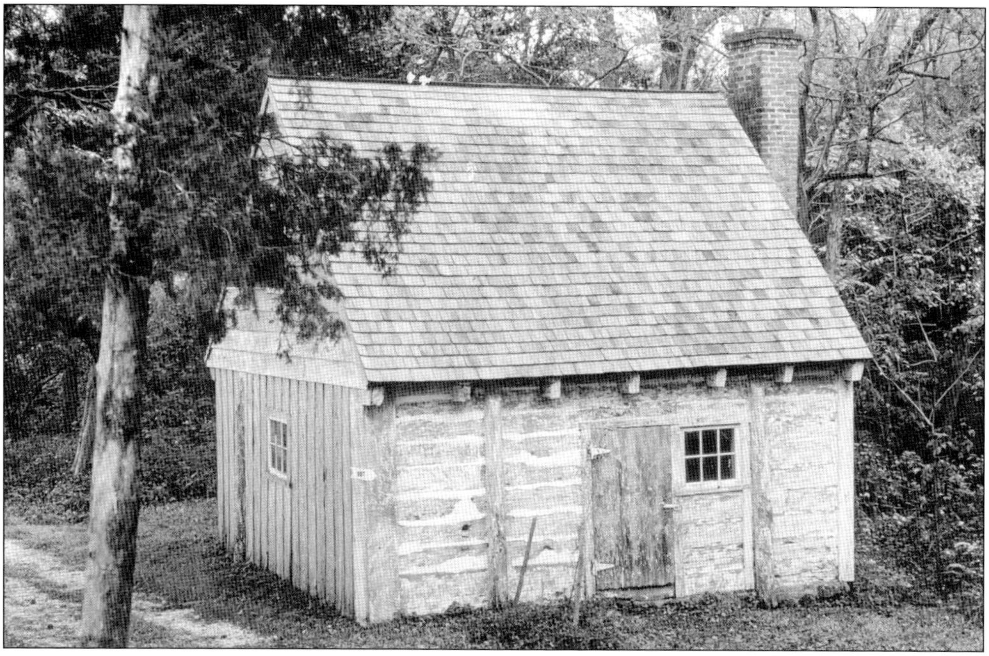

Cabins with few to no windows were not just characteristic of the Lowcountry. This example is found at Sotterly Plantation in St. Mary's County, Maryland. However, in the colder winters the inhabitants may have appreciated less drafty windows. Summers can still be brutal without the ability to air out the cabin, especially after cooking in the fireplace. (Courtesy of the Library of Congress.)

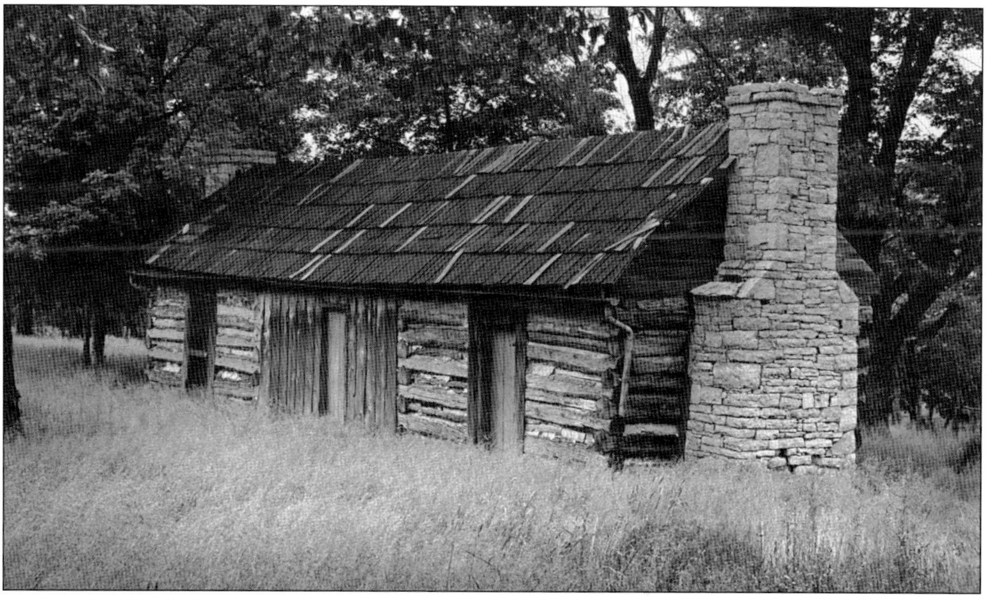

Other plantation-maintained cabins could house several families, such as this cabin from the Cedars in Jefferson County, Missouri. These cabins contain three separate doorways so three different families could be housed in technically one building. These cabins have adequate windows for light and ventilation and may have been used for skilled slaves where brick was rare. (Courtesy of the Library of Congress.)

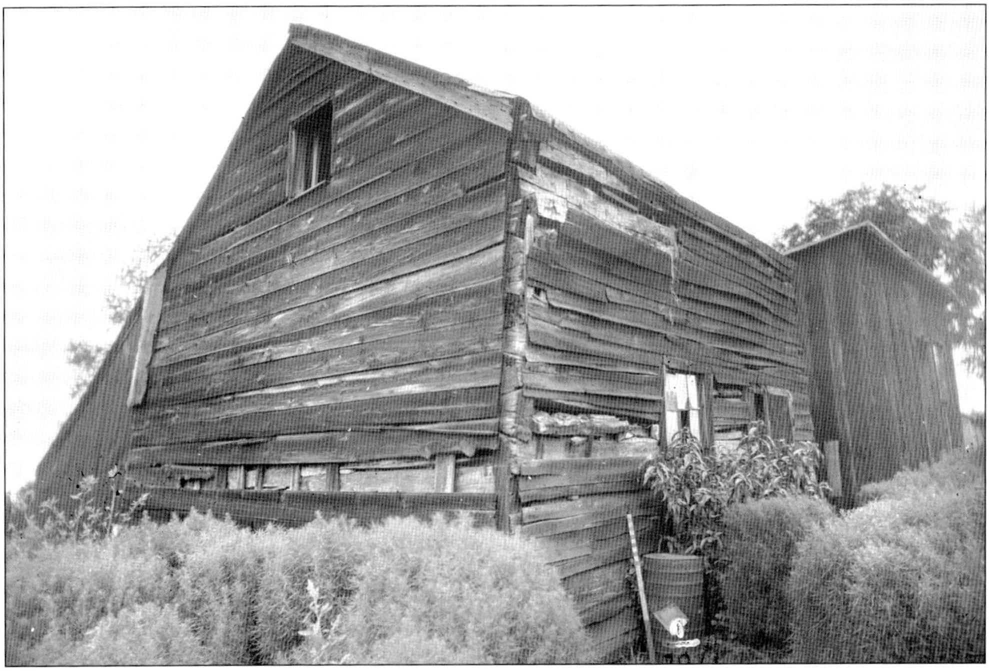

This two-story slave cabin found in St. Charles County, Missouri, shows the use of the loft in the slave cabin. It is interesting to note that one of the only two windows in the cabin is in the loft, allowing little ventilation, especially in the hot, oppressive Missouri summers. (Courtesy of the Library of Congress.)

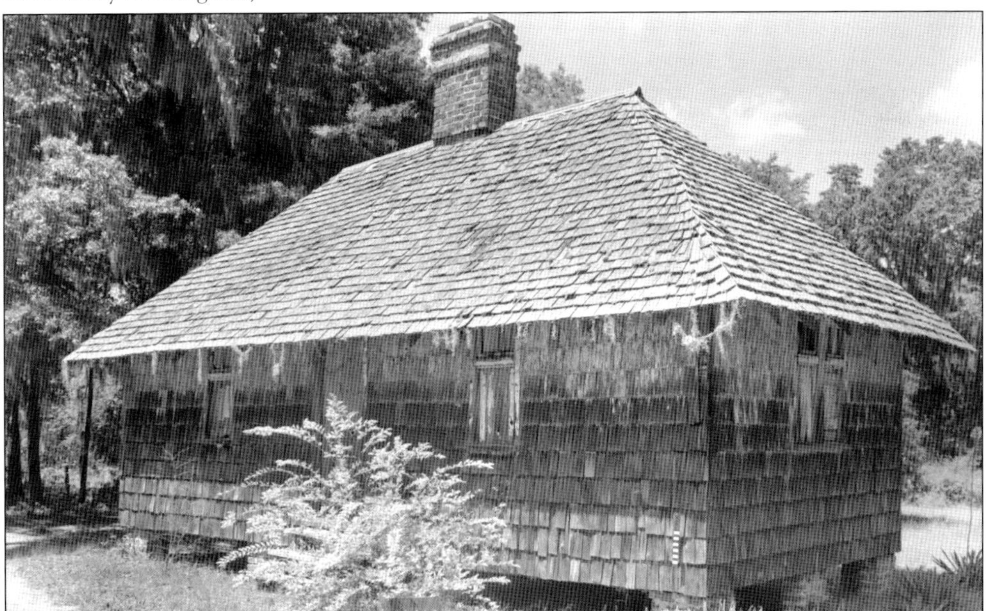

Some cabins, such as this one from Hopsewee Plantation in Georgetown, reflect the heritage that many slaves were able to retain. The African influence that the slaves retained can also be seen in the Gullah culture in the Lowcountry sea islands through their language, basket weaving, and quilts. (Courtesy of the Library of Congress.)

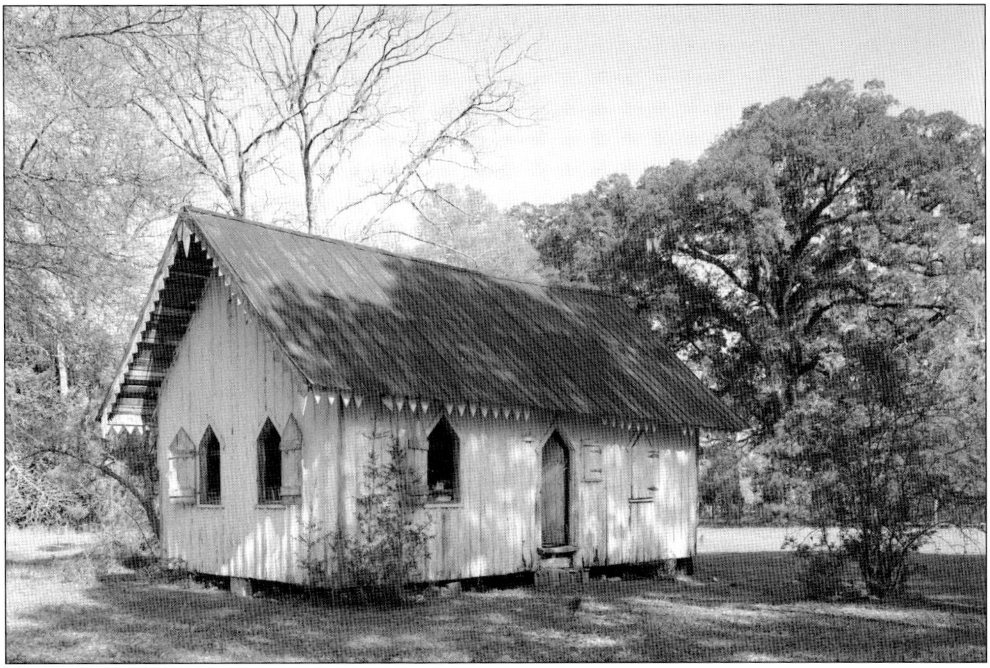

Not all slave cabins had the drab exterior of a wooden shack. This slave cabin, found at Arundel Plantation in Georgetown County, has several interesting architectural aspects not seen in the average slave cabin. The arched windows and doorways, and the fact that there are several windows, make this slave cabin unique. (Courtesy of the Library of Congress.)

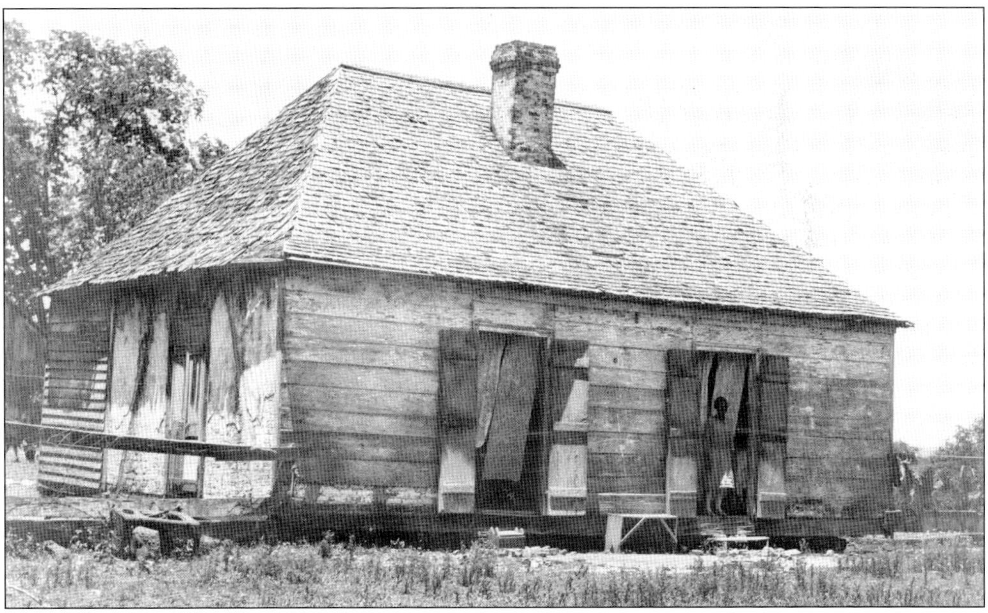

This 1936 photograph was taken at the Barbarra Plantation in St. Charles Parish, Louisiana, and includes one of the residents standing in the doorway. The doorway is covered with a sheet and shows that the current residents are living much the same as their ancestors did. Current owners also do not seem to have made many improvements to the cabins either. (Courtesy of the Library of Congress.)

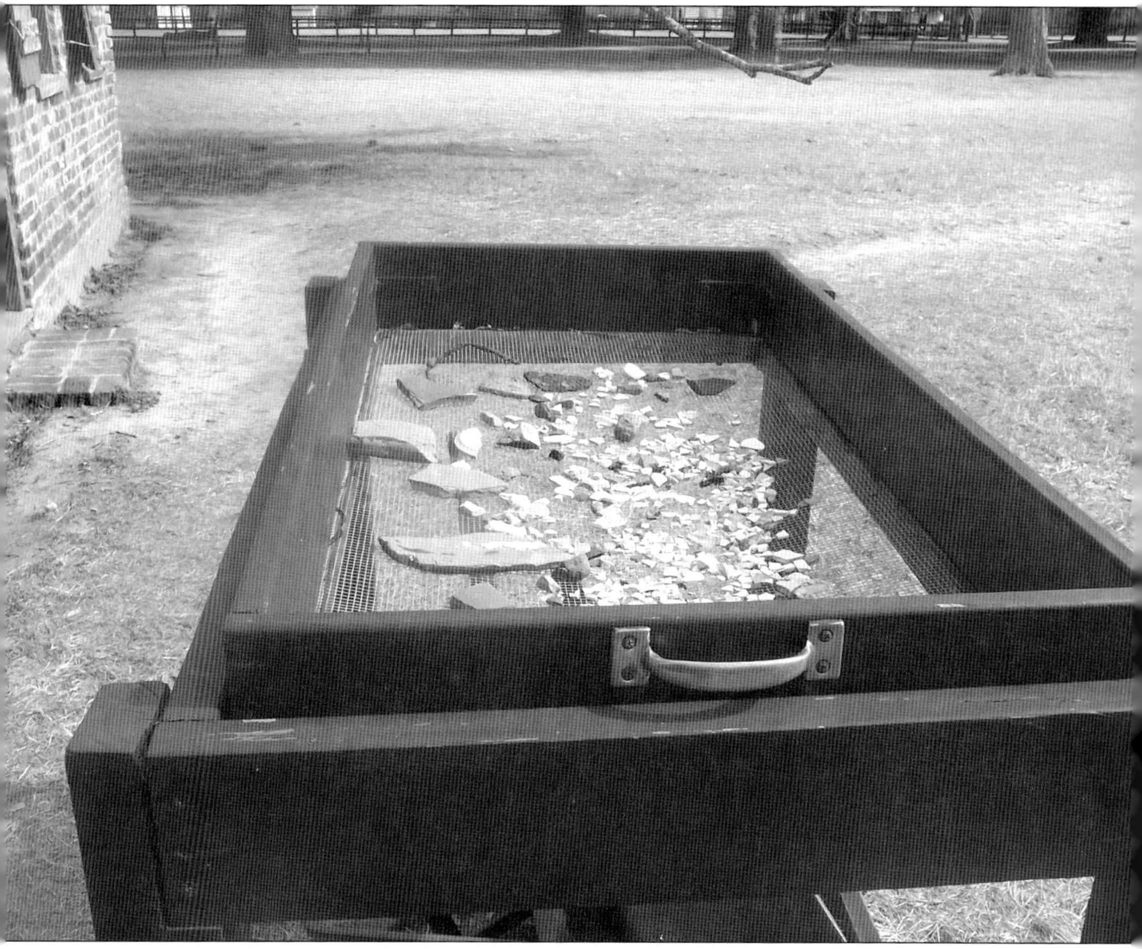

Archeological surveys have been conducted over the years in the slave cabins. Several types of buttons—wooden, porcelain, and oyster shell—have been found, as well as clay marbles, some painted, and glass marbles. Marbles was a common game played by slave children, as were hide and seek and jumping rope. Porcelain dolls, a wooden comb handle, copper thimbles, pieces of dinnerware, and glass bottles have also been found. (Courtesy of Michelle Adams.)

Six

Boone Hall Continues On

Later residents of Boone Hall continued the hard work begun by the Stones. The Stones left Boone Hall in 1940. Thomas Stone resumed his diplomatic work during World War II with the exiled countries of France, Holland, and Belgium. The plantation was sold to Prince Dmitri Djordjaze and his wife, Audrey Emory. They were an interesting addition to Charleston society, but their residency was also short-lived, and the property was conveyed to Dr. Henry Deas in 1955.

Dr. Deas continued the farming operation with the addition of cattle until he sold the property to the McRae family in 1955. The McRaes were able to create a successful agricultural business as well as one of the most visited tourist sites in Charleston. The McRae family also created a relevant educational facility for summer camps as well as school field trips based on South Carolina standards-based educational requirements. Most importantly, they created an informational museum format out of the slave cabins to illustrate the story of the slaves and African Americans as whole who would otherwise not have a voice. A trip to Boone Hall Plantation has truly become an experience that is not soon forgotten.

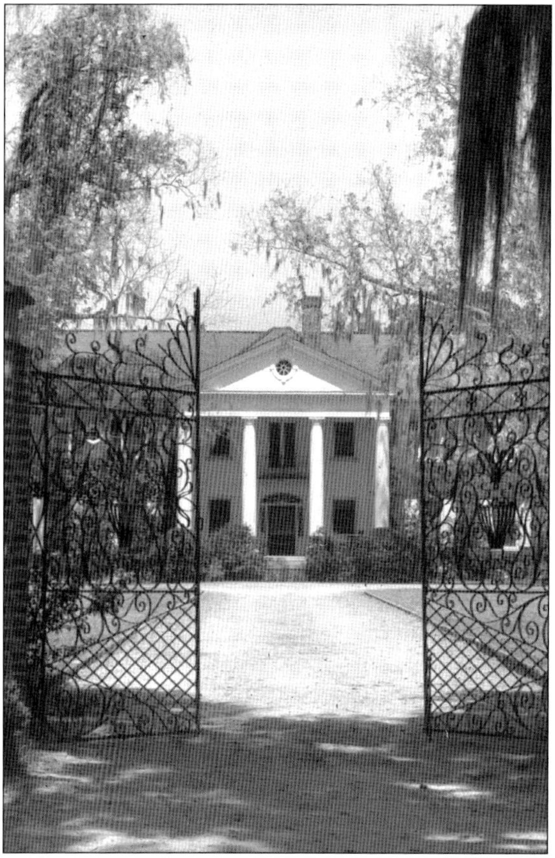

The Djordjaze sale in 1940 included the same acreage that the Stones purchased in 1935. The Djordjazes purchased the property for $150,000, which included the original Boone Hall property, adjoining Laurel Hill Plantation, and part of Elm Grove and Parker's Island, a total of 4,039.5 acres, which also included highland and marsh. Pictured is the plantation house as it looked when the Djordjazes purchased the property. (Courtesy of Boone Hall Plantation.)

Audrey Emory was an American heiress and socialite born in Cincinnati, Ohio. She was the youngest daughter of John J. Emory, a real estate millionaire, and his wife, the former Lela Alexander. In 1926, she married, morganatically, Grand Duke Dmitri Pavlovich of Russia, an exile after the 1917 Russian Revolution. Audrey was elevated to Russian princely rank with the usual name Romanovsky and was granted an additional princely name, Ilyinsky. (Courtesy of the South Carolina Historical Society.)

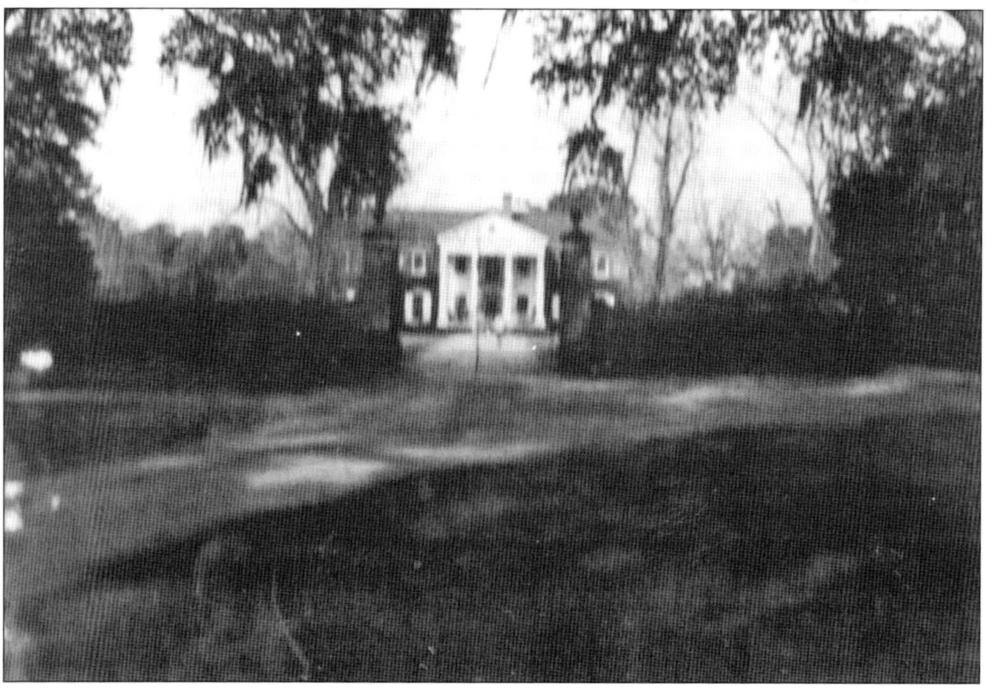

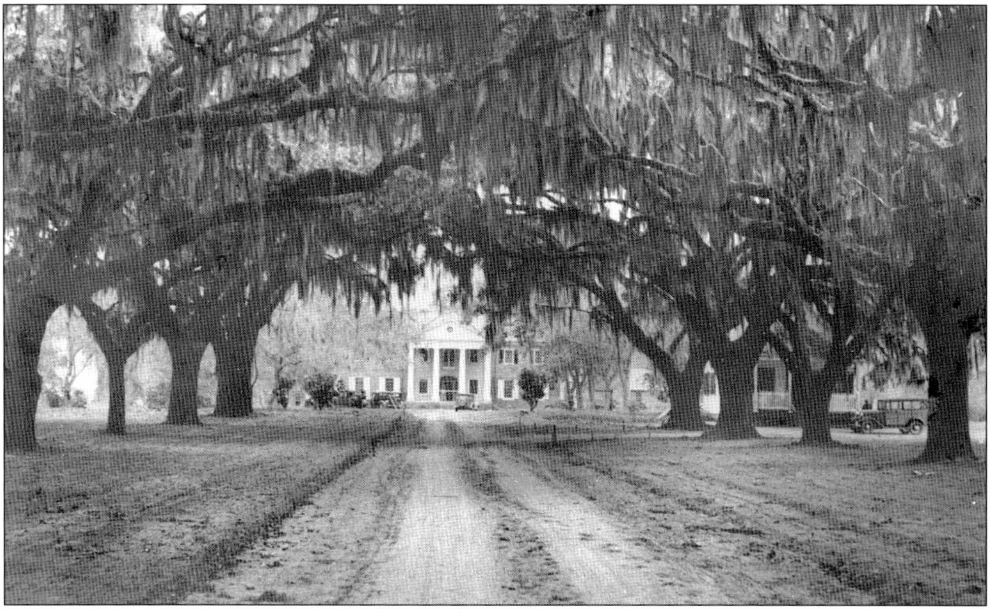

Prince Dmitri Djordjaze was a member of the Russian nobility who became exiled after the overthrow of Tsartist Russia. He was also an executive at the Ambassador Hotel and a race car driver. He was married twice, first to Audrey Emory in March 1937. Together they purchased Boone Hall in June 1940. After their divorce, Djordjaze married Sylvia Ashley in 1954, a onetime English showgirl who was the former wife of Clark Gable and the widow of Douglas Fairbanks Sr. (Courtesy of Boone Hall Plantation.)

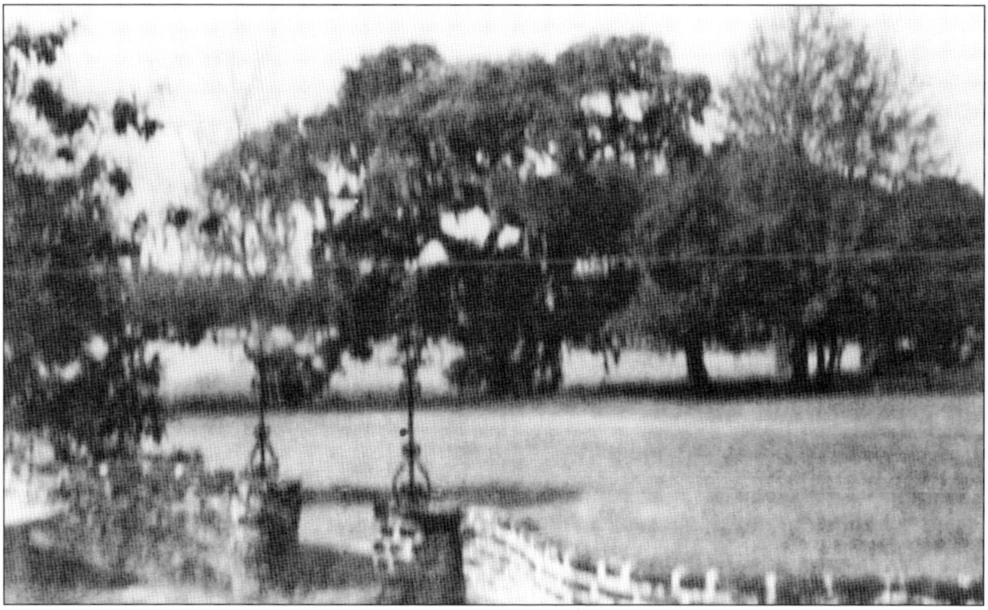

The Djordjazes made several changes to the plantation. They added a patio to the main house, and Audrey added the patio walls in the 1940s. The bricks are laid out in a sunburst pattern and the walls in a serpentine pattern. The couple planned gardens consisting of oval beds to surround the pool, and they also rearranged several buildings, including the caretaker's house, and remodeled the stable. (Courtesy of the South Carolina Historical Society.)

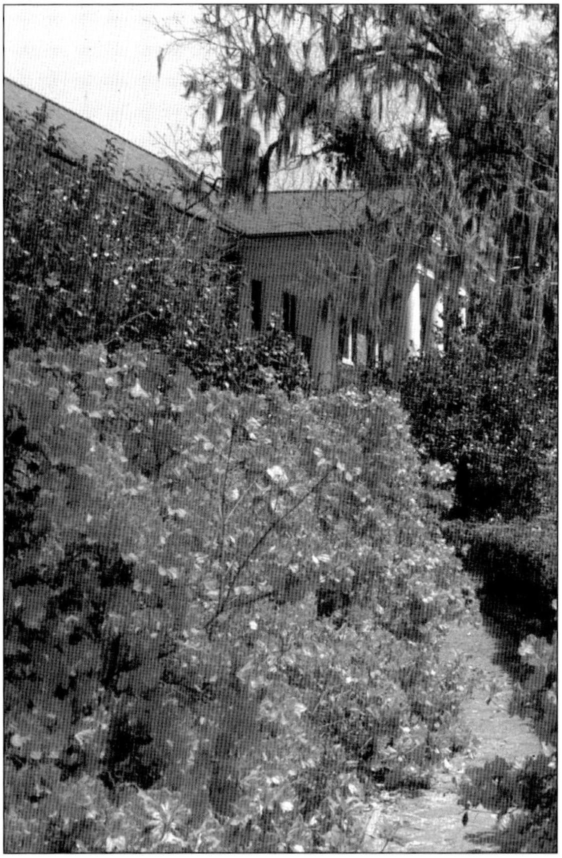

In 1945, Dimitri and Audrey Djordjaze divorced and sold Boone Hall to P. O. Mead Jr. for $120,000. The real estate agent in turn sold the property to Dr. and Mrs. Henry Deas. The Deas raised cattle on the property and remained there until the 1950s, when the property was once again sold. (Courtesy of Boone Hall Plantation.)

In 1955, the plantation was sold for the last time to Harris and Nancy McRae, peach brokers from Ellerbe, North Carolina. Nancy fell in love with the plantation, and her husband purchased it for her. The McRaes moved to the plantation with their daughter, Nancy Elizabeth, and their son, William Harris. They continued to farm the land with a focus on growing peach trees. In 1956, the McRae family opened the plantation to public tours. They also continue to farm, making Boone Hall Plantation the oldest working plantation in America. (Courtesy of Boone Hall Plantation.)

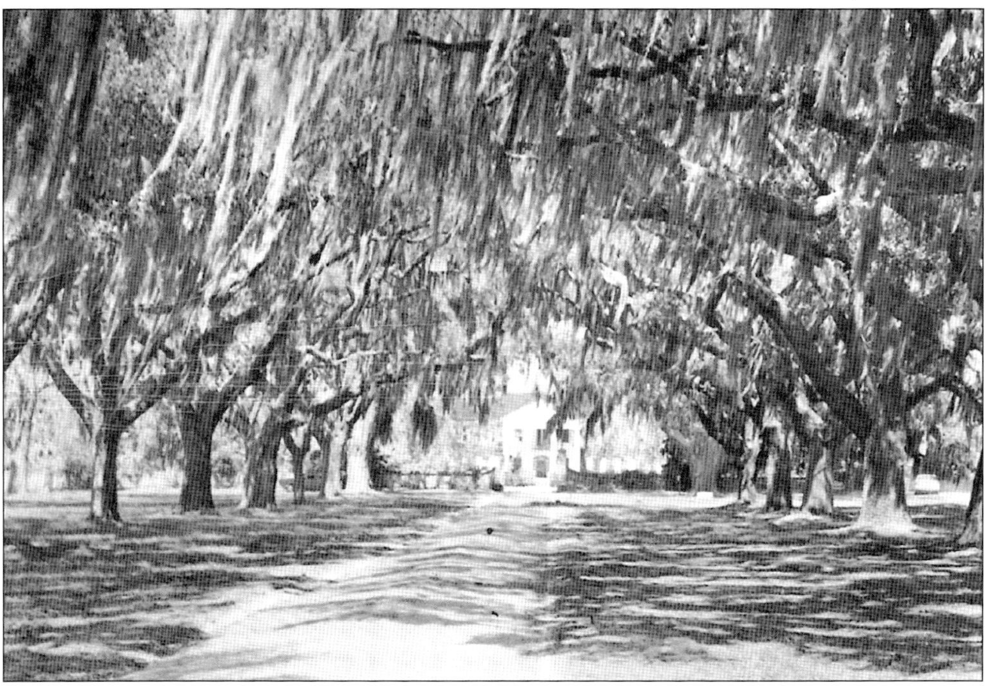

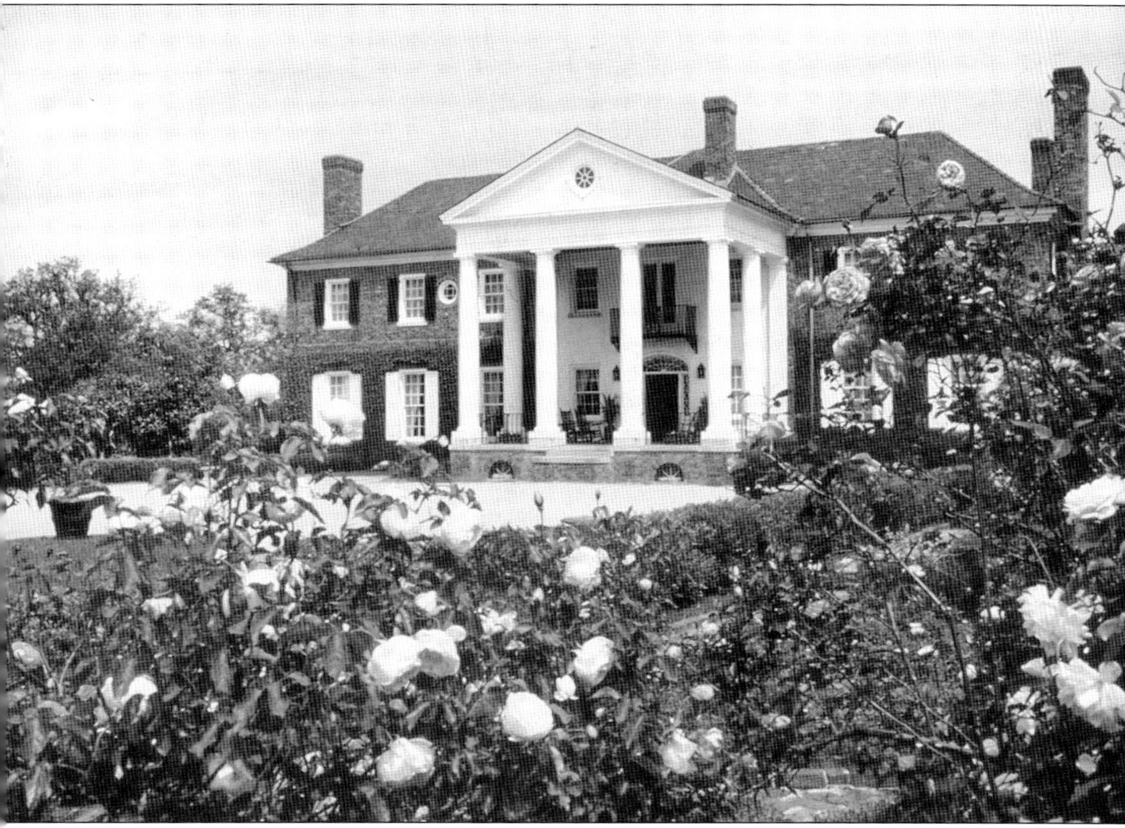

The gardens in front of the house were laid out symmetrically with brick walkways. Antique roses were grown in abundance in the garden due to the expert care by award-winning gardener Ruth Knopf. Roses are classified as antique if they date back to before 1867. Boone Hall's garden includes Noisette roses, a type created in Charleston, and the Duchesse de Brabant, a pink-blooming, fragrant tea rose. (Courtesy of Boone Hall Plantation.)

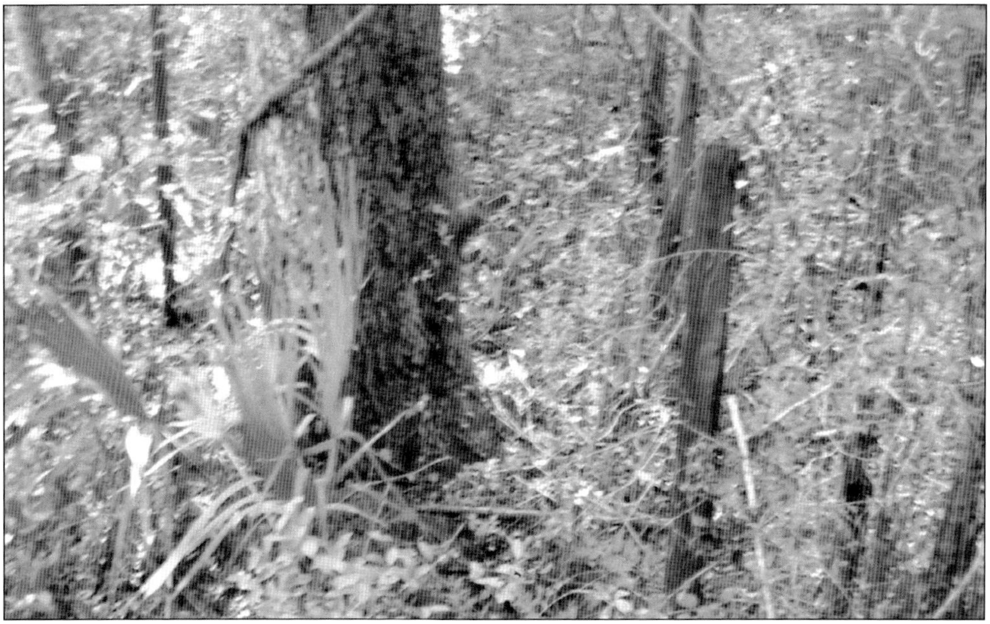

The wildlife is still a main draw when visiting Boone Hall, especially for schoolchildren. Many of the creatures that roamed the plantation several hundred years ago can still be found on a tram ride. Snakes, herons, and turtles still call the plantation home. Those brave enough to drive to the freshwater pond behind the house might just see an alligator. (Courtesy of Boone Hall Plantation.)

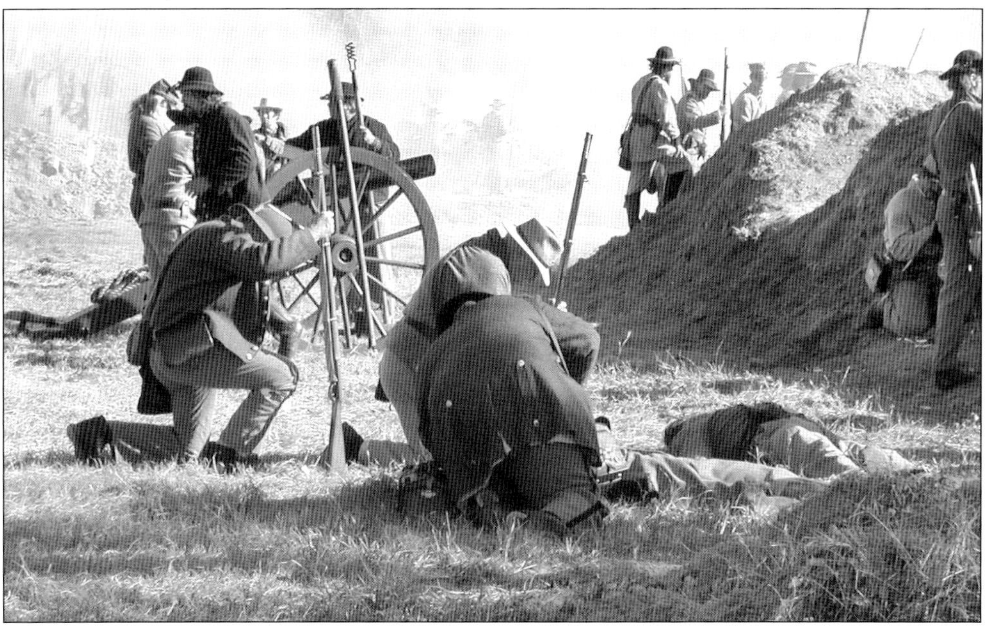

In June 1862, the Battle of Secessionville was fought as the Federal army aimed to take over Charleston. As one of the more significant moments in South Carolina history, this battle is now annually reenacted at the Boone Hall Plantation every November. History buffs and those looking for an exciting time in the Charleston area will definitely want to witness this tremendous show of the history that shaped the land. (Courtesy of Ann Gelwicks.)

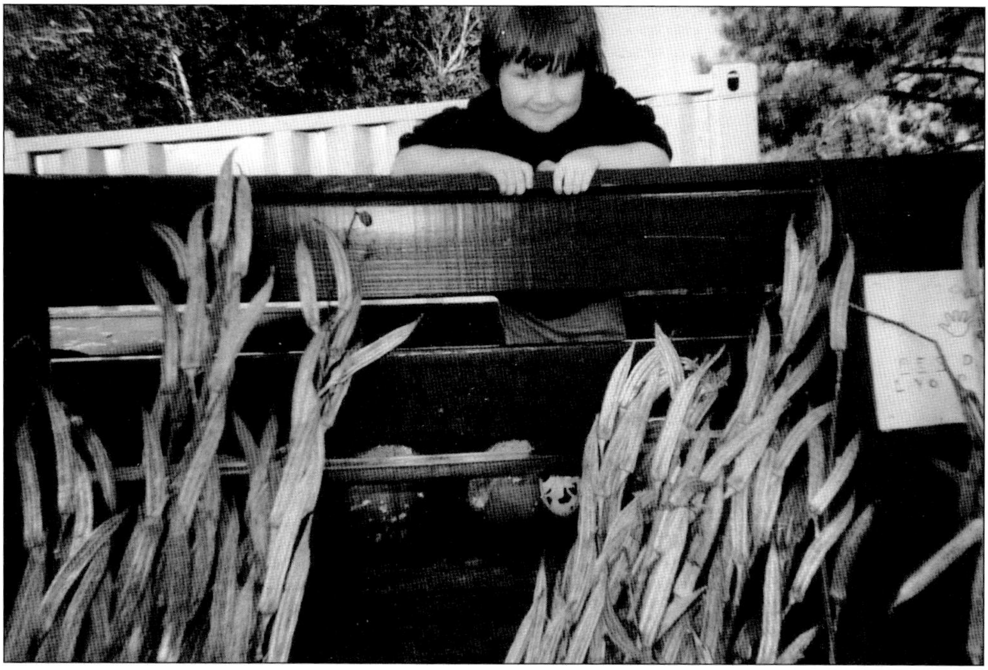

Boone Hall Plantation has served various niches in the community over the years. One popular event happens in the fall with the annual Happy Jack's pumpkin patch, which children in the Mount Pleasant area look forward to. Another aspect that has grown over the years is the annual corn maze, which entertains the adults as well. (Courtesy of Michelle Adams.)

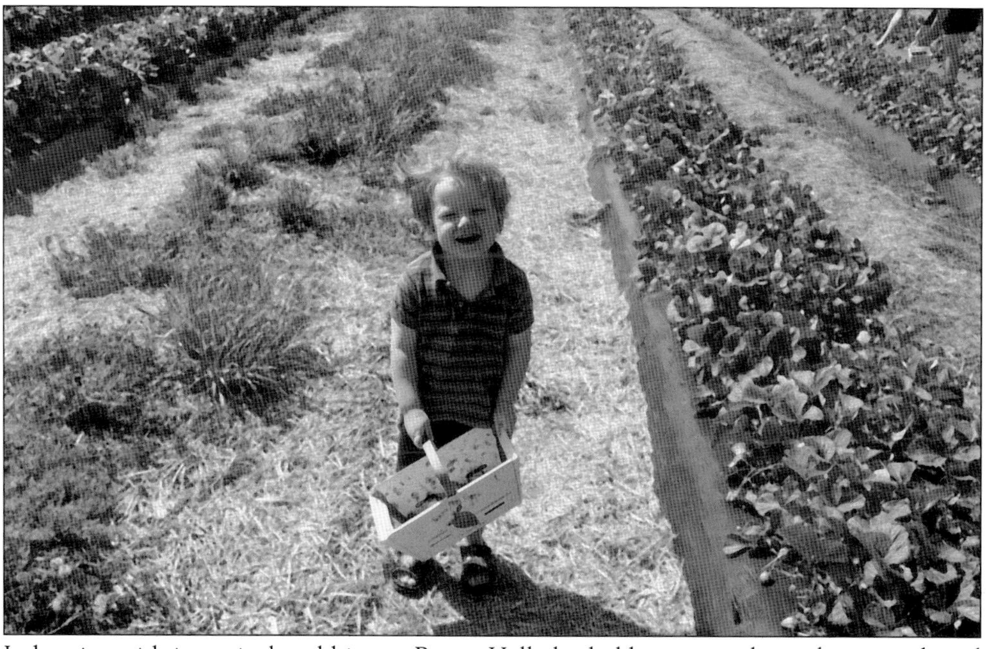

In keeping with its agricultural history, Boone Hall also holds an annual strawberry patch and strawberry festival in the spring. Families from all over enjoy the opportunity to pick their own strawberries and shop for fresh vegetables. Most children come out of the patch with red hands and faces. (Courtesy of Michelle Adams.)

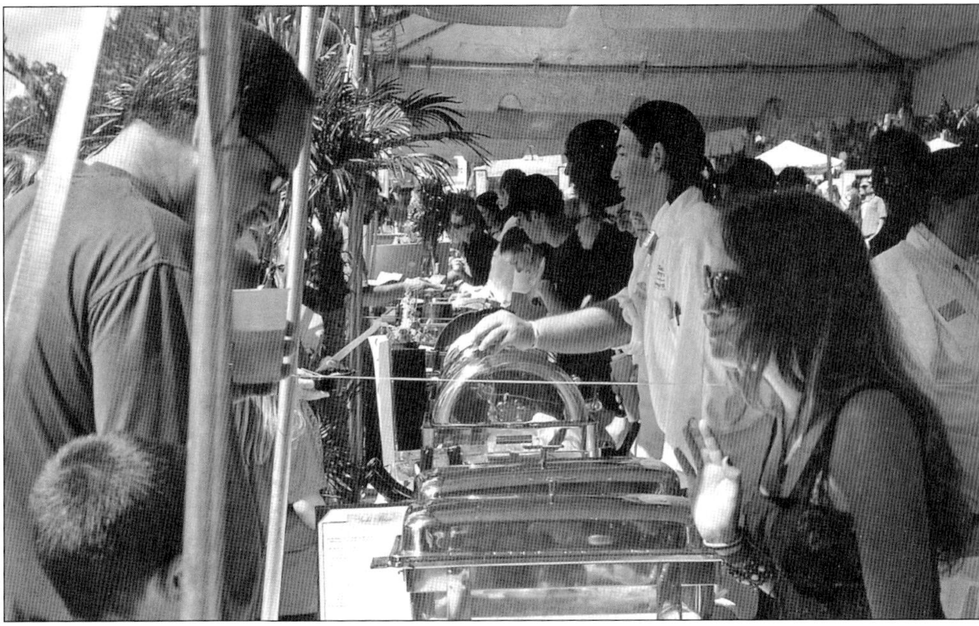

The grounds at Boone Hall Plantation are transformed into the Taste of Charleston event every October by 40 of Charleston's and the Lowcountry's finest restaurants. Proceeds from the event benefit the Ronald McDonald House, the Hollings Cancer Center, and the Charleston County Materials Resource Center. The festival features the famous "Waiters Wine Race," beer and wine tasting, a special Children's Corner, and cooking demonstrations by some of Charleston's finest chefs. (Courtesy of Tony Libby.)

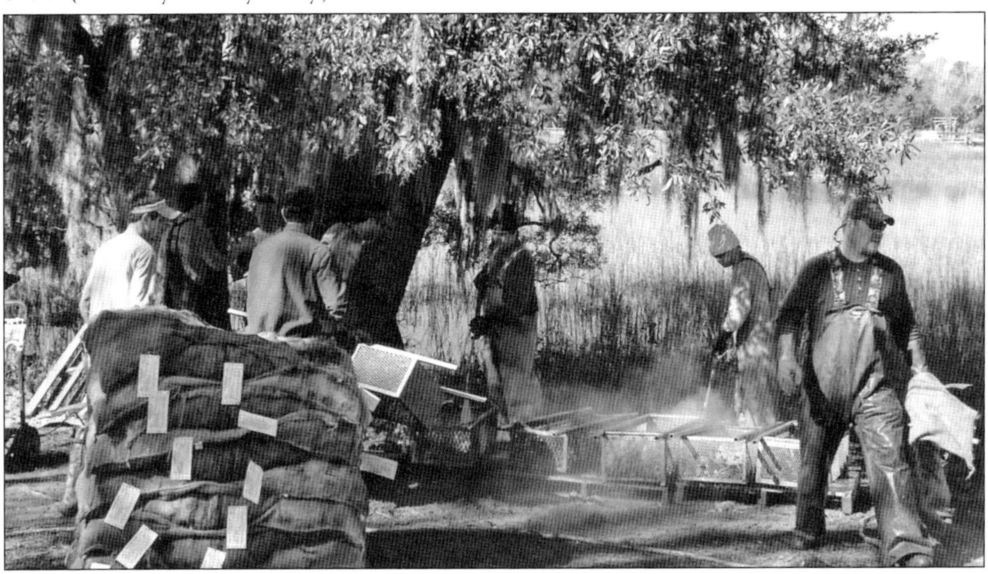

Held by the Greater Charleston Restaurant Association, the Lowcountry Oyster Festival is a Charleston favorite held at Boone Hall every January. Oysters are sold by the bucket for market value and served with cocktail sauce and crackers. Attendees can bring their own knives and gloves or purchase them at the event. Proceeds benefit the Ronald McDonald House, the Hollings Cancer Center, the Travel Council, and the Charleston County Materials Resource Center. (Courtesy of Tony Libby.)

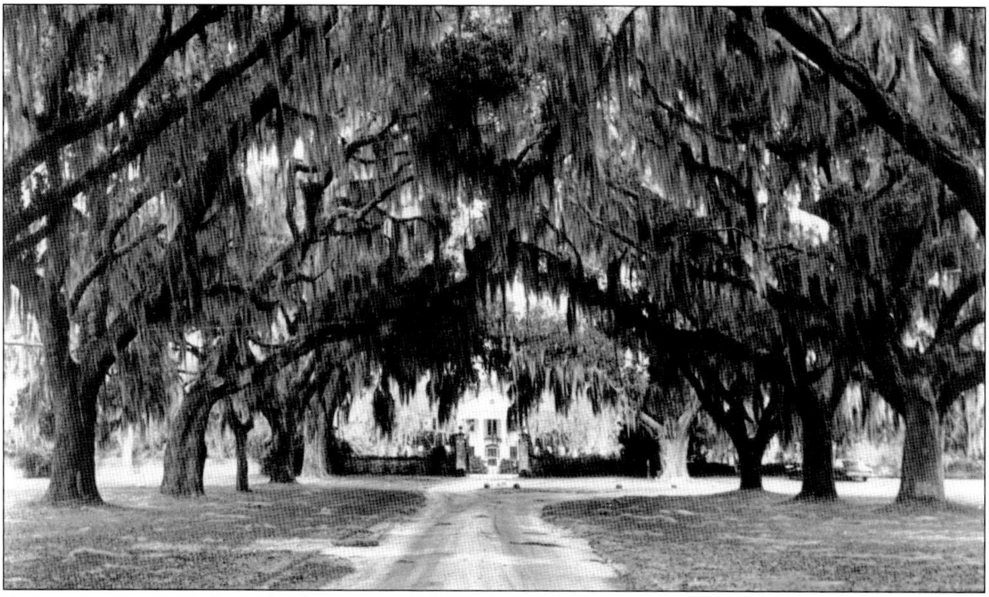

As tourism increased in Charleston, so did the popularity of plantations. Boone Hall was opened to the public in 1956. This photograph was used by the City of Charleston in the 1970s to help promote Charleston as a vacation spot. Boone Hall Plantation was an important part of drawing tourists to the area and helped to boost tourism to the top industry in Charleston. (Courtesy of the Charleston County Public Library.)

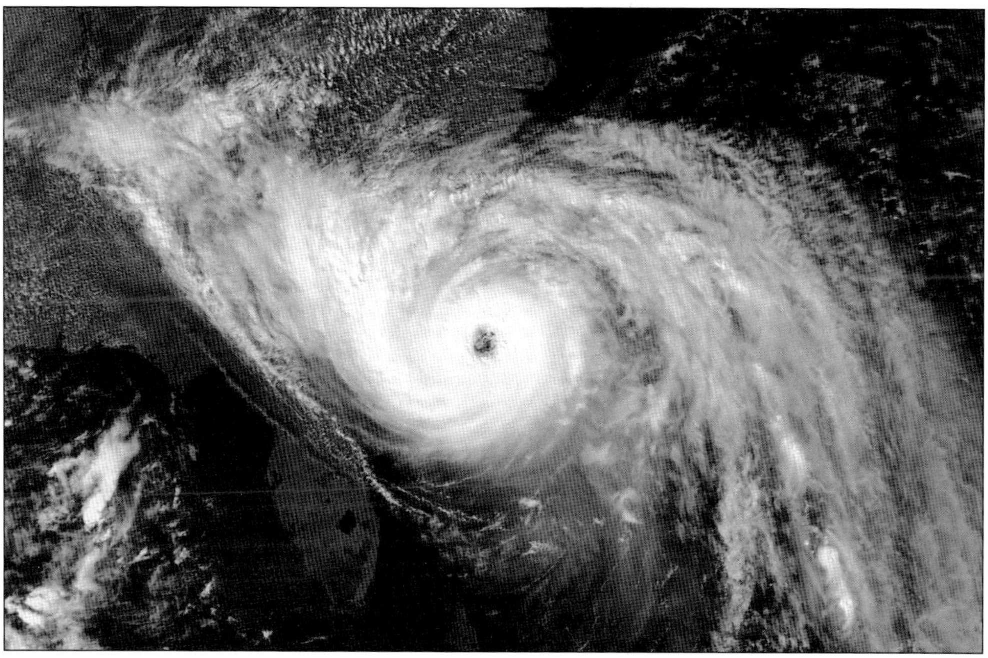

Hurricane Hugo was a destructive category 5 hurricane that struck Guadeloupe, Montserrat, Puerto Rico, St. Croix, South Carolina, and North Carolina in September 1989, killing 82 people and leaving 56,000 homeless. The storm caused $10 billion ($16.3 billion in current value) in damages, making it the most damaging hurricane ever recorded up to that time. (Courtesy of Boone Hall Plantation.)

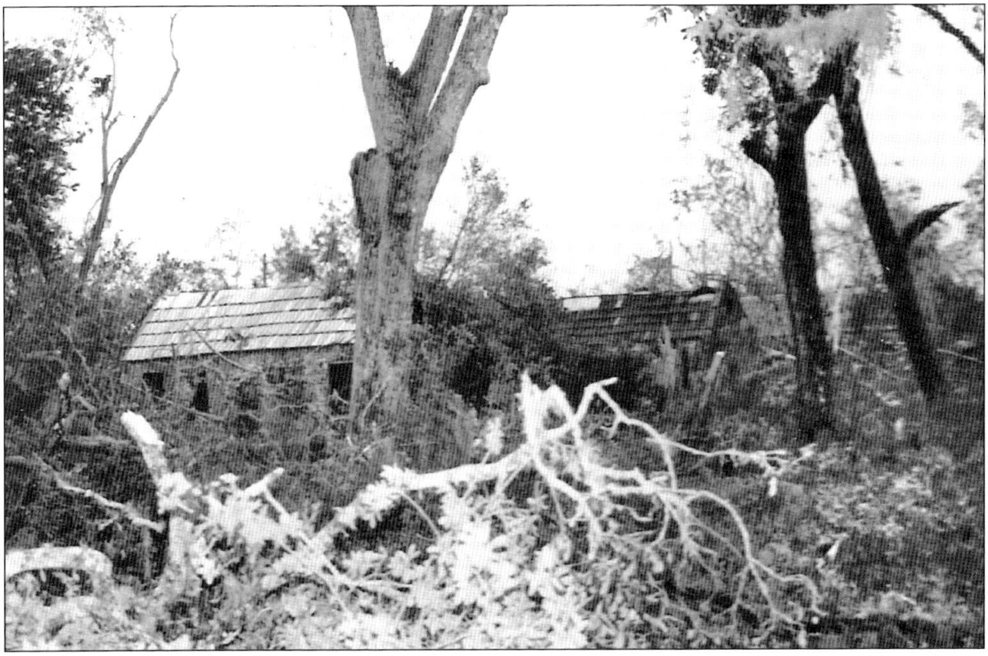

The owners remained with the property throughout the storm, enduring the high winds and rain as the hurricane battered its way through Mount Pleasant. The hurricane caused $1.3 million in damages to the plantation. It took several months of cleanup before the plantation was able to reopen to the public on March 1, 1990. (Courtesy of Boone Hall Plantation.)

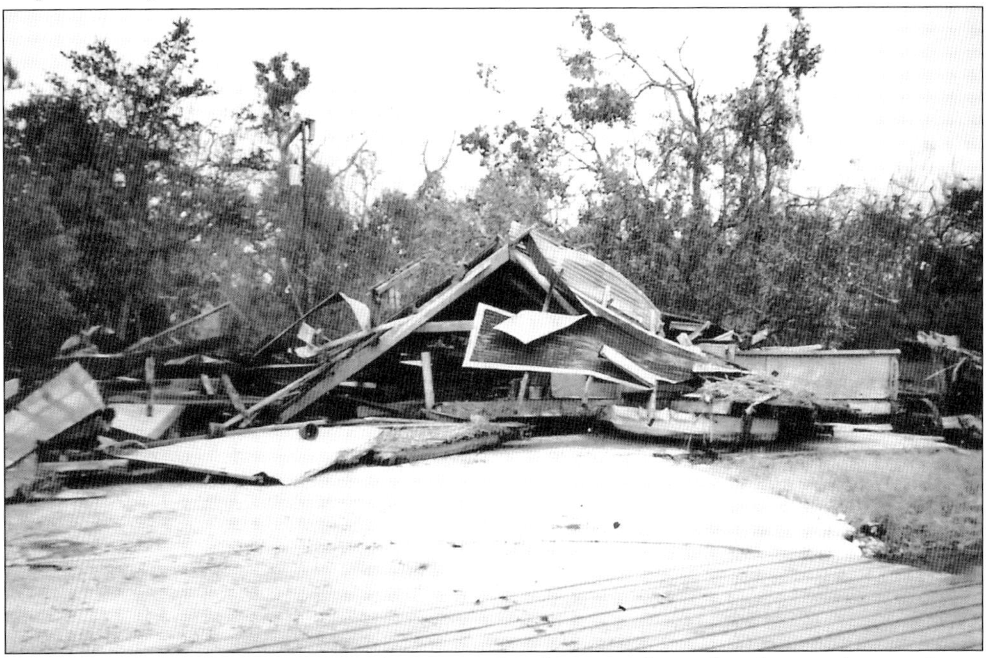

The storm did not cause any major damage to the plantation house but destroyed a significant number of trees and completely closed the plantation to visitors for several months. One of the greatest losses was the complete destruction of the dock house, which was rebuilt following the storm. (Courtesy of Boone Hall Plantation.)

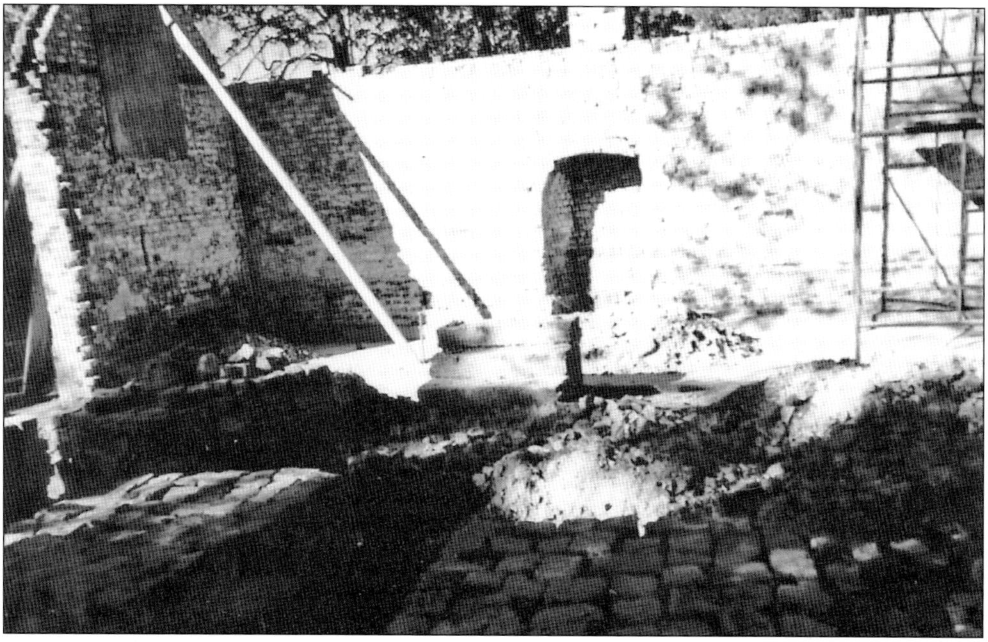

After Hurricane Hugo, it became apparent that the slave cabins needed to be restored. Several were in danger of collapsing and needed support to stay erect. Plans were developed in the mid-1990s to restore the cabins and to provide an educational program detailing the lives of the cabins' former residents for guests and students during their visit to the plantation. The restoration of the slave cabins occurred in 2000. (Courtesy of Boone Hall Plantation.)

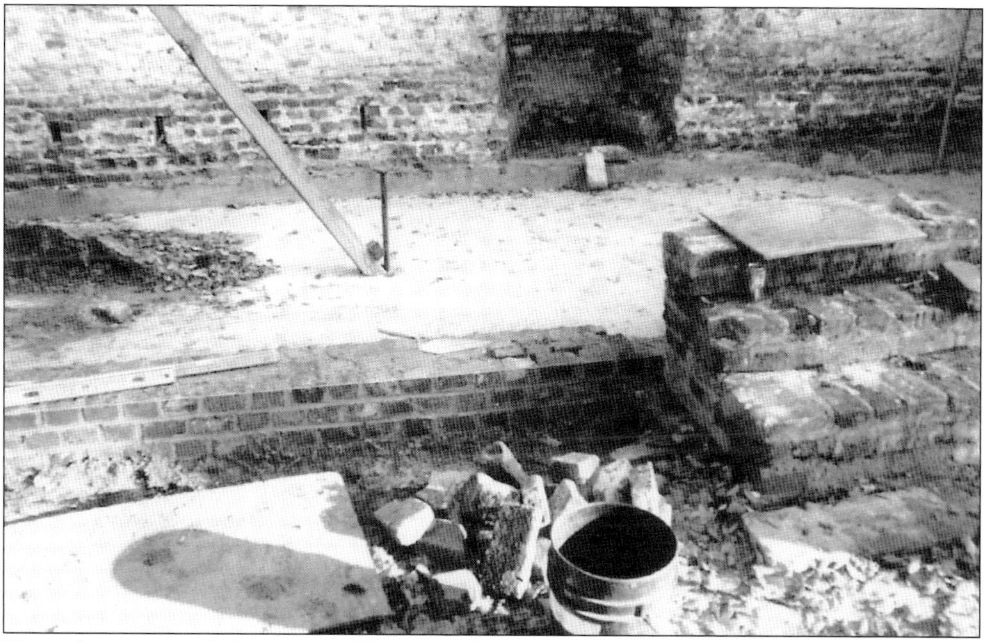

The cabins retained their original brick, and much was learned about the previous residents throughout the restoration process. One of the cabins retained the remains of the excavation process to enable visitors a unique view of the past. It took several months to completely restore all nine of the cabins. (Courtesy of Boone Hall Plantation.)

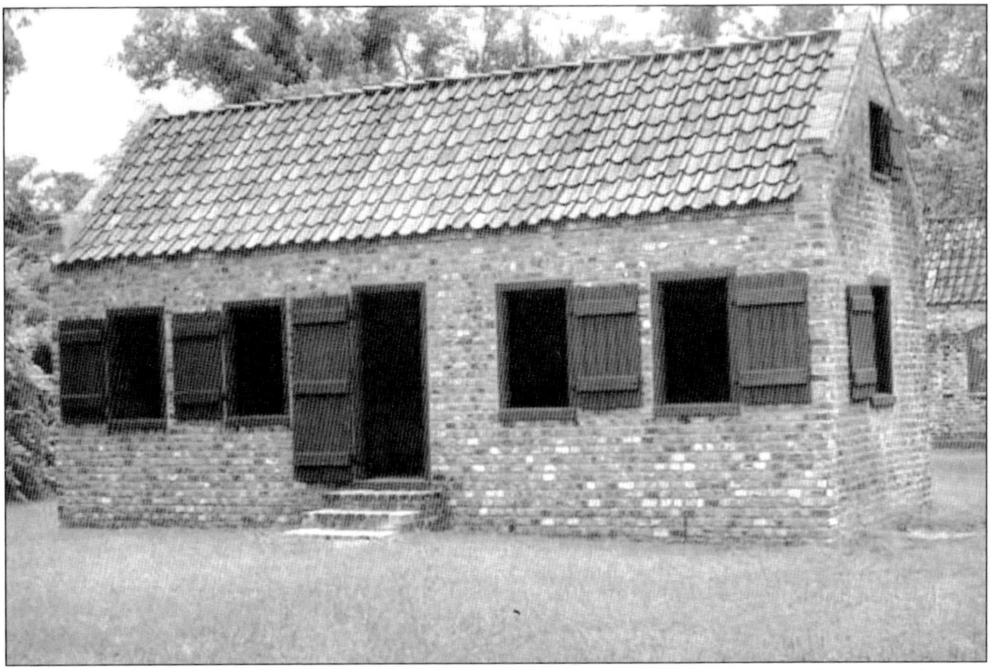

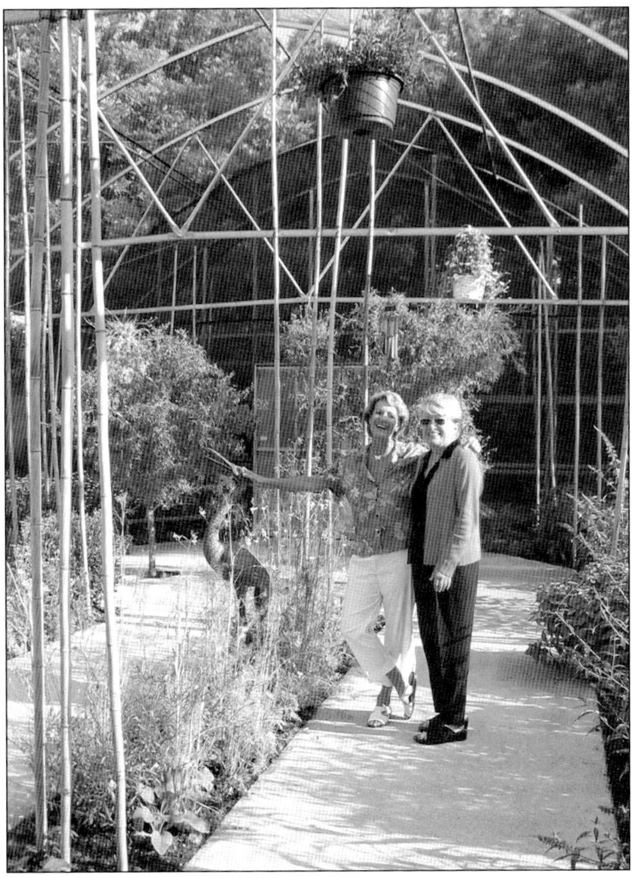

Pictured is a cabin after the restoration. All nine slave cabins were developed into separate mini-museums to add to the overall experience for guests. One cabin displays possible slave furnishings, while other cabins display information on their former tenants and on the institution of slavery itself, as well on the local Gullah culture. (Courtesy of Boone Hall Plantation.)

The Butterfly Pavilion provides guests the opportunity to study the life cycle of the butterfly. Visitors can discover the connection between butterflies and plants in their natural habitat. An interactive media program is also provided to give visitors the opportunity to observe up close the diverse characteristics of each stage of a butterfly's life. (Courtesy of Boone Hall Plantation.)

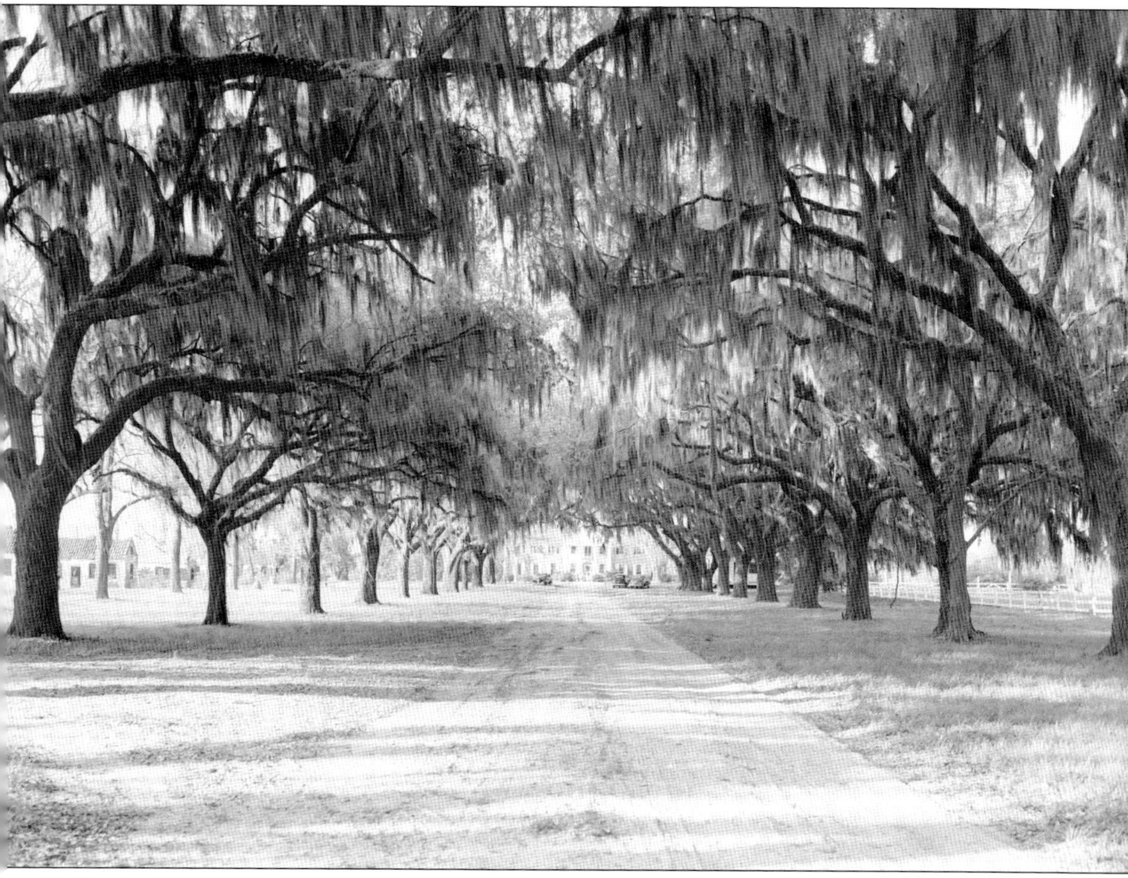

As Boone Hall continues to evolve, it is able to maintain its relevance in today's tourist market through tours and increased exploration of the African American experience on a plantation. Boone Hall has also been able to remain connected with the local community through festivals, educational programs, and Boone Hall Farm, a fresh meat and produce market along Highway 17 that extends its agricultural influence on the area. Boone Hall has been a mainstay of the East Cooper area and will remain so in the years to come. (Courtesy of Boone Hall Plantation.)

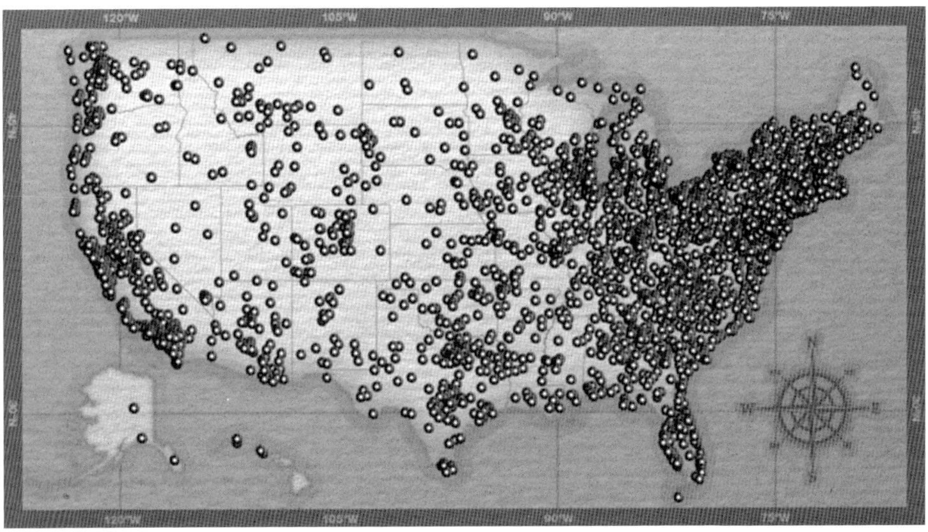